Globalization, Economic Growth and Innovation Dynamics

Springer
Berlin
Heidelberg
New York
Barcelona
Hong Kong
London
Milan
Paris
Singapore
Tokyo

Further Publications by *Paul J. J. Welfens*

P.J.J. Welfens
**Market-oriented Systemic Transforma-
tions in Eastern Europe**
Problems, Theoretical Issues, and Policy
Options
1992. XII, 261 pp. 20 figs., 29 tabs.,
Hardcover, ISBN 3-540-55793-8

M.W. Klein, P.J.J. Welfens
**Multinationals in the New Europe and
Global Trade**
1992. XV, 281 pp. 24 figs., 75 tabs.,
Hardcover, ISBN 3-540-54634-0

R. Tilly, P.J.J. Welfens
**European Economic Integration as a
Challenge to Industry and Government**
Contemporary and Historical Perspectives
on International Economic Dynamics
1996. X, 558 pp. 43 figs., Hardcover,
ISBN 3-540-60431-6

P.J.J. Welfens
European Monetary Integration
EMS Developments and International Post-
Maastricht Perspectives
3rd revised and enlarged edition
1996. XVIII, 384 pp. 14 figs., 26 tabs.,
Hardcover, ISBN 3-540-60260-7

P.J.J. Welfens
European Monetary Union
Transition, International Impact
and Policy Options
1997. X, 467 pp. 50 figs., 31 tabs.,
Hardcover, ISBN 3-540-63309-7

P.J.J. Welfens, G. Yarrow
**Telecommunications and Energy
in Systemic Transformation**
International Dynamics, Deregulation and
Adjustment in Network Industries
1997. XII, 501 pp. 39 figs., Hardcover,
ISBN 3-540-61586-5

P.J.J. Welfens, H.C. Wolf
**Banking, International Capital Flows
and Growth in Europe**
Financial Markets, Savings and Monetary
Integration in a World with Uncertain
Convergence
1997. XIV, 458 pp. 22 figs., 63 tabs.,
Hardcover, ISBN 3-540-63192-5

P.J.J. Welfens
Economic Aspects of German Unification
Expectations, Transition Dynamics and
International Perspectives
2nd revised and enlarged edition
1996. XV, 527 pp. 34 figs., 110 tabs.,
Hardcover, ISBN 3-540-60261-5

P.J.J. Welfens, D. Audretsch,
J.T. Addison and H. Grupp
**Technological Competition, Employment
and Innovation Policies in OECD
Countries**
1998. VI, 231 pp. 16 figs., 20 tabs.,
Hardcover, ISBN 3-540-63439-8

J.T. Addison, P.J.J. Welfens
Labor Markets and Social Security
Wage Costs, Social Security Financing and
Labor Market Reforms in Europe
1998. IX, 404 pp. 39 figs., 40 tabs.,
Hardcover, ISBN 3-540-63784-2

P.J.J. Welfens
**EU Eastern Enlargement and the Russian
Transformation Crisis**
1999. X, 151 pp. 12 figs., 25 tabs.,
Hardcover, ISBN 3-540-65862-9

P.J.J. Welfens
**Globalization of the Economy,
Unemployment and Innovation**
1999. VI, 255 pp. 11 figs., 31 tabs.,
Hardcover, ISBN 3-540-65250-7

P.J.J. Welfens, G. Yarrow, R. Grinberg,
C. Graack
**Towards Competition in Network
Industries**
Telecommunications, Energy and
Transportation in Europe and Russia
1999. XXII, 570 pp. 63 figs., 63 tabs.,
Hardcover, ISBN 3-540-65859-9

P.J.J. Welfens, J.T. Addison,
D.B. Audretsch, T. Gries, H. Grupp
**Globalization, Economic Growth and
Innovation Dynamics**
1999. X, 160 pp. 15 figs., 15 tabs.,
Hardcover, ISBN 3-540-65858-0

Paul J. J. Welfens · John T. Addison
David B. Audretsch · Thomas Gries
Hariolf Grupp

Globalization, Economic Growth and Innovation Dynamics

With the collaboration of
Stefan Jungblut and Henning Mcycr

With 15 Figures
and 15 Tables

 Springer

Prof. Dr. Paul J. J. Welfens
University of Potsdam
European Institute for
International Economic Relations
August-Bebel-Str. 89
14482 Potsdam
Germany
http://www.euroeiiw.de

Prof. John T. Addison
University of South Carolina
Department of Economics
College of Business Administration
The H. William Close Building
Columbia, SC 29208
USA

Prof. Dr. David B. Audretsch
Indiana University
Institute of Development
Strategies (SPEA)
Suite 201
Bloomington, Indiana 47405
USA
Baudrets@indiana.edu

Prof. Thomas Gries
University of Paderborn
Fachbereich 5, Wirtschaftswissenschaften,
Volkswirtschaftslehre, Internationale
Wachstums- und Konjunkturtheorie
Warburger Str. 100
33095 Paderborn
Germany

Dr. Hariolf Grupp
Fraunhofer Institute for Systems
and Innovation Research (ISI)
Breslauer Str. 48
76139 Karlsruhe
Germany

ISBN 3-540-65858-0 Springer-Verlag Berlin Heidelberg New York

Library of Congress Cataloging-in-Publication Data
Die Deutsche Bibliothek – CIP-Einheitsaufnahme
Globalization, economic growth and innovation dynamics: with 15 tables / Paul J.J. Welfens, John T. Addison, David B. Audretsch, Thomas Gries, Hariolf Grupp (eds). – Berlin; Heidelberg; New York; Barcelona; Hong Kong; London; Milan; Paris; Singapore; Tokyo: Springer, 1999
    ISBN 3-540-65858-0

© Springer-Verlag Berlin · Heidelberg 1999
Printed in Germany

The use of general descriptive names, registered names, trademarks, etc. in this publication does not imply, even in the absence of a specific statement, that such names are exempt from the relevant protective laws and regulations and therefore free for general use.

Hardcover-Design: Erich Kirchner, Heidelberg

SPIN 10724088   43/2202-5 4 3 2 1 0 – Printed on acid-free paper

Preface

Since the 1980s as foreign direct investment has increased strongly, new countries opened up as host countries (or became influential as source countries) and innovative forms of interfirm cooperation have been established. This has lead to more intense global competition. Rising foreign direct investment could stimulate economic growth worldwide to the extent that it contributes to technology spillovers, international technology trade, improved use of know-how and a higher overall investment output ratio plus a higher marginal product of capital worldwide. The spatial distribution of foreign investment flows is in turn influenced by regional or local clusters of R&D centers and the availability of human capital or other factors which can be profitably combined with firm specific advantages important for multinational companies (MNCs). Moreover, public support for R&D and the quality of the education system also play a role for attracting MNCs.

In the 1980s and early 1990s international competition increased notorily in the OECD countries, but also worldwide. On the one hand, newcomers from Asian NICs entered medium and advanced technology fields, on the other hand the US, France and the UK as well as Russia reduced their emphasis on military research and development (R&D) after 1990. Hence, the end of the Cold War led to intensified competition in markets for civilian products. The ratio of civilian R&D to GDP has increased in most countries worldwide and there are prospects for a rapid increase in R&D outlays in some NICs and the PR China at the turn of the century. Moreover, the internet has reinforced access to new technological knowledge.

The observable heterogeneity of the global growth process let to a large body of empirical and theoretical research. One of the main conclusions from the empirical literature is that the hypothesis of absolute convergence formerly predicted by growth economists does not hold, i.e. not all countries do automatically converge to the same steady state position. However, if countries are clustered, further statements can be made. Six "clubs" with similar developments in terms of income levels and average growth can be identified: the industrialised elite, the industrialized catching up countries, the strongly catching up countries, the slowly catching up countries, the slowly falling behind and the strongly falling behind countries. Overall a process of "conditional convergence" can be observed for the first four convergence clubs while countries of the last two clubs tend to diverge. Conditional convergence implies that an economy will converge to a steady state that is characterised by a set of fundamentals specific to the country. Meanwhile a thousands of regressions have been run to identify those fundamentals. The most important ones are the investment rate, the human capital endowment, the R&D intensity and the countries integration into world markets. The empirical results therefore strongly support the hypothesis that only countries with sufficient abilities to innovate or acquire new technologies are able to converge in terms of their productivity levels and income.

EU research is not sufficiently specialized and innovations of EU firms often not in the most dynamic patent classes. Some informal coordination of national R&D policies could be useful in the future and the creation of EU-wide R&D networks could be encouraged. However, - disregarding specific exceptions - the creation of an EU-wide R&D network should not be considered if there is no alternative competing network within Western Europe. EU firms could be encouraged to tap the R&D potential in eastern Europe and Russia where skilled personnel often is available at low costs. At the bottom line it is clear that in the face of globalization EU countries have to improve education, training and R&D efforts in order to maintain a global technological leader status. Low equity-capital ratios of firms in many EU countries raises doubts about the EU´s ability to successfully exploit new innovation fields where provision of risk capital is important for survival and expansion of newcomers - more international benchmarking studies are necessary in the future, and one may recommend regular benchmarking in all major policy fields. Capital market policies are important as an indirect way to stimulate R&D in the community.

The most important economic challenge confronting Europe is to restructure economic activity and move out of industries based on the traditional factors of production and into those industries that are knowledge based. The traditional view about the process of structural change is that the large enterprises are the driving force of such structural change. Large organizations have command over vast R&D resources. However, a compelling body of evidence spanning a broad range of countries suggests that small and new firms play a crucial role in triggering structural change. The reason that small and new firms are a driving force behind structural change is that people start firms to pursue ideas that otherwise would not be pursued by the incumbent firms. New firms serve as agents of change, away from the status quo and towards new activities that are controversial and uncertain.

The greatest challenge for achieving efficient R&D policies in Europe is to reduce the barriers impeding the mobility and commercialization of new knowledge. Europe has not performed well in appropriating the returns from the investments made in new knowledge, both in terms of R&D and human capital. Part of this challenge lies in shifting policies away from targeting outputs and outcomes to targeting knowledge inputs.

In recent years, one important characteristic of labor markets in Anglo-Saxon countries at least has been the pronounced widening in skill differentials. The long-standing shift in favor of skilled labor and away from unskilled labor would appear to have accelerated in the last two decades. The supply of skill has increased less rapidly and unskilled wages have declined relatively (and in the US absolutely). There is little disputation in the US and the UK as to the dominance of the relative demand shifts favoring the higher skilled, though there is more ambiguity in continental Europe given intervals of rising skilled worker unemployment. The controversy instead has to do with the sources of these relative demand shifts.

The two candidates are increased international trade and skill-biased (i.e. unskilled-labor saving) technological change, each of which falls under the rubric of "globalization." In both the US and the UK, decompositions of the aggregate change in, say, nonmanual employment have indicated that within-industry movements dominate between-industry shifts.

The presence of MNCs with distributed R&D facilities is a matter of fact. Globalised R&D is increasing from a low level in most countries. The net outflow of R&D is a concern for some countries but whether it is better to make „national" companies work abroad and participate in foreign national systems or to invite foreign companies to the own territory remains largely open. Technology spillovers and knowledge flows certainly accrue in both cases and the debate of the net R&D flows and their benefits is largely a question of employment within the national territory and also tax revenues from local R&D, production and services.

If not the functional specification but the qualification of the employees serves at a benchmarking criterion for the human-capital intensification, then for major OECD countries one arrives at the following assessment. In the first half of the nineties one has to confirm a trend claimed already earlier that the share of employees with a higher education degree (university, polytechnical or related schools) and the share of academic staff (university degrees only) is increasing in the manufacturing sector and in the service industries. This means that there is tendency to employ relatively more highly qualified persons both in the service sector, which is expanding, and in the manufacturing sector with a loss of jobs.

A series of smaller European countries is strongly oriented towards general universities and other non-oriented research and does spend comparatively little money on oriented research. The Netherlands, Italy, Sweden and Germany also belong to this group with a share of less than 50 per cent dedicated for oriented research. The other EU countries and notably the United Kingdom and France spent relatively little on general basic research and put more emphasis on oriented research (in case of the two last-mentioned countries, for armament also). Thus, we have to conclude, country-specific patterns of spending in basic research persist even within the European Union. Reportedly the United States government with its large share of defense research spends least on general basic research, whereas Japan with a small defense R&D budget resembles the pattern of Germany.

To the extent that a supply side R&D policy prevailed in the European Union we have to emphasis that science-based innovation is important in many cases but not in all. In global innovation, down-stream related processes such as effective national lead-markets and demand stimulation and articulation are also important. In this sense, it is recommended that R&D policy should try to warrant that those lead-markets be in the European Union where strong global players are active in. In so far as by non-R&D measures the rapid and stable development of those markets can be facilitated, R&D policy should join in with other European policies in order to achieve the maximum benefit.

PS: The following study grew out of project No IV/97/03 for the European Parliament. The authors would like to thank Nadine Richter, Ralf Wiegert, Albrecht Kauffmann and Tim Yarling for excellent editorial support.

Potsdam, May 1999   *Paul J.J. Welfens (coordinator)*

TABLE OF CONTENTS

1. GLOBALIZATION OF THE ECONOMY AND INCREASING INTERNATIONAL COMPETITION

1.1 Rising International Trade in a Broader Perspective

Economic globalization is a term referring to the fact that trade, investment and technology links are increasing worldwide as is the number of countries which are open to world markets. In addition to this the liberalization of telecommunications – and the rise of the internet which creates a truly global marketplace – has created new opportunities for the international exchange of information and services. Countries able to establish a technological and commercial lead in advanced telecommunications and computer technology are not only in a favorable position to exploit new opportunities, but they can also shape the global economic order. The USA has a clear lead in these fields, but Euroland also enjoys a strong position (e.g. in mobile telephony), while Japan is facing many problems in the wake of the sustained financial market crisis. Japan´s catching-up process in the 1960s, 1970s and 1980s was impressive when Japanese manufacturing industry captured increasing world market shares. However, with the accelerated growth of the modern service industry and the growth of OECD foreign direct investment, Japan´s weakness in service sector productivity became rather obvious as well as the relatively high barriers against foreign direct investment inflows – much in contrast to Japan´s high FDI outflows. As regards the rising number of countries open to the world market, one must take into account the impact of the economic opening-up of the PR of China in the 1980s which went along with rapid structural change and high growth rates of output and exports. After the collapse of the USSR and the socialist Council of Mutual Economic Assistance the formerly socialist countries of eastern Europe and Russia also opened up to the world economy. While the small Visegrad countries (Hungary, Poland, the Czech Republic, Slovenia, and later also Romania) rather successfully embraced the market economy and economic integration, Russia / the CIS faced massive problems in achieving sustained transformation. For reasons which still are somewhat unclear both massive internal policy pitfalls and inadequate policy advice of the IMF / the World Bank – urging fixed exchange rates in the mid-1990s and early capital account liberalization while neglecting institutional reforms and the role of the rule of law (but insisting on traditional IMF medicine of budget deficit reduction and disinflation) – have undermined sustainable transformation and economic opening-up (http://www.euroeiiw.de).

The rapid growth of foreign direct investment (FDI) together with privatization, sectoral deregulation and the removal of barriers to invest creates for many countries favorable growth prospects as the prospects for higher trade growth and accelerated technology transfer have improved. As about one-third of trade in leading OECD countries is intra-company trade and since international technology transfer dominantly is in the form of intra-company deals or cross-licensing, the ability of a country to become an active host country and source country of FDI is crucial for growth. The top ten FDI source countries of 1996 – according to UNCTAD – were the US with $ 74.8 bill., followed by the UK (34.1), France

(30.4), Germany (29.5), Hong Kong (26.4 !), Japan (23.4), the Netherlands (23.1), Canada (8.5) and Belgium/Luxembourg (8.4). The top ten FDI recipients were the US with $ 76.5 bill., China (40.8), the UK (26.0), France (22.0), Belgium/Luxembourg (14.1), Brazil (11.1), Singapore (9.4), Mexico (8.2), the Netherlands (7.8) and Spain (6.5); relative to GDP and overall investment, FDI inflows played not only a significant role in China, Brazil and Mexico but also in Poland, Hungary and Ireland as well as in Belgium/Luxembourg. It also is noteworthy that Germany was not among the top ten recipients of FDI inflows in the 1990s – a poor record for a country facing high unemployment problems which cannot be overcome without strongly increasing the investment-GDP ratio. The above figures point to very strong FDI asymmetries in the world economy, and countries which are unable to nurture domestic entrepreneurship and stimulate two-way FDI clearly stand to be the economic losers of economic globalization.

Taking into account the catching-up opportunities of poor countries, it is therefore important that they not only achieve sustained economic opening-up of trade which then helps to raise per capita output – stimulating then a shift from inter-industry trade towards more intra-industry trade – but it also is crucial that they accept foreign direct investors and create a domestic policy framework that allows firms to develop owner-specific advantages as a basis for successful investment abroad. Here issues of competition policy, capital market development and political stability play a major role – much neglected in many countries. Moreover, with global competition in markets for products with low (unskilled) labor intensity having intensified so much, there are new questions related to the role of skilled labor, R&D and education policy for economic growth and international integration.

The increasing competition in goods markets has reinforced the role of technology competition and innovation since international Schumpeterian rents in medium-technology products tend to fade away faster than in previous decades. Modern computer technology and the rising role of software – relative to hardware – have contributed to the faster diffusion of new technologies worldwide. This could mean that the return on R&D is falling in some sectors, but the general trend should be upwards in civilian markets if one takes into account the R&D-GDP expenditure ratios in major OECD countries. Above all there are strongly increasing R&D expenditures of European countries in the US – with Switzerland, the UK and Germany clearly leading (France and the Netherlands had slightly more than $ 1 bill. and $ 0.5 bill. in the US in 1994) and each representing some $ 4 bill. in 1995 (BEISE/BELITZ, 1997). US manufacturing firms in turn spent some $ 10 bill. on R&D abroad where 26%, 19%, and 11% went to Germany, the UK and France, respectively; some 8% went to Japan. Such developments raise new questions for innovation policies both from a US perspective and from an EU perspective. The EU which still has to find a consistent and efficient policy assignment with respect to national and supranational R&D expenditures has to adjust to this new global reality. How can national innovation policy be effective if there are considerable international "leakage effects"? Will exporters and multinational companies always benefit from positive growth impulses generated by higher R&D abroad? To which extent can tapping the pool of foreign technologies via subsidiaries abroad help to rejuvenate parent companies´ technology basis at home? How important are the imperfections in the technology markets?

Import penetration and export coverage in the manufacturing industry of OECD countries have been growing continuously during the 1970s and 1980s, with growth accelerating in the 1990s (Tab. 1). The export share in industry has increased in the US and other OECD countries, whose exports partly represent exports by US foreign subsidiaries. It is indeed remarkable that the share of the US in world exports is gradually declining while that of US multinational firms has remained relatively constant. Trade increasingly represents trade in upstream inputs (Tab. 2) and international exchange of differentiated products – reflecting a rise in intra-industry trade (Tab. 3). The rise in trade is, therefore, less conflict prone than in the past, during the era of dominant inter-industry trade where the expansion of some sectors was accompanied by the elimination of sectors in which other countries' firms had a comparative advantage. The high share of imported intermediate inputs in some countries implies that trade in finished products is highly dependent on an open trading system which facilitates the exploitation of specialization gains and economies of scale.

As regards trade, globalization shows clusters of regional trade flows, where the EU dominates in western and eastern Europe, the US in the Americas, and Japan – together with the US and China – dominates in Asia. Until the financial market crisis in 1997, the Asian NICs were characterized by robust growth. But the need to correct overvalued exchange rates and excessive asset prices will impair prospects for high growth in the medium term. As is clearly evident from the Asian crisis, insufficient competition within the banking system and the absence of efficient prudential supervision can cause serious regional instabilities and uncertainties which particularly impair long term investment and innovation.

1.2 The Increasing Role of Foreign Direct Investment

Capital Flows
International portfolio capital flows increased strongly in the 1970s and 1980s (Tab. 4), leaving countries vulnerable to sudden reversals in capital flows and to external interest rate shocks. Foreign investment also rose in the 1980s, with foreign direct investment outflows largely dominated by the US, the UK, Germany, France, the Netherlands, Switzerland, Canada, Italy and Belgium. As regards portfolio investment outflows as well as inflows it is possible to discern a series of regional shifts and, sometimes, sudden changes in response to anticipated devaluations or major policy problems. Foreign direct investment inflows have concentrated on OECD countries and China, and, only recently, on eastern Europe and Russia.

While the growth rate in trade among OECD countries exceeded that in foreign direct investment in the 1970s (18.9% p.a. compared to 15.9% p.a.), the 1980s showed a different pattern. The growth rate in foreign investment reached 16.3% p.a., which was clearly above the 6.2% of OECD trade growth. The growth rate in foreign direct investment is likely to exceed that in trade in the 1990s, since eastern Europe's transforming economies increasingly attract foreign direct investment. While it is true that east-west trade in Europe is growing at high rates,

Tab. 1: Import penetration and export coverage in manufacturing

				Average annual growth	
	1970	1980	1991	1970-80	1980-91
	Imports as a percentage of total domestic demand				
United States[1]	5.1	8.7	14.0	5.5	4.5
Canada[1]	25.3	30.7	35.9	2.0	1.4
Japan	4.0	5.5	6.1	3.2	1.0
Denmark	41.1	43.8	52.5	0.6	1.7
France	15.8	21.3	30.9	3.1	3.4
Germany	13.3	19.6	27.3	3.9	3.0
Italy[1]	15.7	19.9	20.9	2.4	0.4
Netherlands	42.0	53.0	66.4	2.3	2.1
United Kingdom	14.7	22.9	30.2	4.5	2.6
Finland	27.9	27.8	30.3	0.0	0.8
Norway	39.8	38.7	43.2	0.3	1.0
Sweden	29.5	35.9	40.6	2.0	1.1
Australia[1]	16.2	21.6	25.4	2.9	1.5
	Exports as a percentage of production				
United States[1]	5.3	9.2	11.0	5.6	1.6
Canada[1]	26.7	30.2	34.5	1.3	1.2
Japan	8.5	11.9	11.4	3.4	-0.4
Denmark	34.6	41.9	54.4	1.9	2.4
France	16.9	22.6	30.2	2.9	2.7
Germany	18.4	25.0	30.0	3.1	1.7
Italy[1]	18.3	22.1	22.5	1.9	0.2
Netherlands	40.9	55.3	68.3	3.1	1.9
United Kingdom	16.3	23.4	28.0	3.7	1.7
Finland	27.5	32.4	35.4	1.6	0.8
Norway	31.1	30.0	36.0	-0.3	1.7
Sweden	29.6	38.0	45.0	2.5	1.6
Australia[1]	11.4	16.1	13.5	3.5	-1.6

[1] 1990 data used instead of 1991

Source: OECD (1997), Globalisation of Industry, Paris, 24.

Tab. 2: International sourcing compared with domestic sourcing

International Linkage Index[1], mid-1980s

	Canad	France	Germany[2]	United Kingdom	Japan	United States
Motor vehicles	0.92	0.34	0.23	0.39	0.06	0.17
Aerospace	0.40	0.28	0.24	0.50	0.57	0.09
Communications/ semiconductors	0.46	0.20	0.22	0.37	0.08	0.13
Computers	0.68	0.43	0.28	0.42	0.10	0.13
Textils	0.33	0.36	0.35	0.51	0.16	0.11
Petroleum refining	0.22	1.10	0.72	0.35	0.75	0.13

[1]Calculated taking into account both direct and indirect (upstream) inputs.For methodology, see OECD (1993)
[2]Electrical machinery includes communications and semiconductors.
Source: OECD (1997), Globalisation of Industry, 29.

Tab. 3: Intra-industry trade indices, all products[1], OECD-Countries 1970-90

	1970	1980	1990
United Kingdom	53.2	74.4	84.6
France	67.3	70.1	77.2
Austria	60.4	73.2	75.2
Spain	41.7	48.9	74.2
Belgium/Luxembourg	61.4	67.5	72.8
Germany	55.8	56.6	72.2
United States	44.4	46-5	71.8
Netherlands	63.4	60.5	69.8
Sweden	52.3	58.2	64.2
Denmark	55.0	54.8	62.2
Switzerland	52.5	59.8	60.2
Canada	52.1	51.5	60.0
Italy	48.7	54.8	57.4
Ireland	48.2	55.1	56.9
Greece	32.4	28.3	50.5
Portugal	39.8	39.5	49.2
Finland	29.4	37.8	45.7
Norway	52.3	42.5	41.9
Turkey	6.7	12.5	34.6
Japan	21.4	17.1	32.4
Australia	20.7	21.6	30.5
New Zealand	10.6	16.3	25.9

[1]Grubel-Lloyd indices calculated on SITC Rev. 2 3-digit level, adjusted for overall trade imbalances.
Source: OECD (1997), Globalisation of industry, Paris, 30.

one cannot overlook that within eastern Europe trade diversion or only modest trade creation is occurring, so that overall trade growth rates for eastern Europe could indeed fall short of those in foreign investment flows. Given the high growth in global FDI flows, roughly amounting to $ 300 bill. p.a. in the late 1990s, one may expect a fast increase in the stock of FDI, which reached some $ 2700 bill. in the mid-1990s (UNCTAD, 1996).

Foreign investment by multinational companies represented in the late 1980s an investment output ratio of about 1% (Tab. 4), which is more than 1/10 of all investment in machinery and equipment in OECD countries. Compared to the 1970s this meant a doubling in the MNC's share of gross fixed capital formation (OECD, 1996) Moreover, multinational companies are among the top users of advanced software, which represents non-physical investment from an economic perspective. As regards productivity growth expenditures on software – together with purchases of computer equipment – are quite important for economic growth.

Tab. 4: International portfolio investment[1]

	1980	1985	1990	1991	1992	1993	1994	1995
	as a percentage of GDP							
United States	9,0	35,1	89,0	95,6	106,6	128,8	131,1	135,5
Japan	7,7	63,0	120,0	91,9	71,8	77,8	60,0	65,7
Germany	7,5	33,4	57,3	55,6	85,2	170,8	159,3	168,3
France	–	21,4	53,6	78,7	121,8	186,8	201,4	178,2
Italy	1,1	4,0	26,6	60,3	92,1	191,9	206,8	250,9
Canada	9,6	26,7	64,4	81,3	113,2	152,9	209,7	192,0

[1] Gross purchases and sales of securities between residents and non-residents.
Source: BIS (1996), 66th Annual Report, Basle, 122.

MNCs will benefit from falling international telecommunication costs, which are expected as a result of early liberalization in the UK and the Scandinavian countries as well as due to the general post-1998 liberalization in EU member countries (WELFENS/GRAACK, 1996; GRAACK, 1997). The international dissemination of technological know-how will be facilitated and accelerate innovation cycles. Rising foreign direct investment in combination with cheaper advanced telecommunication networks will intensify the global techno-logy race and intensify locational competition among EU countries. Few observers consider the rapid rise in global FDI as only a minor problem for leading EU countries (HÄRTEL et al., 1996).

Foreign direct investment inflows only occur if attractive locational conditions (in economic terms) and political stability exist in host countries.

Under such circumstances, FDI inflows can make an important contribution to the restructuring of the economy, structural change and employment growth (WEL-FENS/JASINSKI, 1994). As regions of high medium term growth, Eastern Europe and Asia can be expected to attract high FDI at the turn of the century, while the US and the EU will continue to be the main source and host countries of foreign investment. Japan still is mainly a source for foreign investment. But the need to overcome slow growth might require Japan to reconsider its policy stance vis-à-vis foreign investors, who sometimes complain about an unreceptive host country environment. Indeed, in the era of globalization of the economy – with a higher technological specialization of countries – it can be to the disadvantage of a country if it cannot attract sufficient foreign investment inflows from a diversified source basis.

From a source country perspective it is important that firms have ownership specific advantages, which are mainly rooted in advanced technology, and that the firms' internal international exchange of services is superior to arms-length transactions via the market which is associated with higher transaction costs. The case of telecoms operators provides an example of a sector in which high technological dynamics are observed and where ownership specific advantages are naturally important. Moreover, the recent wave of privatizations in western Europe has removed the political restrictions on EU telecoms operators' ability to invest abroad. Furthermore, the rapid emergence of international alliances in telecoms operation is leading to a high degree of international oligopolistic interdependence and in turn is stimulating waves of foreign direct investment outflows (KLEIN/WELFENS, 1992; WELFENS/WOLF, 1997). New forms of international cooperation which do not involve full foreign ownership are particularly interesting in this context. Subcontracting and joint R&D projects are among the important developments, which will affect growth and employment (ADDISON/WELFENS, 1998).

The enormous importance of MNCs for economic development is due to the firms' large size and high technology intensities – except in some sectors (e.g. food industry, furniture, agriculture). Furthermore, international trade in the case of leading OECD countries consists largely of intra-industry trade – roughly up to 1/3. In the period 1983-92, 43 % of EU-US trade was intra-company trade (OECD, 1996, p. 30). For all these reasons MNCs are crucial for economic growth. Moreover, MNCs have extended networks of supplier firms which depend on the survival and expansion of MNCs. This is not to deny the important role of small and medium-size enterprises which dominate employment in all EU countries. As regards R&D policies the international presence of MNCs allows such companies to critically compare alternative policy approaches and to shift investment and innovation projects to those countries which are receptive to the requirements of technology-intensive firms. Comparing alternative locations will become even more important after the introduction of the Euro since this will create unprecedented transparency with respect to costs and prices in Europe. The marginal investment decisions of MNCs will certainly be influenced by economic policies in alternative location countries. This could lead to some problems for the smaller innovative firms in Europe insofar as the rising pressure from large companies might bring about a decline in the share of public R&D funds allocated to small and medium-sized firms.

1.3 Global Telecoms Networks and New Communication Technologies

Rising trade in goods and services as well as intensified foreign direct investment imply that the global innovation race is intensifying in the economic field. Product innovations typically are relatively expensive and first introduced in high income countries where only a minority of affluent households often will be the pioneer users. Such households are trendsetters for innovative products which gradually will be adopted by broader strata of society. However, as the production process becomes more standardized and logistical demand patterns bring about a wider use of the product innovation in leading OECD countries, prices start falling. The novel product is exported to countries with medium per capital income, and often production is also relocated towards such countries in later stages of the innovation cycle when the home market increasingly will be served by imports from abroad. This pattern of the product cycle trade is likely to intensify as modern telecommunication technologies and improved education and training in NICs facilitate the worldwide relocation of production.

      With privatization and deregulation of telecommunications in the EU – the starting date for the latter being 1998 for voice telephony and network operation – and the further liberalization of telecommunications in the US and Japan in 1997 there are favorable prospects for the telecoms sector to quickly become a global industry with high technological dynamics. System integration in combination with internationalization on the one hand, incorporating latest computer technology on the other hand are the main challenges here. Multinational companies have offered „one-stop shopping solutions" by large international telecom operators or consortia and increasingly use the telecom network to learn about market and technology developments worldwide (WELFENS/GRAACK, 1996; WELFENS/YARROW, 1997; GRAACK, 1997).

      The main global alliances are Global One (headquarters in Brussels) which consists of Deutsche Telekom, France Telecom, and Sprint of the US; Concert, which is composed of BT, MCI of the US and Telefónica (plus the dominant Portuguese operator); and WorldPartners, whose stakeholders are AT&T (40%), the Japanese KDD (24%), Singapore Telecom (16%), and Unisource NV (20%). Unisource NV in turn represents Swiss Telecom, the Dutch KPN and the Swedish Telia. It seems that alliances are not very stable. Cable & Wireless Communications (formed in 1996 by the merger of MCI and three cable TV companies) and NTT constitute two major companies that are still non aligned, and there are new firms ready to challenge established alliances, such as Equant and WorldCom from the US WorldCom launched a successful bid to acquire MCI which had already been envisaged for full takeover by BT having a 20% stake in the US company. The development of Concert thus is uncertain but there is little doubt that besides niche players in the telecommunication market large multinational companies with a global strategy will dominate international markets.

Competition in telephony is developing worldwide via alliances and foreign investment. Foreign investors take advantage of liberalization and privatization. Restrictions in technology trade have been lifted after the end of the Cold War and higher investment in telecommunications is undertaken in eastern Europe as well as in NICs and LDCs. This will lead to improved international communication opportunities for firms from low income countries, which will also have easier access to foreign know-how and knowledge – mainly via internet and new virtual partners. Privatization introduces pressure from capital markets and hence stimulates competition. Market entry by newcomers has a similar effect. In a more internationalized and competitive environment telecom operators have a strong incentive to increase R&D and become more active in patenting.

The telecoms network is a crucial part of the overall infrastructure and a powerful basis for linking firms and households in a way that allows fast communication and data transmission. Telework and telelearning are interesting options for increasing flexibility and productivity in the information society. Indeed, empirical evidence shows that telecommunications currently account for a considerable part of economic growth in Germany (JUNGMITTAG/WELFENS, 1996).

While traditional telephone networks establish a dedicated connection between the two parties of a telephone conversation, the internet uses flexible routing for digitalized packages of communication data (voice gateways and service providers which use leased-line capacities are required for internet telephony.). The US newcomer Global Link will offer internet-based telephony already in 1997, Sweden's Telia will follow after 2000, and many dominant operators are likely to follow suit as the quality of transmission improves and internet telephony becomes cheaper.

International alliances mainly offer their service to multinational companies that require one-stop billing and a seamless network. It is even conceivable that global virtual networks will emerge where the operator does not own a network but combines leased-line capacities worldwide in order to provide services for major customers. The global telecoms market reached about $ 700 billion in 1996 and could reach almost $ 1,000 billion by the turn of the century. Since about 90% of global revenues still come from national telephony, one may anticipate that even global alliances will have to establish a firm foothold in national markets and their corresponding customer bases. Eastern Europe's markets will become fully open for foreign investors only after 2002.

With domestic markets becoming open to foreign investors, the typical west European national operator is reacting to the coming inroads of foreign network operators by entering foreign markets itself. The mutual invasion of markets in western Europe will reinforce competition across European countries; it is likely to bring down the prices charged by traditional network operators as they become more efficient and innovative technologies are introduced ever more rapidly under the pressure of competition and foreign investors. If the intensity of competition in EU countries were to rise while that in eastern Europe were to stagnate, there would be poor prospects for economic convergence in the whole of Europe.

1.4 Russia and China as New Players

Russia
With systemic transformation and economic opening up in the former USSR, Russia is a new player in the global market of civilian R&D. Before 1991 The former Soviet Union had about 4500 R&D institutes, of which some 550 belonged to the Academy of Sciences and focused mainly on basic R&D and military innovation projects. The other R&D institutes were primarily branch institutes under the supervison of the respective ministry and conducted applied research. About 1100 of the branch institutes were privatized in the course of systemic transformation but often find it difficult to survive on their own in the new market environment characterized by very slow economic growth. The Russian federal government has designated 60 top state research centers which can expect solid government support, and it has earmarked 41 priority objectives for R&D, including high-energy physics, fusion power, high-temperature superconductivity, genetics, bioengineering, space exploration, environmental friendly power generation and industrial processes, and technologies, machines and „industries for the future". Government financed R&D fell from 1.9% of GDP to roughly 0.6% in 1995 and increased slightly in 1996. It is expected to reach the US figure of about 0.8 by the end of the century. While there is no doubt that Russia has a pool of excellent scientists, few institutional adjustments have occurred which would allow high-quality research to be translated into process innovations and profitable novel products for domestic and international markets. In Russia foreign firms employ researchers and programmers as subcontractors, but Russia still has to become a normal partner for foreign investors. This can be achieved only if Russia is characterized by macroeconomic stability, institutional adjustment, political stability and the rule of law – which is a formidable list of requirements. It is in the EU's interest to support the transformation process in Russia.

China

The PR China has decided to strongly increase R&D in the future and has, therefore, adopted a series of modernization measures (IWD, 1997, No.3). Government declared that it intends to catch up with leading western countries by the year 2010, namely in fields such as telecommunications and information technology, biotechnology, space flight and research on energy and new materials. From a ratio of R&D expenditures to GDP of 0.5% in 1995 the ratio is to reach 1.5% in 2000. This is still half a percentage point lower than the EU average in the mid-1990s. In 1993 China employed about 2.4 million people as scientists and researchers. Among these were 1.5 million engineers and scientists. On a full-time basis the number of people working in research and development amounted to 650 000, about 1/3 above the figure for Germany.

The PR China has launched a national program for high technology research and development. Some 13000 researchers will be involved in this program which represents some $ 1.8 bill. With the help of the „Torch Program" government intends to accelerate the diffusion process and has therefore decided to support about 12000 high technology firms which have about 800 000 employees. R&D expenditures increased by 50% in real terms in the period 1988-93 and reached some $ 17 bill. in 1993. Between 1986 and 1993 the share of high-technology products in China's exports increased sixfold and reached about $ 5 bill. China recorded 12 000 patents by domestic residents in 1993 which was double the figure of 1990. With ongoing structural change – people leaving the agricultural sector in order to move to industry or the service sector – there exist favorable prospects for a long term acceleration in Chinese rate of innovation. There are, however, three problems: (i) the federal budget faces serious problems with respect to funding; (ii) provincial authorities often follow a rather independent innovation policy so that it is difficult to achieve a coherent overall approach; (iii) the PR China suffers from an aging problem among its researchers and scientists and therefore has to broaden and rejuvenate its R&D personnel. China certainly will try to exploit its new location, Hong Kong, to convince expatriate Chinese researchers to return home – a difficult task in the presence of a natural brain drain on the one hand, and, on the other hand continuous political uncertainties and near-absence of the rule of law and respect for human rights in China.

While it will take time for R&D in Russia and China to develop a successful outward orientation there is little doubt that both countries could become serious contenders in medium technology and high technology in the long run. It is up to EU firms to use the new opportunities for cooperation and subcontracting. National governments as well as the EU Commission could stimulate the international exchange of researchers. It is clear that support for China's and Russia's research system could have a solid commercial pay-off in the long term since technology partners often also become commercial partners.

1.5 Increasing High Technology Competition and Rising Role of Trade and FDI

With improved international dissemination and increasing civilian R&D-GDP ratios worldwide technologically leading high-income countries will face pressure to move up the technology ladder, i.e. concentrate more on leading-edge and high technologies and accept that poorer countries specialize more in low and medium technologies. Multinational companies in EU countries thus will relocate specially labor intensive or weakly technology intensive production to eastern Europe, Asia, Latin America or Africa. At the same time firms from EU countries will try to control and reduce R&D costs by undertaking foreign investment in technologically leading partner countries – mainly the US, Switzerland, Israel, Norway, Australia and Japan (in the long run also in Russia).

For technologically leading countries increasing high technology competition will mean that investment in human capital building and software needs to increase at the expense of investment in machinery and equipment. At the same time innovative firms from high technology countries will face specific risks in the sense that higher R&D (plus software) investment means relatively increasing sunk costs. With shortening innovation cycles and intensifying import competition there are higher investment risks than before. Firms in EU countries will react at the aggregate level with reduced levels of investment – broadly defined – relative to GDP unless other elements of uncertainty relevant for investment are reduced. With European monetary union the exchange rate risk for firms with strong market orientation towards Europe will indeed decline. Using future markets in a better way and with prudent demand management policies – basically with a long term focus (not short-term Keynesian strategy) – demand uncertainty might also be reduced at the sectoral level which should stimulate investment.

To the extent that increasing national and international technology dynamics imply the creation of novel technology fields or reduced sunk costs – as in the service sector – one may anticipate improved opportunities for new firms and newcomers from other sectors. Such newcomers are the more likely to emerge, the more high-quality innovations can be launched by integrating different innovation fields which traditionally were separated. Such newcomers also face better prospects if government standards, consumer preferences and relative price developments strongly favor expansion of so far underrepresented sectors. For example in the automotive industry computer and electronics have gained strongly in importance – measured in terms of the share in overall value-added – so that newcomers from these sectors might one day dominate at least some niches in the automobile market. If electrical engines could gain market shares, firms in the traditional automative sector might indeed become dominated by powerful firms in the electrical engineering sector, and other firms in the automotive industry would have to accept new firms of equal cooperation with innovative electronics firms which in turn would try to retain a larger share of Schumpeterian rents from intermediate products.

International R&D collaboration among OECD countries could become more important in the future as high technology competition will not only raise the share of high technology exports but push countries to increasingly rely on imported high tech equipment and the use of international research networks. With sustaining globalization the international geography of R&D spillovers is also crucial. AUDRETSCH/FELDMAN (1994) argued that industries with knowledge spillovers, „that is where industry R&D, university research and skilled labor are the most important, tend to have a greater propensity for innovative activity to cluster than those in industries where knowledge externalities are less important" so that spatially-mediated knowledge spillovers are important. According to this proximity hypothesis successful innovation in certain fields not only requires that firms are attracted to a given location but also that universities (and competition among universities) and research centers together with a pool of skilled labor are in place.

Globalization clearly is not only related to higher FDI but also to rising international trade. COE/HELPMAN (1993) provided evidence in favor of a trade-mediated hypothesis. Their econometric analysis for 22 OECD countries during 1971-90 showed that a country's total factor productivity is influenced by import-weighted sums of the trade partners' cumulative R&D spending levels as well as by its own „R&D capital stock". These spillovers are rather involuntary and their importance on a global scale should increase with more and more countries opening up to the world economy: Regional economic catching-up of poorer countries thus should be accelerating, and the rising and high growth rates of Latin American countries and Asian NICs indeed seems to support this hypothesis.

There is also evidence on voluntary R&D spillovers in a multilateral setting (LICHTENBERG, 1995), namely that the EC's Eureka program has created significant positive spillovers. The analysis is consistent with the hypothesis of localization of R&D collaboration at the country level. The country analysis estimates are consistent with some patterns of crossnational patenting – this already was noted by SCHOTT (1994) who argued that new technology increasingly is created by collaboration among inventors. The share of US patents that were „coinventions" – with patents issued jointly to several inventors – increased from 40.7% in 1975 to 52.5% in 1991. The analysis of LICHTENBERG showed also that the optimal firm size necessary for commercialization exceeds that necessary for applied research and development. Taking into account globalization this could imply that the optimum firm size for commercialization has increased. Hence, one should expect a wave of national and international mergers and acquisitions.

International trade and international M&As are becoming more significant for optimal innovation and diffusion, so that the role of international organizations responsible for smooth trade and international investment relations is increasing in importance. Moreover, given the rising global integration of financial markets and national economies, there is a rising negative externally risk associated with imprudent national economic policies (e.g. exchange rate policies, banking supervision). Multilateral surveillance thus should be strengthened and at least the range of economic indicators published by international organizations – data to be provided in due time by member countries – should be widened.

One might also have to consider options to improve the functioning of international organizations. Their decisions should be transparent – i.e. be mainly guided by rules and clear policy principles – and efficient (based on a cost-benefit analysis), consistent and speedy. The latter is necessary especially for crisis management. Since international organizations should be active only where one is facing the problem of providing an international public good – which could apply to several countries or, as an extreme, to all countries (e.g. global warming problem), it might be useful to have regional and global organizations. Applying the principle of subsidiarity would require that regional international organizations tackle problems first, except where global externally problems are an issue. It also is clear that the governance of international organizations is often a problem, given the diversity of member countries and the manifold conflicting interests. International leadership is therefore useful. The US assumes this role in many international organizations, although in 1997 the reluctance of Congress to grant fast-track authority for trade negotiations to president Clinton indicates that even the US faces some problems in leadership. The EU could also assume leadership in some fields, but as long as many EU countries face high unemployment rates, especially high long term unemployment rates, the looming internal political conflicts erode the EU's potential for international leadership. To the extent that successful high technology and growth policies of EU countries contribute to full employment in western Europe the EU could become a more active and credible partner in international leadership. Such leadership is at a premium in the world economy, since Japan and Russia have serious problems and hence Asia and eastern Europe could face negative external economic or political spillovers. EU investment in the improved international R&D cooperation might thus result in a double dividend: It could raise growth in the EU and help to stabilize the international system.

1.5.1 Multinational Companies: Regional Concentration and Issues of Innovation

The 1980s were characterized mainly by rising foreign direct investment within OECD countries (STEHN 1992; JUNGMITTAG 1997). The supply in US and many EU markets is based on local production. As regards US firms there is a tendency to serve world markets increasingly via exports of foreign subsidiaries and to rely less on exports of the parent company: The ratio of subsidiaries' exports to overall company exports increased from 37.5% in 1966 to 56.4% in 1991 (MCGUIRE 1995, p.128). While US and Japanese MNCs pursued an international diversification strategy in the choice of the location of subsidiaries, British, French and German firms reinforced geographical concentration, namely on Europe (Tab. 5). What holds for FDI outflows also holds for FDI inflows. It

Tab. 5: Trade and investment in the OECD area

	Annual growth rates of					Percentages of OECD GDP		
	Inter-national investment flows[1]	Trade[2]	GDP	GFCF		Inter-national direct investment flows	Trade	GFCF
1970-80	15.9	18.9	13.8	14.1	1970	0.5	13.0	22.1
1980-89	16.3	6.2	7.2	6.8	1980	0.6	20.0	22.8
1989-90	-2.6	16.6	11.9	10.6	1990	1.2	18.9	21.8
1990-91	-21.7	1.9	5.3	1.8	1991	0.9	18.3	21.1
1991-92	-8.3	7.2	6.8	4.0	1992	0.8	18.4	20.5
1992-93	7.2	-3.6	0.7	-0.5	1993	0.8	17.6	20.3

[1]Average of OECD inflows and outflows.
[2]Average of imports and exports.

Source: OECD (1997), Globalisation of Industry, Paris, 22.

Tab. 6: Intra-regional international investment: 5 largest home and host countries

Percentages of total investment stock at year-end

	1982		1991	1993	
Outward investment to region as share of total outward investment stock					
United States to North America	20.9		15.1	12.8	
Japan to Asia	26.7		15.0	15.5	
United Kingdom[1] to Europe	19.5	(EC 15.8)	30.0	35.0	(EC 32.0)
France[2] to Europe	58.4	(EC 46.4)	65.0	61.3	(EC 55.0)
Germany[1] to Europe	40.7	(EC 32.4)	60.6	57.1	(EC 48.0)
Inward investment from region as share of total inward investment stock					
United States from North America	9.4		8.7	8.9	
United Kingdom[1] to Europe	37.3	(EC 29.7)	40.5	39.6	(EC 31.1)
France[3] from Europe	n.a.		72.3	72.93	(EC 58.8)
Canada from North America	74.8		64.1	64.7	
Germany[1] from Europe	48.8	(EC 30.5)	58.7	61.1	(EC 41.7)

Note: Regions are: North America = United States + Canada;
Europe = OECD Europe; EC = EC(12),
Asia = DAEs + Indonesia, Phillipines, China.
[1]1984 data.   [2]1987.   [3]1992.

Source: OECD (1997), Globalisation of Industry, Paris, 34

remains to be seen whether EU intraregional FDI concentration is a temporary or a more long term phenomenon.

As regards individual industries one may note that international relocation of production and other company activities is rather easy except for a few exceptions in immobile „Schumpeter industries" (KLODT et al. 1994). As Schumpeter industries one may dub those with a high technology intensity. They are mobile in technological terms if R&D and production can be uncoupled in space. By contrast, immobile Schumpeter industries require the continuous cooperation of R&D and production – such as in the aerospace industry – which implies very limited options for dislocating production activities to low income (and low wage) countries. This holds as long as one can assume that top research capacities are only available in high income countries. The obvious exception is Russia but foreign direct investment in this country markedly increased only in 1997. Foreign investors complain about legal uncertainty, weak patent protection and the absence of Russia in the European Patent Agency.

The share of foreign enterprises in manufacturing production and employment has increased in the 1980s (Tab. 6) where Canada and Ireland reached top figures of about 50 and 40%, respectively, in 1988. France, the UK and Italy recorded figures of around 20%, Germany a much lower figure of around 10% in the late 1980s; worse, the share of foreign enterprises in terms of production and employment declined in the 1980s. This is remarkable during a period in which worldwide FDI strongly increased. One may notice, however, that FDI growth worldwide was particularly strong in services and in the provision of infrastructure where governments in Europe, Asia and Latin America adopted strategies of liberalization and partial or full privatization in the 1980s.

Research also became more internationalized in the 1980s (Tab. 7). Compared to the UK, Germany and France could still strongly raise the share in patents of domestic companies, where the invention took place abroad. This could imply losing well-paid jobs in Europe, probably in favor of the US whose efficient and diversified university system is quite attractive to EU firms seeking R&D inputs from abroad. This option is all the more interesting because the US offers a link to a growing dynamic home market. Oligopolistic interdependency could stimulate many EU companies to follow sooner or later the example of industry leaders which established expanding R&D activities in the US early on. The high share of foreign companies contributing to patents in the host countries Germany and France – probably also Italy – could still strongly increase the international division of technology development. This would require that major EU countries become more attractive for technology oriented MNCs from abroad.

Given the bank dominated financial markets on the continent (Tab. 7, Tab. 8) one may doubt whether there are large unexploited opportunities for foreign investors to acquire firms. The British system which is based on stock markets and opportunities for hostile takeovers is more receptive to foreign investors and also more flexible in adjusting the industrial and services landscape

Tab. 7: Indicators of internationalization, selected countries

1993 in percent

Indicators	Ger-many	USA	Japan	France	United Kingdom	Canada
	activities abroad					
Share of exports in gross value added of production (export dependence)	29,9	12,3	11,6	30,2	29,7	44,8
Number of foreign employees relative to domestic employees	23,5	2,4	8,1	32,5	..	..
Direct investment[1] abroad relative to exports	26,2	51,7	32,6	30,9[2]	59,0	34,1
R&D expenditures of companies relative to domestic R&D expenditures	5,0	10,0	2,0	..	.	..
Share of patents of domestic companies where the invention took place abroad	14,9	7,8	1,0	14,3	42,1	33,0
	domestic activities					
Share of imports in domestic demand[3]	25,4	15,9	5,7	28,8	33,7	46,2
Number of employees in foreign owned companies relative	15,9	11,6	1,1	23,9	16,2[4]	48,0
Foreign direct investment[1] relative to imports	19,5	32,2	10,3	20,9	31,7	48,4
Share of R&D expenditures by foreign owned companies in total domestic R&D expenditures	15,8	14,9	8,2	15,2	25,8	40,8
Share of patents of foreign companies where the invention took place at home	17,0	..	..	18,0	41,0	..

[1] stock at the end of the year
[2] direct investment stock in 1992
[3] imports as a share of gross value added in production minus exports plus imports (in percent)
[4] 1990

Source: DIW (1996), DIW Wochenbericht 16/1996, 263

Tab. 8: Share of foreign enterprises in manufacturing production and employment

Percentages

	Production		Employment	
	1980	1991	1980	1991
United States[2]	3.9	14.8 (1992)	5.1	12.3 (1992)
Canada	50.6	49.0 (1989)	37.8	38.0 (1989)
Japan	4.6	2.8 (1990)	1.6	1.2 (1990)
Denmark	-	14.2 (1986)	-	12.4 (1986)
France[2]	26.6	26.9	18.5	22.1
Germany	15.7	13.8 (1992)	9.0	7.2 (1992)
Ireland	46.1 (1983)	55.1 (1988)	37.9 (1983)	44.2 (1988)
Italy	19.2	22.3 (1988)	15.8	17.2 (1988)
Portugal	23.6 (1984)	-	17.7 (1984)	-
United Kingdom	19.3 (1981)	25.5	14.9 (1981)	17.2
Finland	2.5	6.7 (1992)	3.1	6.2 (1992)
Austria		25.7		15.6
Norway[2]	11.5	10.5 (1990)	6.5	7.7 (1990)
Sweden	7.9	18.0 (1992)	6.1	16.9 (1992)
Australia[2]	33.5 (1982)	32.0 (1986)	26.3 (1982)	23.8 (1986)
Turkey	6.2 (1986)	5.9 (1991)	2.3 (1986)	4.4

- Includes minority holdings (equity holdings > 10 or >20 per cent up to 50 per cent) for countries indicated. Percentages are calculated as a share of production from the annual census of production in most cases. This may overstate the share of foreign firms, if small firms (<20 employees) are excluded from the annual census, as small firms are predominantly domestic.
- Includes joint ventures and minority participation (<50%). Values for France are unweighted by share of minority ownership.

Source: OECD (1997), Globalisation of Industry, Paris, 30

in response to changing international conditions. This could be a major advantage for the UK (and the US) in the era of globalization – with intensified pressure for structural change – and should encourage other EU countries to study the virtues of expanding the role of stock markets. For technology-oriented firms access to stock markets is vital and the expected global high technology race favors countries where firms can build up a sound equity capital base (WELFENS, 1997).

1.5.2 Competition, Skill Requirements and Labor Markets in the US

This section addresses the growth in skill differentials at a time when there has been a growth in the share of the skilled workforce, or, equivalently, the phenomenon of (somewhat) increased unskilled worker unemployment at a time of falling relative wages of unskilled workers. This particular concatenation of events is not confined to the US (as we shall see, the UK experience is rather similar) but clearly does not apply for major continental European countries (e.g. Germany).

The increase in the premium for skilled workers at a time when the share of the workforce with higher qualifications has increased is not really controversial, but it is *prima facie* consistent with two different demand-side forces: industrial change on the one hand and technological change on the other. And this is where the controversy resides. Industrial/sectoral change would include such factors as heightened international trade and the growth of the service economy, while biased technological change reflects pervasive skill upgrading across all sectors resulting from an increase in skill complementarities and/or an increase in technological change.

Much US research work has been devoted to establishing which influence – sectoral (or between-industry) demand shifts on the one hand or within-industry movements on the other – is the more important source of the increased demand for skilled labor. (See the surveys by LEVY and MURNANE, 1992; BURTLESS, 1994; RICHARDSON, 1995.) The standard approach has been to decompose the aggregate change in the structure of employment as follows:

$$\Delta E = \sum_{i=1}^{N} \Delta S_i \overline{E_i} + \sum_{i=1}^{N} \Delta E_i \overline{S_i}, \qquad (1)$$

where ΔE is the aggregate change in employment share; $E_i = X_i /L_i$ is the share of group X in industry i employment; $S_i = L_i /L$ is the share of industry i in total employment; and where the bar operator signifies a mean over time. The first term on the right hand side gives that part of the change in aggregate employment that is attributable to between-industry shifts in employment among branches with different skill intensities, while the second term identifies the contribution of within-industry shifts.

Table A1 provides estimates of the two component magnitudes using data for both US and UK manufacturing. The US study by BERMAN et al. (1994) covers no less than 450 four-digit industries, while MACHIN's (1996) British study is for a smaller sample of 100 three-digit industries. In both cases, the "dependent variable" is the change in the employment and wage shares of nonproduction labor.[1]

On the basis of the table, it appears for the US that there has been a long-term shift away from production labor. Thus, using the employment share measure, the shift toward nonproduction labor was at the rate of 0.069 percentage points per year in the earliest period, increasing to 0.299 points per year in the intermediate interval and to no less than 0.552 points per year in the most recent period. As can be seen, similar results are obtained when using the wage share.

As for the decompositions proper, both studies indicate that the within-industry movements dominate the between-industry changes. This is particularly obvious in the British case: the percentage contribution of the within-industry component to the total change is 82.0 percent for the employment share and 82.9 percent for the wage share. For the US, the corresponding values for 1979-87 are

70.1 and 60.5 percent, respectively. Moreover in the US case there are clear signs that the within-industry component accounts for the bulk of the acceleration in the share of nonproduction worker employment between the 1970s and the 1980s.

On this evidence at least, the suggestion is one of pervasive skills upgrading rather than sectoral shifts that might be associated with international trade or deindustrialization. Further historical perspective is added in a recent study by JUHN and MURPHY (1994) who construct demand indices for a wider range of skill groups. The indices measure the percentage change in the demand for a particular skill group (the five quintiles of the wage distribution) as a weighted average of percentage changes in employment shares of different industries and occupations, where the weights conform to the group's initial employment distribution across these industry and occupational categories. (Note that the indices are adjusted for relative wage changes, without which there would be understatement of demand shifts in groups with rising relative wages.)

It is shown that the relative demand for workers in the highest quintile of the wage distribution grew faster than the demand for the bottom quintile in the 1940s and to a greater extent than in either the 1970s or the 1980s. In short, there is nothing new about demand shifts in favor of skilled workers. What is new, however, is the changed relation of the between-industry and within-industry components. In particular, during the 1980s the within-industry component accounted for the entire (11) percentage point differential in demand growth between the highest and lowest quintile workers. In the 1940s, by contrast, the within-industry component accounted for just 6 of the 15 percentage point change in relative demand for skill. That is to say, the within-industry component has accelerated in the 1980s. JUHN and MURPHY (1994, 358) conclude that "factors such as changes in product demand and international trade had only minor influence during the 1980s." Instead, the facts are consistent with labor-saving (i.e. biased) technological change.

Tab. 9 presents some beginning- and end-period summary statistics from the above study. The table also reveals that there has been some hollowing out of the income distribution; that is, there has been a decline in the demand for those in the middle quintile. This is another stylized fact of the US income distribution. More importantly, however, the authors infer from these facts that there has been "a growth in the demand for the type of skills that are more inelastically supplied in the economy" (JUHN and MURPHY, 1994, 357).

JUHN and MURPHY also briefly examine changes in the relative supply of skill over their sample period, concluding that such changes cannot account for differences in the growth of wage inequality; for example, the growth in the relative supply of skill was slowest of all in the 1940s. But a more compelling analysis of the supply side is offered by BLACKBURN et al. (1990) who seek to explain the deteriorating position of high school dropouts and high school graduates using a conventional demand and supply framework. On the demand-side, a shift-share analysis of the change in average wages received by less skilled workers is used (supplemented by a logarithmic earnings regression model with year dummies). This reveals that between 70 and 80 percent of the increase in the earnings gap between high school dropouts/graduates and college graduates over 1979-87 occurred within industries, again underscoring the relative unimportance of changes in the allocation of labor across industries.

Tab. 9: Changes in Relative Demand[1] for Men by Wage Percentile, U.S. Nonagricultural Sector

	Interval	
Percentile	1939-49	1979-89
Total employment shift		
1-20	-.07	-.08
21-40	-.00	-.08
41-60	.04	-.09
61-80	.07	-.07
81-100	.08	.03
Employment shifts across industries only		
1-20	-.03	-.03
21-40	.01	-.04
41-60	.03	-.06
61-80	.05	-.07
81-100	.06	-.04
Employment shifts across occupations only		
1-20	-.04	-.05
21-40	-.02	-.04
41-60	.00	-.02
61-80	.02	.00
81-100	.02	.07

[1]see text for definition of relative demand construct
Source: Juhn and Murphy (1994), Table 10.4, p. 356

The authors next attempt to ascertain the contribution of supply-side factors as well as institutional factors (specifically, minimum wages and declining unionization) to these within-industry shifts. The supply side analysis focuses on shifts in the relative supply of workers with different educational qualifications. BLACKBURN et al. first examine the increase in the differential between college trained and high school dropouts/graduates between 1979 and 1987, assuming there were no shifts in relative demand. Despite the growth in the proportion of college graduates in the workforce, the ratio of college educated among those aged 25 and 34 actually declined after 1979. The suggestion is then that part of the increase in the observed differential(s) after 1979 could be due to this falling supply of young college graduates. And it is found that the decline could explain up to 30 percent of the growing differential of college educated younger workers. In other words, this amount of the differential potentially attributable to shifts in relative demand is in fact due to a supply shift.

Next, assuming that the rate of increase in relative demand was the same in the 1980s as in the 1970s (when the differential was fairly stable despite a sizable growth in the college educated population), the authors estimate how the slowed growth in the relative supply of college educated workers in the 1980s contributed to the change in differentials between the periods 1979-87 and 1973-79. It is reported that the deceleration in the growth of college educated manpower can explain much but by no means all of the increase in the growth of the wage gap. In other words, the suggestion is that shifts in relative demand in favor of the college educated accelerated in the 1980s.

Lastly, BLACKBURN et al. report that although the effect of (declining) minimum wages had minimal effects on differentials, the 13 percentage point fall in union density may have contributed up to one fifth of the drop in relative wages received by low skill workers during the decade of the 1990s.

The interest of this study is twofold. First, it is able to demonstrate that an accelerated shift in demand favoring more skilled workers and a reduced growth in their relative supply combined to increase wage inequality in the 1980s. Second, in the process it quantifies within a unified framework the contributions of a number of factors making for declining wages among the unskilled. That analysis while clearly supportive of biased technological change does not accord it exclusive domain.

We now return to the interpretation of the dominance of within-industry over between-industry shifts in explaining changes in the structure of US employment and in wage inequality. As we have noted, the conventional view is that biased technological change largely underpins these developments. This view is on balance shared by the labor and trade literature.[2] However, the biased technological change argument has not gone unchallenged. Much of the criticism has focused on the point that the evidence is actually less supportive of the biased technological change story than it is destructive of the alternatives. In other words, there is an absence of direct evidence favoring the technology hypothesis. This is sometimes referred to as the "labeling problem," namely, that "biased technological change" is a label for our ignorance. This problem is attenuated though by no means eliminated (not least because the skill requirements embodied in specific technological advances are unobserved) in several new studies that seek to proxy technology. These studies are reviewed later.

The technology explanation is that autonomous changes in production methods have caused changes in relative demands and hence factor prices. A second line of criticism has focused on this assumed exogeneity. Might not technological change be caused by factors such as deregulation? If so, one has to be wary of attributing changes in wages and employment to technology. Ultimately, the argument may be widened to include trade itself, although there are few signs to suggest that trade does in fact stimulate productivity gains (SCHERER, 1992). (A related issue is that major changes in technology may have followed rather than led changes in employment.) A third criticism is that the data analyzed typically pertain to manufacturing. Is it safe to deduce economy-wide effects from results that largely relate to manufacturing alone?

We will return to criticism of the biased technological change argument below (section 2.5). In the interim, we have first to consider differences in labor market responses between the US and (continental) Europe. The conventional representation is that wages are inflexible in Europe and conversely so in the US. Thus, technological change (or increased trade) that shifts demand away from unskilled labor translates into quantity adjustments in the former and price adjustments in the latter. An initial observation in this regard is that unskilled worker unemployment has also risen in the US. Thus, for example, TOPEL (1993) finds that nearly all the increase in unemployment between the peaks of 1967/68 and 1987/89 has fallen upon unskilled individuals. The number of weeks unem-ployed among those in the lowest decile of the wage distribution rose by 3.7 weeks as compared with 0.2 weeks for those in the top four deciles. At the same time, the change in logarithmic wages for those in the lowest decile was -0.30 as compared with 0.04 for the top four deciles. These are the facts of market clearing in the US.

Next, turning to the European situation, do wage inflexibilities lie at the heart of the matter? Answers to this question hinge on two issues. First, is the relative shift in demand explanation appropriate to the European case? And, second, assuming that it is, what is the scale of the required flexibility. It should come as no surprise to learn that we do not know as much as we would like about either issue. In any event, on the former question, NICKELL and BELL (1995, 1996) argue that the demand shift away from unskilled labor is capable of explaining only a fraction of the overall rise in European unemployment from the 1970s to the late 1980s – 19 percent of the average rise in Germany, the Netherlands, and the UK. Adverse neutral shocks are claimed to have assumed much greater importance than relative shifts in demand.[3]

On the second question, estimates of the substitution elasticity between skilled and unskilled labor in Germany, reported by STEINER and WAGNER (1996), suggest that reductions in relative earnings on the US scale would have countered the trend decline in unskilled worker employment (partly indexing biased technological change), if not actually restoring past employment levels. By the same token, the fall in the employment share of unskilled workers due to an inflexible wage structure *per se* is modest.

Finally, we turn to manpower projections for the US. Official forecasts up to the year 2005 show not only above-average growth in occupations that require a bachelor's degree or other post-secondary education or training but also above-average employment growth for many occupations requiring less formal education (SILVESTRI, 1993). For example, the number of operators, fabricators, and laborers is expected to increase by 1.6 million, or 10 percent. This is to be sharply contrasted with German projections that point to a 50 percent decline in unskilled worker employment by 2010 (TESSARING, 1994). The US estimates of changes in occupational employment have been broken down into their industry shifts component on the one hand and those changes resulting from the changing occupational structure of industries on the other. For major occupational groups, most of the change is attributed to projected changes in industry employment. This is especially true for the service occupations. Only in two (out of 9) broad occupations – administrative support workers (including clerical) and professional specialty occupations – are significant shares of employment changes attributable to expected changes in the occupational structure (SILVESTRI, 1993, Table 7).[4] There is the suggestion of some dissonance between official manpower forecasts and the notion of the accelerating technological change story, although it should be noted that technological change underpins official estimates of both industry employment shifts and occupational structure changes.

1.5.3 Environmental Problems, Innovation and Optimal Global Growth

A problem associated with globalization and rising foreign direct investment is that governments in OECD countries increasingly hesitate to raise the prices of natural resources in a way that is necessary for inducing an efficient factor allocation. If emission-intensive production is relocated from OECD countries to soft countries among NICs and LDCs which then raise their exports to the OECD massively, the environmental aspect of higher foreign investment is that higher capital mobility undermines efforts to internalize negative external effects of production. From a theoretical point of view there exists a need to estimate the negative external effects of all production and consumption in order to determine appropriate Pigou taxes. In the field of international resource taxation some minimum international coordination will be necessary if any effective Pigou taxation is to be imposed. One might, of course, also discuss alternative instruments, such as trade in emission certificates.

The increasing global output growth and the continuing growth in international trade contribute to national and global environmental problems. Emissions and discharges represent negative external effects so that one should employ models of endogenous growth with negative external effects (GRADUS/SCHMULDERS, 1993; BOVENBERG/ SCHMULDERS, 1993). These models do not take into account the additional aspect of R&D and its impact on growth and sustainability – a problem which is covered in an innovative paper by BRETSCHGER (1997a,b,c). His main focus is on the link between a growing stock of knowledge which partly substitutes for natural inputs, namely in one- or n-sector models of growth. Various aspects of this substitution process are analyzed in models of expanding goods varieties.

A one sector model is quite misleading because it cannot express the fact that an economy adjusts not only in terms of the factor mix in output but also in the sector mix where sectors use the inputs with different intensities. Hence BRETSCHGER (1997c) introduces a research sector in the model to generate knowledge capital and endogenous growth. The three sector model is quite useful although simple in its setup: with R&D, traditional goods are produced under constant returns to scale, and high technology consumer goods are assembled from differentiated intermediate inputs. Interestingly, it can be shown that a decrease in the supply of natural inputs can even increase the steady state rate of growth. Incentives for pro-ecological substitution processes on the input side have to rely on the price mechanism in a market economy.

In EU countries industries and consumers often are opposed to rising prices of natural resources, and sometimes industry representatives point to the globalization challenge as an excuse for not pursuing resource-saving technologies more decisively. Stricter environmental standards are criticized on the grounds that it would raise production costs, and that, as long as competitors do not impose stricter standards as well, it would put EU industries at a disadvantage. As a matter of fact higher prices for some natural resources are indeed appropriate in many cases and may induce innovations both in the technologically leading North and stimulate international relocation of production in favor of the South. It is clear that inflexibilities in labor and capital markets in the North – i.e. high structural adjustment costs – reinforce industry's resistance to stricter environmental policies. This holds even for the case where such policies would strongly emphasize support for environmental-friendly R&D. In this case few firms would benefit from "green R&D projects" while most multinational firms would need to adjust production, output mix and the firm-internal international division of labor.

1.6 MNCs' Role for Environmental Policy and Social Policies

The role played by multinational companies in environmental progress is rather ambiguous in the medium term but probably positive in the long run. Mobile real capital clearly implies that profit-oriented firms will try to relocate pollution intensive production to countries with soft environmental standards. If the goods produced under soft standards are then exported to the parent country we have a case of ecological dumping in a wider sense. In a strict sense this would only amount to ecological dumping if the host country allows foreign firms – e.g. in export processing zones – to have higher discharges than domestic producers producing for the home market. Given different national and individual preferences for a clean environment one should politically tolerate the mobility of real capital as long as minimum environmental standards are not violated and as long as international cooperation among governments is not undermined. The positive impact of MNCs depends on the intensity of international technology transfers, which certainly is relatively modest in the case of foreign ownership restriction in the host country. The technological and ecological modernization of foreign direct investment could be reinforced by gradually removing barriers to foreign majority ownership. Majority ownership is the minimum requirement that technology intensive firms expect if modern technologies are to be transferred internationally.

Quite important for global technological development is the technology policy in major source countries of foreign direct investment. If governments in source countries – leaders in technological development – impose strict environmental standards and use market-based instruments in environmental policy MNCs have strong incentives for pro-ecological technological progress. Given that within the international network of firms mainly proven technologies are applied, the divergence between the standards/technologies applied by the parent company and those applied abroad will be limited. If one assumes that there is a maximum range, the continuous upgrading of environmental standards in OECD countries is crucial.

Given the high growth rates in eastern Europe and many NICs global environmental problems are increasingly compounded by the economic success of countries catching up with OECD countries. While it is certainly important that EU countries do not impose arbitrarily trade restrictions on goods produced under "dirty environmental conditions", consumers nevertheless have a right to obtain adequate information. Countries could be assigned an environmental quality label – possibly differing between sectors or products – so that consumers can take into account implicit environmental standards when they decide to purchase goods. Information about foreign environmental conditions are a collective good from the perspective of all importers and consumers. Therefore governments or international environmental agencies have a role to play in the creation of a certification procedure. This does not rule out that environmental rating of countries is organized by private firms or specialized NGOs.

What holds for environmental rating of countries could also apply to social standards. Countries should be encouraged to introduce social standard labels which indicate the degree to which minimum levels in social security have been achieved. Assuming that consumers from rich countries are willing to pay more for a good from a country with a favorable rating the poorer countries will have some incentive to introduce some social protection. Consumers are, of course, free to ignore ecological rating or social rating results.

MNCs contribute to the development of social security systems through the technology transfer effects and efficiency gains brought about by foreign direct investment: with higher economic output and higher tax revenues there are improved opportunities for governments to develop some minimum social protection. At the same time it is clear that MNCs will view social security protection as a locational disadvantage to the extent that it raises labor and production costs, respectively. This could encourage high income countries with excessive social security systems to trim these safety nets.

It is clear that a basic level of social protection is productivity-enhancing since it allows young people to attend schools – otherwise they might have to start working at a very early age in order to pay for medical care for their ill parents –

and since unemployed workers can take a longer time to search for a new job after being laid off. A longer search time (within reasonable limits) should facilitate the matching of labor demand and labor supply in a world with heterogeneous labor.

Some critics have argued that the growing importance of MNCs will lead to much reduced corporate tax rates which in turn could force governments to reduce the level of social security protection. The risk of a downward spiral can be contained by international minimum standards which should be low enough to allow differentiated upgrading across countries and over time. A serious problem in the field of social security systems could be that the rise in the number of countries since 1990 leads to efficiency problems in international policy coordination and in supranational/multilateral organizations which are getting bigger and bigger. While there is some risk of a downward spiral one should not overlook that MNCs – i.e. locational competition – also have economically positive effects by helping to avoid excessive social security systems. Given the poor organization of the taxpayers in most EU countries an excessive social security system – gradually developed under the pressure of political competition – can indeed be a serious problem in OECD countries with high per capita income.

There are various arguments which lead to the conclusion that globalization will create impulses in favor of the reform of European social security systems (WELFENS/HILLEBRAND, 1997). International organizations could play an important role in setting international minimum standards.

1.7 Theory of Globalization: Trade and Growth Theory in a Technological Perspective with FDI

The fact that in the 1990s a record number of countries were members of the leading international organizations is mainly explained by political developments and the demise of the socialist system in eastern Europe. However, it also has to do with the visible failure of development policies in Latin America that focused on import substitution. The successful outward-oriented policies of Asian NICs certainly have encouraged the worldwide shift towards external economic liberalization. The direction of technological progress in the field of computers and telecommunications has also facilitated globalization in the sense that the creation of large multinational companies with a global presence – production on all continents – is not necessarily associated with an increasing degree of centralization in the economy. While the parent company will always assume some headquarters functions, several dozen subsidiaries abroad can be managed in a rather decentralized fashion provided that adequate communication technologies are employed.

Given the many imperfections of the market for information the gradual increase in the R&D-GDP ratios in OECD countries and NICs has encouraged an increasing number of firms from ever more countries to become multinational companies. At the same time regional integration – e.g. in Western Europe – has created larger markets, which in some sectors has implied a larger minimum optimum plant size. This is stimulating international mergers & acquisitions. In the EU aggressive US investment bankers are also actively contributing to this development in the 1990s.

A theory of globalization still has to be developed in full, but one may at least point out basic theoretical building blocks that can help explain globalization. Moreover, it is necessary to check to which extent the standard body of economic theory has to be revised. While there seem to be many necessary changes the adjustments in conclusions need not be equally encompassing.

From a methodological point of view the gravity equation is important in explaining rising international trade, but – suitably modified – it could be equally important for the analysis of foreign direct investment. New growth theory also is important for the analysis as it has emphasized the importance of spillover effects and scale economies in technology intensive sectors and in sectors which are human capital intensive. Since foreign direct investment often occurs in clusters in certain regions, the new growth theory helps explain foreign investment developments in the 1980s and early 1990s, which saw a rather uneven regional allocation of inflows.

Putting the main emphasis of globalization on foreign investment raises the question how traditional economic trade analysis changes in a world of trade *and* foreign direct investment. Following the Dunning approach to FDI the main basis for successful outward foreign investment is provided by ownership-specific advantages, which typically are in the form of technological (or organizational) advantages. A conclusion to be drawn here is that in the case of economic sectors with FDI the level of technology differs between the home country and abroad. The standard Heckscher-Ohlin model, therefore, is no longer valid as it is based upon identical (macroeconomic) production functions at home and abroad.

The standard neoclassical theory offers elegant models for a world without differences in technology levels – and without economies of scale and innovation. Even without international factor mobility there will be, according to this theory, equalization of relative factor prices across countries and finally, a convergence of absolute factor prices. This analysis can be slightly modified by taking into account the heterogeneous labor skills as well as education abroad and at home. However, in reality the world is not neoclassical in this traditional sense. The global economy is characterized by product differentiation and scale economies as well as network effects on the demand side (the marginal utility of user C positively depends on users A and B also having access to the respective good, e.g. a telephone network). Taking this into account will lead to a more diverse set of models.

Some of the above challenges were picked up by NELSON/WINTER (1982) who stressed the need for analyzing bounded rationality in a world with innovation and suggested an evolutionary paradigm. More recently new trade theory – emphasizing differentiated products, innovation and scale economies as well as transport costs – added new aspects (BRANDER/ SPENCER, 1984; VENABLES, 1985; HELPMAN/KRUGMAN, 1985) while still neglecting the technological dynamics of overlapping research fields (GRUPP, 1997). With economies of scale and innovation, i.e. differentiated products, the neoclassical free trade doctrine has to be modified. It is still true that in a two country, two commodity model free trade will benefit both countries, but the gains from free trade can be rather unevenly spread depending upon which product country I and II specialize in. The choice of product innovations and of technologies can influence the respective gains from trade.

Multinational companies have hardly been integrated into traditional macroeconomic analysis. Foreign ownership creates a need to distinguish between gross national income and gross domestic product. GNP in a pure source country is gross domestic product plus profits accruing to foreign subsidiaries. WELFENS (1996) has emphasized that economic convergence in the sense of narrowing per capita GNP across countries cannot be expected if the international distribution of industrial property rights is rather uneven. Assume, for simplicity, that the production functions abroad and at home are identical and of the Cobb-Douglas type (with the output elasticity of capital equal to ß, and of labor equal to 1-ß). Furthermore, assume that the GDP in the two countries with equal populations is the same (Y at home = Y* abroad), but all capital at home and abroad is owned by the home/source country so that national income of this country amounts to Y+ßY. National income abroad is then Y-ßY. This leads to a GNP per capita ratio of 2 for the home country relative to the foreign country. In reality a more complex production function will have to be considered, and foreign ownership of capital typically is a two-way phenomenon. Furthermore, traded goods are not homogeneous, and trade balances will not always equilibrate. Without going into complex details the main message of globalization in the context of foreign ownership and innovations is the following:

● Profits at home and abroad are needed to increase the firm's equity capital which in turn is required to finance risky innovations and investments. Countries which impose high income taxes and corporate taxes are likely to face locational shifts of major companies, which will opt for a higher share of production and R&D abroad.

● Profits will be higher the more Schumpeterian economic rents can be appropriated by innovative firms. Such rents crucially depend on product innovations, process innovations and first-mover advantages in scale-intensive industries. To the extent that government procurement falls on scale-intensive goods large countries could have an advantage over countries with smaller home markets.

● First-mover advantages in world markets are important especially in scale-intensive sectors. For firms from all countries, especially the smaller ones, this points to the importance of free access to foreign markets.

- The ability of a country to accommodate foreign multinational companies is crucial for economic growth and full access to the international trade network-part of which is intra-company trade. A hospitable legal framework for foreign firms is not sufficient to attract high FDI inflows; complementary factors also have to be available in relative abundance. Positive long-term growth prospects plus political stability should be in place.

- The ability of a country to be a major source country of FDI is important if the country is to have access to global technological progress. With more subsidiaries located in technologically leading countries the parent companies' opportunities to tap the foreign pool of advanced technologies increase. This creates a particular problem for national R&D policy because with a rising presence of foreign multinational companies the "leakage effects" rise; i.e. as more and more foreign firms either directly benefit from R&D programs or imitate the technologies of rivals in the host country, considerable international external benefits will accrue. This could lead to suboptimal public R&D expenditures as governments do not take into account the positive external benefits of induced innovations. International cooperation could only partly solve the problem.

Scale economies can explain the regional concentration (location in space) of production. Product differentiation allows firms to appropriate economic rents in oligopolistic markets. Regions which specialize in product varieties with a high income elasticity of demand will particularly benefit if static or dynamic scale economies are also present. While transportation costs typically lead to a homogeneous location pattern of production, scale economies imply concentration effects. Following KRUGMAN (1991) scale economies are particularly important for industrial goods so that the expansion of industry – a rising share of industry in output – will reinforce concentration patterns. Innovation, product varieties and trade were theoretically analyzed by GROSSMAN and HELPMAN (1991). ROMER (1990) emphasized the role of accumulation and technology spillovers in his approach to endogenous economic growth.

With firms from the US and EU countries shifting industrial production to low income/low wage countries, one may expect that concentration effects in the dominant service societies of North America and Western Europe become less pronounced at the turn of the century, while concentration effects – i.e. the problem of agglomeration – become more important in eastern Europe, Asian NICs as well as in Latin American NICs. This could imply that environmental problems become regionally more concentrated in the world economy, especially since the newly industrializing countries experience high growth rates and rapidly increasing traffic. Indeed the world economy has a problem to the extent that transportation costs do not fully reflect economic costs, where road transport probably has high negative external effects which are not properly internalized. A Pigou tax could be a useful instrument for stimulating pro-ecological innovation in the automotive and truck industry. To the extent that greenhouse problems are accentuated by rising international transport and trade, one might consider a multinational R&D program on "green transportation technologies". The willingness of NICs to contribute to such programs will increase only gradually, namely as a consequence of rising per capita incomes and changing individual preferences. International real income convergence thus could facilitate international political cooperation to the extent that less divergent preferences in UN countries ease the bargaining process in the field of environmental policy. This positive North-South perspective could be undermined by more intense policy conflicts within Europe where the goal of full employment and high growth is not easily compatible with ecological improvement.

Those countries and regions in the world economy which are main exporters of such products and major source countries of foreign investment will record particularly high per capita GNPs. It is, however, doubtful that massive net foreign direct investment outflows have no negative consequences on employment in the source countries and hence could not cause higher unemployment and intensified social conflicts between workers and wealthy owners of domestic and foreign capital. A strategic policy focus thus should be to make sure that the country is not only an attractive host country for foreign investors but also an active source country.

Since successful foreign investment abroad can only be expected if the parent company has ownership-specific advantages – special management know-how and technological leadership in some fields – fostering innovation is crucial. Moreover, a strict domestic competition policy is required in order to generate sufficient domestic pressure in the tradables and nontradables sector to develop highly competitive firms.

1.8 MNCs' Impact upon National Economies and the EU

The main impacts of multinational companies on economic development are positive since existing basic economic models of foreign direct investment show a global economic gain from free flow of capital. With rising capital mobility locational competition certainly is intensified. Therefore high capital mobility should encourage governments to pick up political best practice solutions from competing locations with high economic success. By helping to accelerate learning in the political system, MNCs are a catalyst for change. Those countries where governments learn rather slowly will suffer from capital outflows and – in the case of flexible exchange rates – a currency devaluation. This will raise the pressure for political reforms. However, the crucial question is whether political competition among parties is truly functional and efficient. Only with functional competition may one expect that FDI implies systemic competition in a meaningful way, namely by contributing to the diffusion of political solutions from abroad.

One major problem of mobile real capital is that the tax basis in countries with a high tax rate will be strongly eroded; indeed with rising intra-company trade there are all kinds of options to use transfer prices to reduce taxes in some countries and to allocate tax payments in a rather arbitrary way to the country with the company headquarters or to countries with subsidiaries facing more favorable tax conditions. In Europe there is some need to rationalize and harmonize national tax systems. Harmonization should not mean primarily that tax rates become equal but that definitions of the tax basis and fundamental rules in tax policy are equal, and, of course, that arbitrary political decisions are avoided. It is an open question to which extent EU countries really should have a minimum corporate tax rate. While some minimum tax rate might be considered in order to make sure that sufficient tax revenues for financing basic infrastructure are available, one should also consider the positive role of tax competition within a clearly set framework of credible rules. Government will be forced to consider for each project whether the "tax price" is matched by adequate provision of benefits for society.

Rising intra-EU foreign direct investment can be expected as a consequence of the single market and monetary union. While the single market encourages the exploitation of economies of scale – therefore of local concentration of production in favorable locations able to serve the whole EU market – monetary union will create a fully integrated capital market with increased competition among banks and many financial innovations. Under such conditions international (intra-EU) mergers and acquisitions will become easier. Since few reasons remain after 1999 why mobile real capital should not flow to locations within the EU in which the marginal product of capital is highest, the convergence of marginal products across Euro countries and the (near) equalization of real interest rates across regions is to be expected. Different tax regimes within the EU will, of course, remain a factor that could cause differences between rates of return across Euro countries.

Higher intra-EU foreign direct investment will contribute to accelerated technology transfer within the Community. This in turn should stimulate real convergence of per capita productivity and per capita GDP in the Community. If this effect is strong enough to offset regional concentration effects emphasized in the new growth theory, there could be opportunities to reduce EU structural funds and to allocate a higher share of the EU budget to the promotion of R&D projects.

1.9 Foreign Direct Investment in the Triad and Eastern Europe

FDI inflows contribute to higher investment, economic growth, and technology levels plus higher exports in the long term, in turn stimulating rising foreign direct investment outflows. High foreign investment inflows will only develop if there is political stability, well-developed infrastructure, and a profitable, expanding market. In Spain, the share of foreign investment in total domestic capital formation increased from average annual shares of 5.2% in the period 1981-85 to 9.9% in 1986-1990, while the outflows relative to domestic investment reached

1.8% in the period 1986-1990. The US had inflows of 6.1% and outflows of 2.9%; Canada 5.9 % in inflows and 5.1% in outflows in the same period (see Table 10, 11). Germany and Japan, which have both been suffering from an economic crisis in the 1990s recorded only around 1% in foreign investment inflows but much higher outflows. (In Japan the problem of foreign investment is aggravated by language problems for foreign investors and extreme problems in hiring skilled personnel, which typically prefer to work for Japanese companies). The Republic of Korea has become an important source country for foreign investment but is still not really open to foreign investment inflows. Effectively, however, the widespread use of subcontracting to Korean firms (mainly with orders from US and Japanese firms) is a silent form of foreign investment. In the period 1990-94 foreign investment outflows and inflows in Taiwan amounted to 7.5% and 3%, respectively relative to domestic investment, while Singapore's respective figures were 10% and 28%, (IWD, 1997). The top ten source countries of foreign investment in the period 1990-95 were the US ($309.7 billion), Japan ($167.8 bil.), France ($150.8 bil.), the UK ($143.5 bil.), Germany ($130.8 bil.), the Netherlands ($78.1 bil.), Hong Kong ($77.7 bil.), Switzerland ($46.4 bil.), Sweden ($40.8 bil.), and Italy ($36.4 bil.).

In the Visegrad countries, foreign investment inflows in the early 1990s contributed to up to 10% of gross domestic investment, while the figure for Russia was about 1%. Clearly, foreign investment can be only expected on a broader scale if privatization in combination with competition has led to the emergence of an efficient supplier network and of interesting options for mergers and acquisitions. Other prerequisites include political stability, sound prospects for growth, and high profits. Lack of foreign investment has to be seen as a crucial bottleneck to higher economic growth in Russia.

The top ten recipients of foreign investment in the first half of the 1990s were the US ($238.6 billion), the UK ($118.0 bil.), China ($117.8 bil.), France ($108.2 bil.), Spain ($65.5 bil.), Belgium/Luxembourg ($56.0 bil.), the Netherlands ($47.1 bil.), Canada ($37.3 bil.), Australia ($37.1 bil.), and Sweden ($32.1 bil.). China's high foreign investment inflows in the 1990s are largely from Chinese expatriates and also reflect the booming prospects of the whole Asian region. Russia's options are different and require more domestic reforms including prudent regulatory reform as a prerequisite for attracting high and sustained foreign investment inflows.

Foreign investment in post-socialist countries rapidly increased in 1994/95, when Hungary and the Czech Republic sold part of their national telecommunications operator to foreign investors. Assuming that foreign investment contributes to an acceleration in the modernization of the telecommunications sector, one may expect a positive foreign-investment multi-plier effect: a modernized telecommunications network generally improves the prospects for attracting foreign investors to whom reliable telecommunications links to world markets are crucial. The CEFTA group – Poland, the Slovak Repu-

Tab. 10: Foreign Direct Investment (FDI) relative to Gross Domestic Capital Formation

		1981-1985	1986-1990	1991	1992	1993	1994	1995
		yearly average						
Germany	I	0,6	1,1	1,0	0,6	0,4	0,2	1,7
	II	3,2	5,9	6,0	4,3	3,7	3,7	6,7
	III	20,4	19,9	23,0	23,1	21,8	22,0	21,7
France	I	2,0	3,9	5,9	8,2	9,0	7,1	7,3
	II	2,4	7,9	9,4	11,8	8,8	9,5	6,4
	III	20,4	20,5	21,2	20,1	18,5	18,0	18,0
Italy	I	1,2	2,2	1,1	1,3	2,3	1,3	
	II	1,9	2,4	3,2	2,5	4,5	3,1	
	III	21,8	20,0	19,8	19,1	16,9	16,4	
United	I	5,5	13,9	9,4	9,0	10,2	6,8	17,9
Kingdom	II	11,8	19,3	9,4	11,5	18,1	18,6	22,8
	III	16,4	18,8	17,0	15,6	14,9	14,8	15,0
Netherlands	I	6,1	12,7	10,7	12,1	12,7	8,7	13,2
	II	15,4	20,2	22,9	22,1	19,5	26,0	15,5
	III	18,8	21,0	20,4	20,0	19,3	19,3	19,7
Belgium	I	7,9	15,7	24,9	27,0	28,6	18,7	
	II	1,5	14,9	16,7	27,3	13,1	1,5	
	III	16,6	17,8	18,9	18,8	17,8	17,3	17,6
Denmark	I	0,8	2,9	7,3	4,6	8,5	23,1	15,0
	II	2,0	5,6	8,7	10,1	6,8	19,2	10,7
	III	16,7	18,8	16,5	15,6	15,0	14,8	16,0
Schweden	I	1,5	3,9	13,7	0,0	14,0	23,3	42,8
	II	7,3	21,2	16,7	1,0	5,6	24,6	32,2
	III	18,8	20,3	19,4	17,0	14,2	13,6	14,5
Spain	I	5,2	9,9	9,9	10,5	8,6	9,8	5,4
	II	0,9	1,8	3,5	1,7	2,8	4,0	3,1
	III	20,4	20,7	23.8	21,9	19,9	19,8	20,8
Switzerland	I	4,1[a]	5,3	5,4	2,2	1,7	6,3	
	II	9,4[a]	10,3	11,1	9,9	16,8	17,9	
	III	23,5	26,1	25,6	23,7	22,5	22,8	23,1
United	I	2,8	6,1	2,5	1,9	4,1	4,4	4,8
States	II	1,1	2,9	3,6	4,5	7,5	4,8	7,7
	III	19,2	18,0	15,3	15,6	16,3	16,3	17,2
Canada	I	1,0	5,9	2,4	4,2	5,0	7,2	11,0
	II	4,7	5,1	4,9	3,4	5,8	7,4	5,9
	III	20,9	21,3	19,5	18,7	18,1	18,5	17,3
Japan	I	0,1	0,0	0,1	0,2	0.0	0,1	0,0
	II	1,5	3,9	3,0	1,5	1,1	1,4	1,6
	III	28,6	29,8	31,8	30,7	29,8	28,6	28,4.

I)   FDI inflows relative to domestic investment.
II)   FDI outflows relative to domestic investment.
III)   investment relative to GDP.

[1] Based on national accounts.   [a] 1983 to 1985.

Source: SVR (1996), Reformen vorantreiben, Jahresgutachten 1996/97 des Sachverständigenrats zur Begutachtung der gesamtwirtschaftlichen Lage, p. 67

Tab. 11: Foreign Direct Investment in Transformation Countries 1993 -1996[1]

Hostcountry/ -region	1993	1994	1995	1996	01.07.96[2]
		Stock figures in million US- $			
CEFTA[3]	8701	13891	18958	30659	32568
Poland[4]	1370	2307	3789	7843	9045
Slovak Republic	231	366	547	726	803
Czech Repuplik	1598	2166	3029	5587	6045
Hungary	5502	8342	9965	13740	13868
Slovenia[4]	...	710	1629	2762	2806
Balkan region	581	844	1547	2115	2498
Bulgaria	65	192	412	517	610
Rumania[5]	516	652	1135	1597	1888
Baltic region	166	487	978	1483	1551
Estonia[6]	59	221	442	646	680
Latvia	33	75	294	485	496
Lithuania[7]	74[5]	192[5]	242[5]	352[4]	375
Eastern middle Europe					
total	9448	15222	21483	34257	36617
CIS countries	8	4537	6045	9866	11225
among these:					
Kazakhstan	...	1271	1910	2769	3244
Russian Federation	...	2783	3365	5875	6550
Ukraine	...	219	484	891	1083
Belarus	8	264	287	331	348

(...) = not available
[1] At the beginning of each year
[2] preliminary
[3] Central European Free Trade Association
[4] Figures are expressed in national currencies calculated on year-ended exchance rates
[5] Cumulated foreign shares of nominal capital owned by firms with foreign participation
[6] Cumulated flow figures of the balance of payments
[7] New system of data collection since 1996
Source: UN-ECE 1996; Calculated by the DIW on the basis of national statistics

blic, the Czech Republic, Hungary, and Slovenia – reached a stock of foreign investment of $32.6 billion in mid1996 while Russia, according to the UN Commission for Europe, had a stock of $6.6 billion – roughly the same as the Czech Republic and about half of the Hungarian stock value of $13.9 billion (DIW, 1997). Russi-a certainly could increase its share in global FDI flows, which sharply increased after 1985. Foreign investment relative to gross domestic capital formation reached up to 15% in some EU countries in the late 1990s (SVR, 1996, Tables 10, 11). Telecommunications is a good starting point since successful joint ventures and foreign investor operations could prove the usefulness of foreign capital in a straightforward way for firms and households. Because a modernized network would facilitate the expansion of the business sector, the rise of exports and the spread of internet use for firms, government authorities, and private households, the benefits of rapid telecommunications network development are obvious. Some effects are summized in Fig. 1 and 2.

Fig. 1: Telecommunications, Innovation and Growth

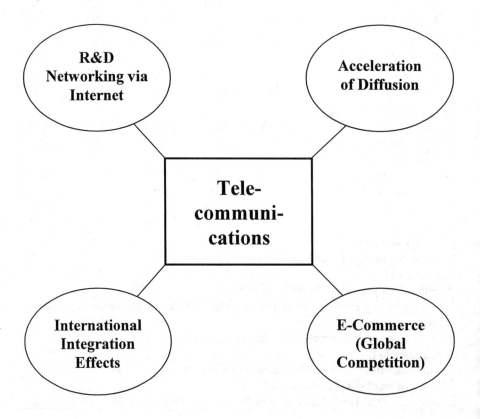

Fig. 2: Telecommunications and R&D

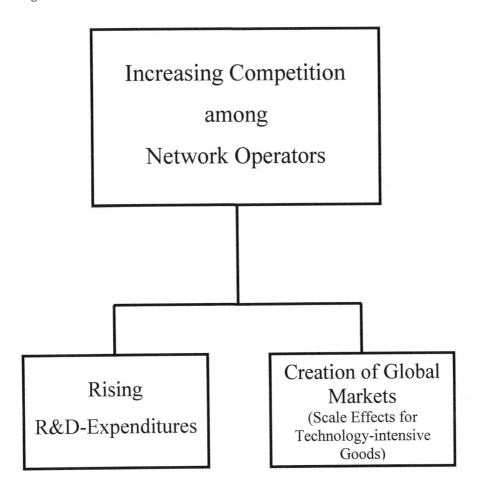

2. HUMAN CAPITAL ACCUMULATION, GLOBALIZATION AND GLOBAL PRODUCTIVITY GROWTH

2.1 Empirical Characteristics of the Global Growth Process

We start our discussion by introducing some empirical facts about the processes of growth and convergence in the world economy. We will argue that the experience of growth and development was extremely heterogeneous for different groups of countries over the last three decades. Most important are differences in the levels of income per capita and average rates of growth. We will propose show that both characteristics can be used to identify different groups or "clubs" of countries characterized by comparable developments and experiences. In addition we will present some data suggesting that each group of countries can be characterized by similarities in a set of fundamental factors of growth. Further we will investigate recent econometric work on growth and technological upgrading which can serve as a starting point for the theoretical discussion in the following sections.

The probably most striking empirical fact of the world economic development is the variety of average growth rates across countries. A first impression of this heterogeneity can be taken from Fig. 3. The figure shows the distribution of average growth rates for a sample of 123 countries over the period from 1960 to 1992. Since the figure covers a period of thirty years the variety in average growth indicates substantially different growth regimes. The lowest average growth rate is –2.2, the highest 7.3, and the mean is 1.9 percent. The difference of roughly 10 percentage points between the highest and lowest average growth rate indicates the heterogeneity of growth experience across nations over the last three decades. Only 51 countries, about 41 percent, have growth rates in between one percentage point above or below the mean. For 14 countries the average growth rate is even negative. Roughly 16 percent of the economies were not able to increase their income per capita in absolute terms.

The distinction of countries by average growth rates is helpful as a first step towards theoretical reasoning. Average growth rates are the natural starting point to identify different groups of countries characterized by similar growth experience. We can identify diverging countries, slowly growing and fast growing countries. Fig. 3 suggests that the first group of countries contains all economies that are not able to grow at all. These economies obviously diverged in absolute terms. The second group can be identified as the bulk of countries near to the mean. Since the standard deviation is 1.9 this group roughly covers average growth rates from zero to about 4 percent. The third group consists of those countries with very high average growth rates above 4 percent.

Although helpful, the identification of different groups of countries by average growth rates is not sufficient to discuss similarities in growth experience. Instead we have to consider additional empirical characteristics. Most important is the level of income per capita. Suppose two countries have different average growth rates of e.g. 2 and 4 percent. If the country with the higher growth rate also has a higher income level, both economies will diverge. But, if the country with the lower income level has a higher growth rate both economies will converge.

Fig. 3: Average growth rates (1960-92)

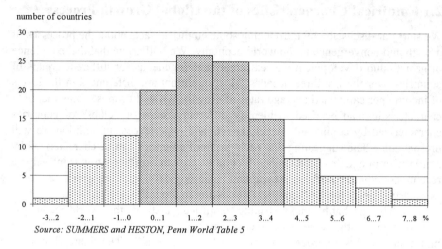

number of countries

Source: SUMMERS and HESTON, Penn World Table 5

Fig. 4: Average growth rate of income vs. initial income per capita

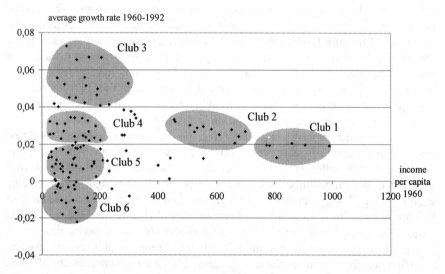

Source: SUMMERS and HESTON (1993), Penn World Table 5

The idea of convergence and divergence is extensively used in recent empirical and theoretical studies on growth. In most studies two different concepts of convergence are considered, σ-convergence and β-convergence. For additional definitions of concepts see QUAH (1993). If there is a negative correlation between the average growth rate and the initial income per capita, β-convergence will occur. In this case economies with lower income levels tend to grow faster

Fig. 5: Development of human capital of six clubs

average years of schooling, 1960, 1985

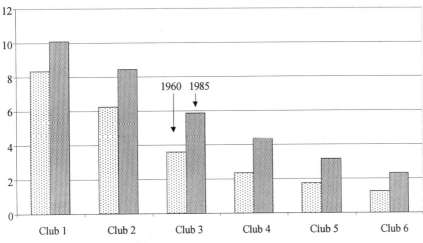

Source: BARRO and LEE (1993)

Fig. 6: Average years of schooling and internet host density

internet host density per 10000 inhabitants (log scaling)

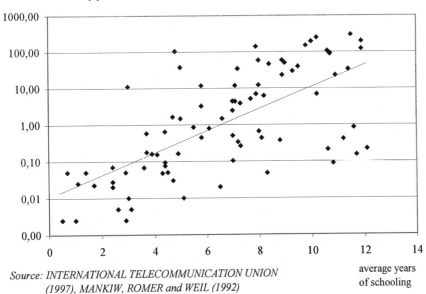

Source: INTERNATIONAL TELECOMMUNICATION UNION
(1997), MANKIW, ROMER and WEIL (1992)

Fig. 7: Average R&D intensities of six clubs

average expenditure for R&D as % of GNP (1981-1992)

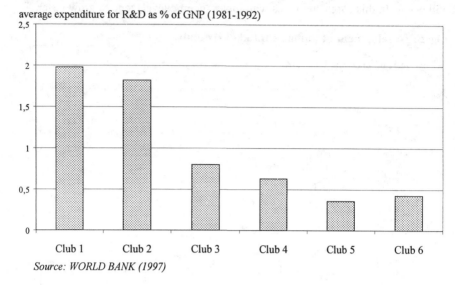

Source: WORLD BANK (1997)

Fig. 8: Average investment shares of GDP of six clubs

average investments per GDP (1960-1992)

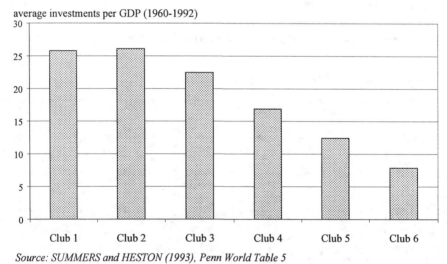

Source: SUMMERS and HESTON (1993), Penn World Table 5

than rich ones. σ-convergence is said to occur, if the dispersion of income per capita within a group of countries tends to fall over time. Both definitions are related, since β-convergence is a necessary condition for σ-convergence.

To get an idea whether the hypothesis of (absolute) β-convergence holds Fig. 4 plots the 1960 level of income per capita against the average rate of growth over the period 1960 to 1992. Again Fig. 4 supports the heterogeneity of the global process of growth. There is obviously no simple correlation between the initial level of income and the average rate of growth. FUENTE (1997) calculates the fitted regression line in this diagram. Since it has a positive slope, he argues that this is a sign for divergence instead of convergence. The positive slope indicates that on average rich countries get richer and poor countries get poorer. However, the fit is very poor. Hence, the regression does not support the hypothesis of convergence for the whole group of countries. If we had (absolute) convergence, we would expect the points to gather around a negative sloping line and economies finally converging to the same level of income. For that case poorer countries would generally tend to grow faster than richer countries. Instead there is a considerably small number of countries with high initial levels of income and similar growth rates but a very high number of countries with low initial levels of income and very different growth experiences. The further the countries are behind the higher is the variance of the average growth rates. While the average growth rate is negative for some backward countries it is as high as five to seven percent for other countries.

The non-appearance of (absolute) convergence for broad samples of countries is now widely accepted in the empirical literature (see FUENTE (1997) for a detailed discussion). Not all countries will eventually converge to the same steady state. Therefore a further refinement has proved to be useful, the distinction between absolute and conditional convergence. Absolute convergence means that all economies are able to reach the same level of income and productivity no matter what initial condition they have. Conditional convergence means that a process of catching up occurs only within a group of countries characterized by similar initial conditions. Thus, only countries or regions with comparable fundamentals will approach similar levels of income per capita and productivity. Countries with different fundamentals will converge (or diverge) to different steady states. Following BAUMOL (1986), we have to cluster the countries in a first step and to analyze countries with similar developments in a second step.

Any clustering of such a heterogeneous scatter data is difficult. Using the initial income per capita and the average growth rates given in Fig. 4, countries that are close together in the scatter diagramm will form a club. Therefore, economies of a specific club will have similar developments of the level of income per capita. Regardless on how these countries have formed clubs there will always be countries that do not belong to any of these clubs. In addition to our above classification the figure shows that we can divide countries with average growth in between zero and four percent in at least four additional subgroups. Altogether a total of six groups can be identified:

Club 1, „the industrialized elite", consist of the leading countries which have the highest initial income per capita in 1960. The members are Australia, Luxembourg, New Zealand, Sweden, Switzerland and the USA. The average growth rate of these countries is about 2% (for New Zealand it is lower). The economies from Club 2, "the industrialized catching up countries", have a lower initial income per capita, but a higher average growth rate than the leading elite. Thus, the income levels of these economies tend to converge to the leading countries. Typical members are Canada, (West) Germany, Netherlands, France and Italy. Countries from the remaining four clubs have similar initial income levels, but are distinguished according to their average growth rates. Club 3, "the strongly catching up countries", has the highest average growth rate. Typical members are the newly industrialized countries (NICs), like Korea, Hong Kong, and Taiwan, or countries like Japan, Malta, and Portugal. The economies of Club 4, "the slowly catching up countries", still have a higher average growth rate than the leading economies, but they are not as dynamic as the NICs. Here we find countries like Egypt, Tunisia, Syria, Turkey and Brazil. Economies of the remaining two clubs have lower average growth rate than the leading elite and hence, tend to diverge. Countries of Club 5, "the slowly falling behind countries", have positive average growth rates, but less than two percent. In this club are e.g. Bolivia, Cameroon, Congo, Ecuador, India and Kenya. Finally economies like Central Africa R., Haiti, Mali, Niger, Zaire, and Zambia have negative growth rates and form Club 6, "the strongly falling behind countries". These economies diverge in absolute terms.

There are other methods of identifying clubs. SOETE and VERSPAGEN (1993) use the technique of cluster analysis and calculate the clubs by considering research and development (R&D) intensities, the average share of investment in national income and initial level of catching up potential in addition to average growth rates. Thus, they use conditioning variables to form the different clubs. In contrast, we analyze the development by clustering countries with a similar performance and investigate the conditioning variables witch have to be seen as the source of this performance in a second step.

As a first stylized fact we can formulate that the industrialized countries (Club 1 and Club 2) and newly industrialized countries (Club 3) have a tendency to converge. The first view suggest that poorer economies of these clubs have higher growth rates than richer economies. A number of empirical studies confirm that for these countries the conditional convergence hypothesis holds (see e.g. SALA-I-MARTIN (1996), QUAH (1996) or FUENTE (1997)). The lower the countries income per capita the higher is the growth rate. But, it has to be emphasized that the evidence for β-convergence is strongly dependent on the chosen group of countries. This aspect is demonstrated by FUENTE (1997). Using data for 16 countries from MADISON (1987) a strong negative correlation between the average growth rate of the economy and the initial income per capita can be found. This does not hold though for a less homogeneous group of 23 countries suggested by DE LONG (1988). Using that sample, the situation is less obvious, the correlation between the average growth rate and the initial income is rather weak. But, it has to be emphasized that the negative correlation between the initial income level and the average growth rate for the sample of 31 countries which form the clubs 1 to 3 is very clear.

Much less research is devoted to the development of the countries of Club 4 to 6. Now we take a closer look to the conditioning variables to be able to explain why some countries are able to catch up and others are falling behind. As will become clear in the theoretical discussion below the conditioning factors cannot only be used to characterize the different clubs, but they are also the main sources for growth opportunities of economies. The development of economies depends on their endowment with particular production factors and the rate technological progress. These variables determine the capability to absorb or invent advanced techniques. The fundamentals mainly considered to be responsible for upgrading are the stock of human capital, the R&D intensities, the investment rate, and the openness of a country. Other parameters like fiscal policies (EASTERY and REBELO (1993), LANDAU (1986), or BARRO (1991)), political stability (e.g. PRZEWOSKI LIMONGI (1993) or FISCHER (1992a)), financial systems (KING and LEVINE (1993)), social and demographic factors (e.g. SOETE and VERSPAGEN (1993)) are sometimes added. But, before discussing the characteristics of the economies it has to be mentioned that the fundamentals change over time. Dividing the whole period in two smaller periods SOETE and VERSPAGEN (1993) show that several countries managed to switch from catching up countries to the leading elite while other countries switch from leading to catching up countries. Fundamentals change and therefore, growth opportunities of countries change.

Stock of human capital:

Fig. 5 a shows the average of human capital endowment for each group of countries proxied by average years of schooling in 1960 and 1985. Different results can be obtained from the figure: First, average years of schooling are the highest for the industrialized countries.

Second, average years of schooling increased in all clubs from 1960 to 1985, most significantly in clubs 2, 3 and 4. Comparing the average stock of human capital of the clubs 3 to 6 which have similar initial per capita income level, the data suggest a correlation between the average growth rate and the stock of human capital. But the high level of human capital of clubs 1 and 2 also suggest that the stock of human capital is crucial to sustain high levels of income in later phases of the convergence process as well as for the technological leaders. Thus, human capital seems to be crucial for growth opportunities. The empirical literature widely supports this view (see especially BARRO (1991), MANKIW, ROMER and WEIL (1992), FAGERBERG (1994), GUNDLACH (1995) and FUENTE (1997)). AZARIADIS and DRAZEN (1990) find that human capital proxied by the literacy rate is a crucial factor for growth, especially for low income countries. Another interesting result was derived by WOLFF and GITTLEMAN (1993). The authors used different proxies for human capital and found that first and secondary education significantly determine the growth rate while higher education does not. BENHABIB and SPIEGEL (1992) argue that instead of using proxies like enrolment rates, literacy rates or average years of schooling the impact of human capital should be measured by estimating the impact of human capital in technology.

Several empirical studies support this view. The most important conclusions to be drawn from this literature is that human capital and technological progress are complements in the processes of growth and development (see OECD (1996)). Especially the adoption of advanced techniques is restricted by the availability of human capital. Fig. 6 plots the internet host density per 10.000 inhabitants against the average of years of schooling for more than 90 countries. The correlation coefficient is 0.47, a rather high value. The interaction between human capital and growth opportunities is also supported by ANTONELLI (1998), who finds a high correlation between the usage of business and communication services within major European economies.

R&D intensities:

Figure 4 shows the average R&D intensities of the six clubs. Again the most obvious regularity is the decreasing rate of R&D activities from leading to backward countries. The industrialized countries (club 1 and 2) have the highest intensities. More over the difference between these countries and those of the lower income groups is substantial. The differences in R&D expenditure indicate that innovation activities are more important for highly developed countries compared to those lagging behind. Within the groups of low income countries the average R&D intensity is higher for the NICs (club 3) than for the remaining economies. But, the differences between these group are surprisingly small. The intensity of club 6 is even higher than for club 5. This is partly due to the non-availability of data for many economies of the clubs 3 to 6. Nevertheless, the data suggests that R&D is most significant and important for industrialized countries being in competition for innovation and less important for backward countries trying to imitate or adopt technologies already existing. There are only a few empirical studies investigating the direct effect of R&D for growth opportunities, but the results are supportive. For example LICHTENBERG (1992) finds that R&D determines the level and the growth of productivity and FAGERBERG (1988) finds evidence that the importance of innovation activities increases compared to imitation as countries converge to the technological frontier.

Gross Investment rate:

The accumulation of physical capital is another important factor for growth. Figure 5 shows the average rate of gross investment for the six clubs between 1960 and 1992. Again the picture is clear: The investment rate of the industrialized countries is the highest and the rate continuously decreases along with the average growth rates of the economies of the clubs 3 to 6. The result that economies with high average growth rates are characterized by relative high investment rates is not surprising. Investments are important for growth opportunities, since new technologies diffuse through new investments. For countries at the technological frontier (club 1 and 2) permanent investments are necessary to hold their position as technological leaders. For countries with similar levels of income (club 3 to 6) higher investments translate into higher rates of growth. The positive relation between growth and investments is also supported by the empirical literature (see especially DE LONG and SUMMERS (1991, 1992), LEVINE and RENOLT (1992), FAGERBERG (1994) and QUAH (1996)). It has to be added that the different conditioning variables interact. For example, including physical investments reduces the direct impact of education to growth (see e.g. BARRO (1991)). However, although it is widely accepted that growth and investment rates are correlated it is not widely accepted that investments are the source for growth. While DE LONG and SUMMERS (1992) find evidence that investments are the source for growth, other authors argue that investments are not the driving forces but the vehicle for growth (see e.g. FISCHER (1992b)).

Openness:

Another factor relevant for growth opportunities is the degree of economic integration. But the problem is to find adequate measures of openness. For example, export or import shares are frequently used as a measure. However, these measures for openness have to be seen critically, because they suggest that small countries tend to be more open than big countries. Another method is to estimate how much prices within a country differ from world market prices. A country is open with respect to this criteria, if the prices inside the country permanently equal world market prices. But it is extremely difficult to compare different countries by means of this proxy. Empirical results about growth and openness are mixed. On the one hand a number of studies exist which strongly support a positive correlation between growth and openness. See e.g. EDWARDS (1993) or FAGERBERG (1997) for a survey. But these studies often do not take into account additional variables. LEVINE and RENELT (1992) argue that the regression coefficients turn out to be insignificant, if additional variables are included into the regression. Thus, the direct impact of openness to growth is not unambiguously supported by empirical studies. It is widely accepted that participation in trade and liberalization alone is not sufficient to be able to gain from globalization. However, several studies suggest that investment in capital and openness are positively correlated (see ROMER (1990c), DE LONG and SUMMERS (1991) or LEVINE and RENELT (1992)). It has also been found that the impact of human capital to growth depends on openness (see LEVIN and RAUT (1992)). Thus, economies with sufficient domestic abilities to compete for ideas and techniques seem to be able to gain from globalization.

To summarize, even though all countries are different, we tried to identify general characteristics of global growth. Of course, there will always be countries that develop in a different way suggested here. However, our discussion is sufficient for the hypothesis that cross-country convergence occurs and for some countries, while this tendency does not hold for other countries. We intended to introduce some empirical facts about the processes of growth and convergence in the world economy that can serve as a starting point for the theoretical discussion. After this empirical review we have to take a closer look to the theory of convergence and divergence. In the following paragraph we will investigate the implications of recent growth theory and its applications in more detail. We will thereafter consider the role of globalization to the process of technological catch up.

2.2 Local Characteristics, Global Integration and Growth

The variety of growth processes of different countries or clubs of countries needs to be explained theoretically. The natural way to analyze long run developments is to apply approaches of growth theory. Thus, in this paragraph we will investigate, if traditional and new growth theory are able to explain the characteristics of the global growth process discussed in the previous section.

The traditional neo-classical growth theory of the SOLOW (1956, 1957), SWAN (1956) type regarded technological progress as exogenously given. Technologies are equally available without costs in every country. As a result global convergence is predicted. Countries are expected to converge to steady states determined by the rate of technological progress, savings and population growth. Testing the traditional Solow model MANKIW, ROMER and WEIL (1992) found that the effects of the saving rate and population growth are overestimated. Further, the traditional model is not able to explain observable differences in the level and growth rate of income across countries unless unreasonably high capital shares are used. Thus, the predictions of traditional neo-classical growth theory do not correspond with the stylized features of the global growth process.

Therefore, MANKIW, ROMER and WEIL (1992) introduced a new interpretation. They augmented the standard Solow model by including accumulation of human capital. The emphasis to include human capital is not knew. KENDRICK (1976) estimated that more than half of the capital stock of the USA in 1969 was human capital. Introducing human capital MANKIW, ROMER and WEIL (1992) show that the extended model provides a good explanation of the differences in the countries economic performance. Due to human capital the impact of the saving and population growth rate decrease. Or, to be more precise, if human capital accumulation is included and countries have different rates of accumulation and population growth, the implications of this extended Solow model cannot be rejected easily by the empirical facts.

Considering the empirical results we found that both, the endowment of human capital and the investment rate, seem to be important factors determining growth opportunities. Especially catching up countries of the club 3 do have high endowments of human capital endowments and high investment rates while falling behind countries tend to have low human capital and low investment rates. Several empirical studies in labor economics suggest that human and real capital are poor substitutes in the production process. In a survey on human capital

HAMERMESH (1986) states: "Perhaps the most consistent finding is that non production workers (presumable skilled labor) are less easily substitutable for physical capital than are production workers (unskilled labor). Indeed, a number of the studies find that non production workers and physical capital are p-complements. This supports ROSENS' (1968) and GRILICHES (1969) results on capital-skill complementary hypothesis" (HAMERMESH 1986, p. 461). Later studies also correspond with these findings. BARRO (1991) reports that investments in education and physical capital are positively correlated. From various studies by BARRO (1991), DE LONG and SUMMERS (1991) or LEVINE and RENELT (1992) we also know that the significance of education in growth regression is reduced when investment in physical capital and other elements are included. Therefore FAGERBERG (1994) concludes that countries do not invest in either education or physical capital, but in both assets.

These characteristics of human and real capital interactions are emphasized in further theoretical discussions. GRIES (1995a,b) studies the role of human capital accumulation for the international allocation of goods and capital. If human and real capital are poor substitutes, the domestic abundance of human capital will determine domestic investments:

A skill relates to the ability to use a certain technology. The ability of handling a technology often is the skill. On the other hand, technologies are embodied in capital goods: A certain capital good embodies a certain technology by the productive properties of the machinery. Hence the technology defines the link between human capital and real capital. This fixed link implies, that a country with a certain human capital stock and structure will efficiently employ the adequate stock and structure of real capital. Accumulated local human capital determines the local requirements of real capital. A country is identified by the country's "characteristic endowment", namely the local abundance of human capital and labor. The endogenously determined human capital accumulation determines comparative advantages, the pattern of specialization and trade, and the direction of real capital flows. If the stock of accumulated human capital is small, little real capital is needed in domestic production. For a given world interest rate the required real capital is absorbed from internal and external sources. The domestic excess supply (demand) of real capital is provided to (taken from) the world markets. Thus, a region that accumulated little human capital will attract little real capital. The lack of domestic opportunities to invest will channel wealth accumulation to world markets. A capital outflow can be observed even for a poor region with little capital endowment.

To conclude: The above studies confirm the empirical support for the extended versions of the traditional neo-classical model. Therefore, this type of models were rehabilitated. Nevertheless, the global public good character of the technologies remains a serious problem in these theories. The aggregate production function describes the aggregate technology of a country. The aggregate technology covers the know how of a country in all fields of economic activities, - in production, management services etc.. Even if there are some fields where the same technology is used in the industrialized world and other countries, the technical capabilities are different for the economy on aggregate. The free access to the worlds technology for all countries by a perfect and instantaneous diffusion cannot be a realistic assumption about the worlds economic conditions. Hence, two different approaches appeared, "new growth theory" and the "technological gap approach to economic growth".

The key factor in the "new growth theory" is again human capital. But unlike in the extended versions of the traditional theory, human capital is not just accumulated. The new growth theory has identified human capital as an important factor that induces positive externalities, scale economies and innovations.

On aggregate spillovers between firms and the multiple use of techniques and skills in different fields give human capital almost the character of a public good. These positive externalities affect the production processes and generate increasing returns to scale at the aggregate level. With some special additional assumptions about the production of human capital or the creation of new technological knowledge, these models can generate endogenous growth processes. Technological progress is now endogenously generated.

While a model of endogenous growth was already discussed by UZAWA (1965), the idea of human capital externalities was developed by ROMER (1986, 1990a, 1990b), LUCAS (1988) and later broadly extended and modified by AZARIADIS and DRAZEN (1990), KING and REBELO (1990), REBELO (1991), GROSSMAN and HELPMAN (1991b) and others. Several causes for increasing returns to scale are introduced (BACKUS, KEHOE and KEHOE (1992)): Arrow's learning by doing (ARROW (1962)) was used by LUCAS (1988, ch.5) or YOUNG (1991). The introduction of R&D or education sectors to induce endogenous growth was suggested by LUCAS (1988, ch.4), STOCKEY (1991) or ROMER (1987, 1990a,b), GROSSMAN and HELPMAN (1991b), AGHION and HOWITT (1992). A sector of intermediate goods as engine to endogenous growth was added by GROSSMAN and HELPMAN (1990) and others – "love of variety for inputs" (HAMMOND and RODRIGUEZ-CLARE (1993)). In these models the economies are supplied with new technologies generated in a specific R&D sector. The firms profit maximizing behavior leads to R&D activities and technology growth as an endogenous process. Economic rationality drives production and trade of new technologies and innovations. The industry sector purchases new technologies from the R&D sector. And the new technologies are transformed into final products produced for a market with imperfect competition.

The discussion of endogenous growth was extended to almost all fields of economics: BARRO (1990) and ZIESEMER (1991) analyzed the government sector and HECZOWITZ and SAMPSON (1991) developed a business cycle model. Increasing returns to scale as a factor that might favor developing strategies like the "big push" were brought into the discussion by MURPHY, SCHLEIFER and VISHNY (1989b).

There is also an increasing amount of literature discussing the effects of international integration to growth processes (see YOUNG (1991)). The first papers in this field investigated growth effects from integration for symmetric countries (GROSSMAN and HELPMAN (1991a), RIVERA-BATIZ and ROMER (1991a,b)). In the symmetric case, integration will have positive growth effects. Integration increases total knowledge and due to rather special assumptions the growth rate in both countries will increase. In contrast, RIVERA-BATIZ and XIE (1992, 1993) found that in the asymmetric case integration can reduce growth rates. The latter result is not too surprising. In countries with human capital abundance, integration will intensify the production of manufactured human capital intensive goods. This increasing production of manufactured products will shift skilled labor from the research sector to manufactured industry. The reduced human capital in the research sector decreases growth rates. Thus, following new growth theory effects of globalization for growth cannot be unambiguously predicted.

After some years of discussion, looking carefully at the now existing bunch of literature of the "new growth theory", the most innovative contribution is the modeling of innovations on a firm level. With the endogenous "production" of technological progress diverging growth processes in different countries can be explained. The internal accumulation and allocation of resources – especially of human capital – determines the R&D activities, the technological ability and finally the productivity growth rates of a country. Therefore, growth opportunities are determined endogenously and the countries preferences determine the growth position. The mechanics of new growth theory suggests, why growth processes may differ and divergence can be observed.

Confronting the implications of "new growth theory" with the global growth process, there are doubts about the explanatory power of this type of models. New growth theory tries to identify differences in productivity growth by different activities of innovations. New technologies are either exclusively developed and used in one country (no international integration) or available without costs from the other country (integrated world).

Looking at the time series of most OECD countries which are now members of the industrialized clubs the picture looks very similar for most of them. The development of the per capita income relative to the United States plotted in figure 6 shows that the countries started at a low per capita income position. At the beginning of the process, the relatively high growth rates led to a fast improvement of relative income positions. There was a fast upgrading. But, when the economies came closer to the US income level their growth rates came down to a level similar of the US. A similar process can be observed for countries forming club 3. In Fig. 9 Japan is now catching up towards the income level of the US and thus, had higher growth rates than the industrialized countries. This process does not coincide with the predictions of new growth theory.

For the group of industrialized countries the idea of endogenous innovations by firms in imperfect competition may be somehow attractive, even if the mechanics of innovative processes still is doubtful. (In order to increase the productivity growth rate the country needs only to devote more resources to R&D

Fig. 9: Development of income per capita relative to the USA

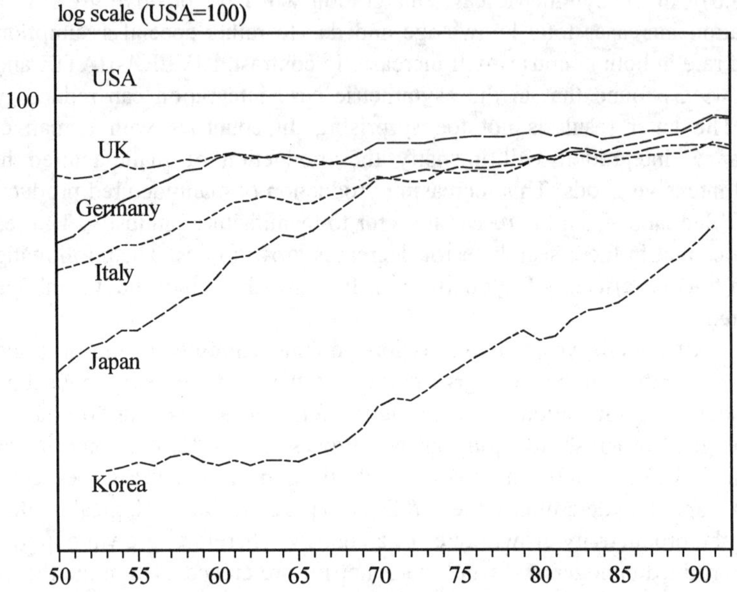

log scale (USA=100)

Source: SUMMERS and HESTON, Penn World Table 5

activities).

But, the real world is different. Looking at the global growth process, it is hard to believe that the countries present differences in growth rates are of a steady state type. If we compare high growth rates of Japan or other economies forming club 3 with the lower growth rates of the industrialized elite clubs, "new growth theory" fails to explain this phenomena. The rate of productivity growth is actually higher in economies of club 3 than in the industrialized countries. And this holds, even though these catching up countries are characterized by much lower R&D intensities than the industrialized countries (see Fig. 7). The process of using human capital in research and development to invent new technologies which "new growth theory" focused on is not relevant for backward economies. Rather, catching up countries or developing countries will basically try to get hold of existing knowledge and known technologies by devoting resources to adopt or imitate these technologies. Only when economies have successfully caught up and have sufficiently closed the existing technological gap, innovation processes and thus, new growth theory is able to describe the development of these economies.

As a result, Mankiw came to the conclusion: "Like many theories, the theory of endogenous growth has its place but has been oversold by its advocates.

[...] Even more if knowledge is undeniable important for economic growth, theories of the creation of knowledge may be of little help in explaining international differences in growth" (MANKIW (1995, p. 300). And Fagerberg resumes: "One important result is, that there is little evidence of higher marginal productivity of physical capital in high income countries. [...] The available evidence also suggests that the social and private returns to investments in physical capital are not sufficiently different. [...] On balance, therefore, the existing evidence does not seem to give much support to the suggestion made in the first versions of the new growth theories." (FAGERBERG (1994, p. 1169)).

New growth theory gives new insights for explaining the growth process of the industrialized world (club 1 and 2). But, new growth theory fails in explaining the variety of the global growth process. On the other hand a major result from new growth theory is to emphasize the importance of human capital for any kind of technology related activities. Because of its special properties human capital is responsible for the existence of positive externalities, increasing returns to scale and continuing growth, which can be determined at the preferred rate. Human capital is the key-factor for the growth process. – And this result should be also used to explain diffusion processes of technologies, which will probably give a better understanding of the global growth mechanism. Thus, we turn to the ideas and the implications of the technological gap approach now.

2.3 Human Capital Requirements for Technology Upgrading in a Global Economy

Looking at the global growth situation a large group of countries is in a process of catching up towards the industrialized world. Catching up takes place in terms of the improvement of fundamentals like human capital endowment as well as with respect to the technological capabilities. While the adjustment to the steady state by factor accumulation is sufficiently discussed by the extended traditional growth theory, the theoretical literature has spend much less attention to the process of technological upgrading. Catching up through technological upgrading does not play a significant role in the theoretical literature, even if empirical studies emphasize the importance of technological development. However, as the empirical data about growth and convergence show, a process of technological upgrading is not guaranteed. In fact, despite of some upgrading countries a large number of economies seems to stagnate or even diverge in terms of relative productivity and income per capita. Thus the question ahead is why some countries successfully manage to catch up while others are not.

To enhance their technological knowledge upgrading countries are mainly forced to adopt techniques developed outside of the country. The most important factor is that technologically backward countries can rely on techniques already existing. The imitation of existing techniques instead of own innovation is the distinguishing feature between the growth processes of technological leaders and follower. Generally speaking countries at the middle or the lower end of the technological ladder face an advantage of backwardness (ABRAMOWITZ (1979, 1986, 1992, 1993), GOMULKA (1991)). The underlying idea is that technologically backward countries have a second mover advantage compared to innovating countries. This idea was first stated by VEBLEN (1915) and adopted by GERSCHENKORN (1962). The advantage of backwardness is partly due to the fact that imitation is generally associated with lower risks, lower human capital requirements, and lower research expenditures than innovation activities. The potential to use existing and mature technologies for products in later phases of the product cycle offers the chance for a process of technological catch up due to imitation. This is especially true for countries at the middle or upper stage of the technological ladder. These countries may easily transform technological advantages into higher growth rates of productivity and therefore rapidly converge to the technological frontier of the leading economies.

Over the past decade a large number of studies were addressed to the question about the factors determining the process of convergence and technological upgrading. Meanwhile the empirical literature points out to a number of factors that are frequently found to be positively correlated with economic upgrading. The theory has to identify the way how the diffusion of technologies is likely to take place. Which channels and determinants will be most important for adopting foreign technologies successfully?

As the technology is taken from abroad there must be a channel to get hold of the international technologies. The idea that trade and economic integration tends to increase growth is supported by a number of empirical studies (see e.g. MICHAELY (1977), KRUEGER (1978), BALASSA (1978), WORLD BANK (1987), HELLIWELL (1992), EDWARDS (1992) and DOWRICK (1994)). There are more ambiguous findings and the subjective classification of trade regimes as well as the sensitivity of coefficients may be criticized (LAL (1993), LEVINE and RENELT (1992)). Nevertheless, the overall conclusion from the empirical literature tends to support the positive influence of integration to growth.

The empirical findings are further supported by theoretical considerations. Trade and imports as a diversified bundle of goods enable the country to get hold of modern technologies incorporated in imported goods. As a result a high degree of integration and high export shares are important preconditions for technological convergence. Another important argument why integrated economies usually face higher growth rates is that of higher competition in the markets of goods and services. Since competition is one of the predominating motivations for the adoption of advanced techniques, outward oriented economies are forced to use more modern and more efficient techniques than economies following a strategy of import substitution. A closely related argument is based on the neo Millian considerations that trade is one of the dominating sources of technology transfer. Developing and newly industrializing countries are forced to import technology intensive intermediates and products. Although these products are mainly used for production purpose, they also offer a substantial chance to accumulate foreign knowledge by means of reverse engineering and imitation. Even in branches not able to compete with international suppliers positive spill over in terms of personnel and organizational knowledge frequently occurs. Therefore trade flows generate substantial external economies and thus strongly interact with the technological gap of a country. The reverse implication is that a lack of foreign exchange may heavily burden or even prevent the process of economic and technological upgrading.

Nevertheless, a high degree of integration is not sufficient for upgrading. Backward economies must not only have access to modern technologies but also bring up resources necessary to efficiently absorb techniques available from abroad. Any technique is characterized by a variety of factors like the capital intensity, the scale of production, the mix of skilled and unskilled workers, and complementary services, just to mention a few. In general, technologies coming from industrialized countries will often not match the conditions of less developed countries. Therefore the degree of technological congruence and capability compared to the leading countries becomes a central issue for the process of technological upgrading (ABRAMOWITZ (1992, 1993)).

The probably most important factor responsible for the technological capability is the stock of real and human capital available to the economy. The predominating role of human capital endowments can be explained by several theoretical ideas. Many of the points made by the "new growth theory" concerning the role of human capital for innovations will hold for imitations as well. Sufficient human capital is a precondition for a successful adoption and use of advanced technologies in a country. This proposition is supported by a number of empirical studies (see e. g. FAGERBERG (1994)). The conclusion that can be drawn form the empirical literature is that the countries who tended to catch up are those with a high initial level of human capital and high investment rates (BAUMOL et al. (1989), BARRO (1991)). VERSPAGEN (1991) also finds that countries with low social capabilities (proxied by education) run the risk to be caught in a low growth trap. In addition, the complementarity of human capital to technology in the processes of research and production is commonly suggested in the literature (see OECD (1996) for a discussion).

If a country meets sufficiently favorable conditions – integration and sufficient human capital – a process of technological upgrading begins. Because the country can rely on technological knowledge already available from outside, it will be able to realize higher productivity growth rates than countries at the technological frontier. As a result the countries technological gap will diminish. This process of catching up can be roughly divided into four different phases prominently exemplified by the economic development of the eastern Asian countries. At the beginning the process of upgrading will be relatively slow due to the missing technological congruence as well as the low endowment with human capital compared to the leading economies. But in a second phase, if the country is able to assimilate higher incomes into the additional accumulation of physical and human resources, the process of upgrading may become self sustained or even accelerate. After a period of rapid convergence the third phase starts. This phase is characterized by a slowdown of technological progress and growth. The slowdown is due to counteracting forces rooted in the process of upgrading. Although the country is now able to adopt more and more advanced techniques the set of technologies available for imitation will continuously diminish as the technological gap becomes closed. Therefore resources necessary for imitation will increase relative to gains in productivity. The last phase is characterized by a process of convergence and essentially determines the final technological position relative to the leading countries. Countries which do not bring up the internal and external conditions for upgrading are unable to use their comparative advantages as technological followers. Therefore, these countries will stagnate or even diverge.

The idealized paths of convergence and divergence are graphed in Fig. 10. The formal model developed by GRIES and WIGGER (1993) given in Box 1 can be used to derive the time paths shown. The horizontal axes in Fig. 10 denotes time. The vertical axes shows the technological position of a country relative to the industrialize elite denoted w. The technological position of the group of industrialized countries is normalized to 1. Therefore the timepath of these economies is a horizontal line. The remaining two paths correspond to a converging and a diverging economy respectively. Both economies are assumed to have identical initial relative technological positions w_0. But as a result of different human capital endowments both economies differ with respect to their technological capabilities. The human capital endowment of country 1 is assumed to be lower than the critical level necessary for successful upgrading by means of imitation. Therefore the economy is not able to close the technological gap and diverges. Country 2 has sufficient human capital and is able to adopt technologies developed by the industrialized elite. As can be seen from the figure the different phases of catching up will result in an s-shaped path of convergence.

The time path shown is supported by empirical studies about catching up. For example, VERSPAGEN (1991) has tested the hypotheses of catching up for a sample of 100 countries. His findings do not only confirm that education is crucial for upgrading but give also support to the hypothesis of nonlinear upgrading. Similar results are derived in GOMULKA (1971), BARRO (1991) and CHATTERJI (1992).

Fig. 10 also shows that the final position of the upgrading country is lower than 1. Although both, the leading as well as the upgrading country eventually grow with identical rates, they differ with respect to their income and technology position at any point in time. The hypothesis that a country is not able to fully close the technological gap by means of imitation alone is an important conclusion from the theoretical model above. The prediction of the diffusion model thus differs from the prediction of the neo-classical growth model. In the latter it is assumed that costless technology diffusion will enable all countries to participate the technological frontier in the long run. This result does by imitation

Fig. 10: Convergence and divergence

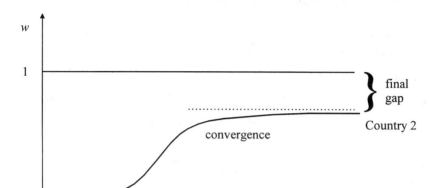

the country is forced to lag behind the industrialized elite. Therefore the only way to fully close the technological gap is to develop the ability to switch from imitation to innovation. This idea is supported by a number of empirical studies. FAGERBERG (1988) finds that innovation activities become the more important the closer a countries position actual position relative to the technological frontier. FAGERBERG (1987) also shows that converging countries are characterized by similar levels of R&D activities. AMABLE (1993) also find support for the existence of convergence clubs and the remainder of a final gap towards the leading elite. Since the technological capability as well as the ability for own innovation activities crucially depend on the educational composition of the workforce human capital is again likely to be the most important factor with this respect.

The diffusion model discussed above can be extended in a variety of ways. It is well known that foreign direct investments (FDIs) are another important source to adopt advanced technologies. But in reality only a few countries are obviously able to support their process of upgrading by means of foreign real and human capital investments. The reason is that technologically backward countries are not only characterized by higher returns on investment compared to industrialized countries but also by a high default risk due to unstable technological and social environments. The premium necessary to compensate this risk will tend to counterbalance the return differential or – in the worst case – exceed it. This might explain why most FDIs take place within the industrialized

Box 1: Model of Technological Upgrading

Basic Equations

Human capital endowment $H = H_Y + H_W$ (1)

Final good production $Y = WL^\alpha H_Y^{1-\alpha}$ (2)

Technology production $\dot{W} = H_W \, Im\Theta$ (3)

Efficient human capital Allocation $(1-\alpha)WL^\alpha H_Y^{-\alpha} = p_W \, Im\Theta$ (4)

R&D investments $p_W \dot{W} = \gamma(Y + p_W \dot{W})$ (5)

Utility function $U = Im^\delta C_Y^{1-\delta}$ (6)

Technological progress in the industrialized world $\dot{V} = nV$ with $n = const.$ (7)

Technological gap $\Theta = 1 - w$ (8)

Solution

Logistic equation for $\dot{w} = (\Psi - n)w - \Psi n^2$ (9)

$w = W/V$ ($\Psi = \Psi(H)$) with $\Psi' > 0$

Solution $w = \dfrac{\Psi - n}{\Psi + \left(\dfrac{\Psi - n}{w_0} - \Psi\right)e^{-(\Psi-n)t}}$ (10)

Critical level for upgrading $\Psi(H) > n \Leftrightarrow H > \Psi^{-1}(n)$ (11)

Final technological position $\lim_{t\to\infty} w(t) = 1 - n/\Psi(H)$ (12)

The model describes a technologically backward economy integrated into the industrialized world. The economy consists of two sectors, a final good production sector and a R&D sector. The factor endowment of the economy is human capital H and unskilled labor L. Unskilled labor is fully employed in the final good sector. The final good production function is of the Cobb-Douglas type. The technological progress of the economy is a result of technology encoding and the imitation of foreign designs. The technology production

elite. In addition to the industrialized elite only a few countries are actually able to substantially attract international capital flows, especially the Eastern Asian economies forming club 3. This observation suggests that capital flows also interact with the technological gap of a country. FDIs will generally tend to speed

---

Definition of Variables

H Human capital Endowment

H_W Human capital used in research

H_Y Human capital used in production

L Unskilled labor

Y Final good production

W State of technological knowledge

$\dot{W}$ Technological change

w_0 Initial relative technological position

V Knowledge in the industrialized world

w $= W/V$, Relative technological position

n Rate of technological progress in the industrialized world

Im Imports

C_Y Consumption of the domestic product

τ ad valorem tariff rate on imports

p Relative price of imports

p_w Shadow price of copied technologies

γ Fraction of GNP spent for research

U Utility

Θ $= 1 - w$, Technological gap

---

function (3) is positively related to human capital and technology intensive imports while inversely related to the relative technological position (advantage of backwardness). Equation (4) gives the efficient allocation of human capital in production and research activities. The expenditure for research activities are assumed to be politically determined as a constant fraction of GNP (equation (5)). The demand for imports is derived from utility maximization. The utility function is given by equation (6). The rate of technological progress in the industrialized world is assumed to be constant and denoted n. The technological position is determined as the ratio of the technological abilities relative to the industrialized world w. The model equations can be used to form up a logistic equation for w. The solution is given by equation (10) and graphed in figure 7. Condition (11) determines the critical level for upgrading and equation (12) gives the final technological position as a function of human capital endowment.

up the process of technological upgrading because they raise the rate of capital accumulation and offer additional access to advanced techniques. GRIES, JUNGBLUT and MEYER (1998) use a dynamic model of technological upgrading to show that the reduction of the risk premium is likely to dominate the diminishing return differential as the technological gap decreases. Therefore upgrading economies have a good chance to attract additional capital through FDIs which in turn tend to speed up the process of catching up. The model also shows that FDIs are less important for the final level of convergence. The final gap will depend on the fundamentals determining the potential to absorb technologies, especially human capital endowments.

2.4 Upgrading and Change in Competitive Positions

The process of upgrading discussed in the previous chapter will also affect comparative advantages and the structure of the economy. The permanent shift in factor endowments described in the open economy version of traditional neo-classical growth theory as well as the permanent improvement of the relative technological position of the country will permanently cause a change in the position of comparative advantages. The change in relative factor endowment will change the Heckscher-Ohlin trade position and the technological catching up will change the Ricardian comparative advantage.

The dynamics of Heckscher-Ohlin trade as discussed by FINDLAY (1973 and 1985) is an extension of the neo-classic open economy model. Like in the traditional neo-classical theory the technology is given. Technological progress is assumed to be exogenuously given and available without costs. The difference between countries is not caused by various technological capabilities, but only by differences in factor abundance. A backward country starts with a low capital and high labor abundance. According to Heckscher-Ohlin theory this backward country will realize comparative advantages in labor intensive industries. Hence the country will tend to specialize towards the labor intensive sector. In a dynamic world the economy will accumulate capital. As long as the country has not reached the steady state position the relative factor abundance will permanently change. According to this change in relative factor abundance the comparative advantage will also adjust towards more capital intensive industries. The pattern of trade and specialization will adjust. This process continues until the country reaches its final steady state position. The domestic accumulation process in an integrated world will determine the time path of comparative advantages and thus, the structure of production. As long as countries are in different stages of development and have different factor abundance, Heckscher-Ohlin trade will be expected. Once the countries reach their steady state position relative factor abundance as well as income positions will converge (if the saving rate is not to different). Therefore, Heckscher-Ohlin trade becomes less important.

Another approach of dynamic trade theory is focusing on the dynamics of Ricardo trade. In this approach the factor abundance is given and technologies available in various countries are different. GRIES and JUNGBLUT (1997a, b) introduce a model with two sectors of final goods – a traditional and a modern sector. According to the Ricardian theory the technological backward country will have a comparative advantage in the traditional sector and specialize in production

Fig. 11: Structural adjustment during the process of upgrading

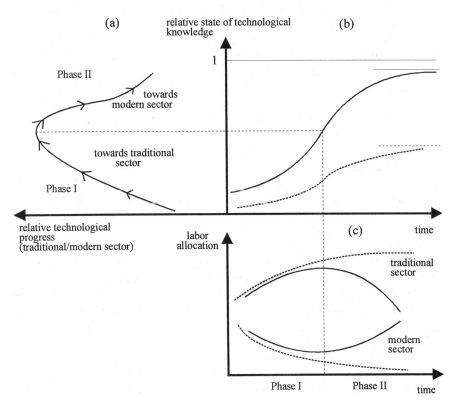

of this sector. The leading country will have comparative advantages in the modern sector. Economic integration gives the backward country access to technologies used in the industrialized world. As this model is an extension of the basic model presented in the previous section (see Fig. 10 and Box 1) the relative technological position of the country changes as the country catches up. Thus, comparative advantages change permanently.

The diffusion of general technological capabilities into the productivity of the two industries is regarded to be non-symmetric (see Fig. 11(a)). The introduction of non-symmetric technological diffusion does not change the aggregate s-shaped pattern of catching up (compare Fig. 10 and 11(b)). Both sectors as well as the aggregate economy will show substantial growth. The economy is on a path of upgrading. On the other hand, at the sectorial level the processes of upgrading differ substantially. Production and factor allocation in every period directly depend on the country's relative technological position. The non-symmetric productivity gains during the process of upgrading generate a permanent pressure on structural adjustments.

The permanent structural adjustment process implies some interesting interpretations. In phase I the productivity gains of the traditional sector exceed those of the modern sector. The non-symmetric diffusion of technologies will generate additional comparative advantages. The improved trade opportunities will increase the production of the traditional sectors and factor absorption (see Fig. 11(c)). Furthermore, the relative shift of productivity will induce the reallocation of human capital from the modern towards the research sector. Both, the improved trade opportunities as well as the human capital reallocation will increase the overall rate of research. As a result the growth opportunities increase and the process of catching up accelerates.

Phase II is generally characterized by reverse reactions with important implications for the catching up process. The structural reallocation process will turn in favor of the modern sector, as might be generally expected for upgrading countries. The relative productivity gain in the modern sector will reduce comparative advantages and relatively cut back the speed of imitation which is governed by the relative technological position and determines trade opportunities. Labor as well as human capital is reallocated towards the modern sector (see Fig. 11(c)). The reduction of trade opportunities and the human capital reallocation towards the modern sector will both reduce. Further, the imitation of foreign designs becomes increasingly difficult as the technological gap diminishes. These reactions will slow down the process of upgrading until the country has reached the final position of catching up.

From this approach we can draw three major conclusions: 1. A catching up process generates permanent requirements of structural adjustment. 2. There might be a "structural turn pike" phenomenon. Efficient catching up may in a first phase turn towards the traditional sector, reinforce comparative advantages, strengthen trade positions and improve technological capabilities. In a second phase the structural adjustment reverts towards an increasing weight of the modern sector as generally expected for a process of catching up. 3. The speed of catching up may be overestimated in the first phase, if growth rates are simply extrapolated. In a second phase, decreasing trade advantages and reallocation of human capital from the imitation sector towards the modern sector will slow down the catching up process. Finally it is worth to mention a second possible case described by the dashed lines in Fig. 11(b) and (c). In this second case of structural adjustment the final gap will be on such a low level that there is no switch towards the modern sector. The level of catching up again determines the production structure. Countries with low steady state positions will move towards, and finally stay in the traditional sector.

A combination of both approaches – the dynamics Heckscher-Ohlin and the dynamic Ricardian trade – probably gives the most comprehensive view: backward countries are characterized by low real and human capital supply and low technical capabilities. With the human capital accumulation relative factor abundance as well as technologies will improve and cause permanent changes of comparative advantages in the process of catching up. With a permanent change of comparative advantages the structure of the economies will also change permanently. The countries will move towards the production of new industries and move out of the production of old industries. Thus, catching up implies continuous structural change until the countries reach their final steady state position. Further, during the process of upgrading Heckscher-Ohlin and Ricardo trade is dominant, hence trade is inter industry trade. When the countries approach their final steady state position the fundamentals tend to converge. Due to converging fundamentals (factor endowments and technological abilities) comparative cost advantages of the Heckscher-Ohlin and Ricardo type disappear. The result is a continuous change from inter industry to intra industry trade. The countries of the industrialized club do not show major differences in factor abundance and technologies and therefore trade is not dominated by comparative cost advantages. For these countries intra industry trade and the underlying theories are more important.

The above theoretical discussion on globalization, catching up and trade should be consistent with empirical findings. Confronting the dynamic approach with the development of world trade, we have to ask: Can we observe Hechscher-Ohlin and Ricardo trade pattern for catching up countries while observing intra industry trade for countries close to their steady state position? At least, this result would be the prediction of traditional dynamic trade theory.

In an extensive study for more than a hundred economies LEAMER (1984) found that the trade pattern could be explained quite well by endowment based theory of the Heckscher-Ohlin type. In this study only four classifications in manufacturing industry were distinguished. Therefore, only the broad pattern of trade was analyzed. As WOLFF (1997) points out, "Those results are consistent with the argument that the broad pattern of exports – primary versus secondary goods, heavy versus light manufactures – can be explained by general factor endowments, but the specific pattern of exports of manufactures at a more disaggregated level depends on industry-specific factors captured in the TFP [total factor productivity] measure" WOLFF (1997, p. 3).

DOLLAR and WOLFF (1993) investigated the idea of convergence of productivities, resource abundance and trade pattern for nine OECD countries. On an aggregate level strong evidence for convergence of capital labor ratio and aggregate total factor productivity was found. If industries are investigated more disaggregated, the picture becomes less clear. For advanced OECD countries an analysis of manufacturing industry exports does not suggest any convergence on a disaggregated level. Specialization towards specific industries has continued at the industry level for advanced OECD countries. Thus, economies close to their steady state specialize production towards those products where they initially had advantages.

In addition of Heckscher-Ohlin trade theory and convergence of factor abundance, the technology gap, or neo-Ricardian propositions were also tested empirically. A study of OECD countries by DOSI, PAVITT and SOETE (1990) came to the conclusion that on industry level the relation between export performance and innovative activity is strongly confirmed. The importance of R&D activities for trade advantages was also found by VERSPAGEN and WAKELIN (1993).

GUSTAVSON, HANSSON and LUNDBERG (1997) confirmed the importance of endowments and technology differences. "Our main conclusion is that *both* sets of variables seem to be important. Factor endowments of countries, in combination with factor requirements of industries, seem to be significant determinants of trade and specialization." (GUSTAVSON, HANSSON and LUNDBERG (1997, p. 31))

Comparing these empirical results with the predictions of theory, we find predominantly consistence: Factor abundance and total factor productivity converge. Factor abundance and technology differentials do matter as determinants for the broad trade pattern. Dynamic Heckscher-Ohlin and neo-Ricardo trade theories at least give first ideas of the engines of global growth and competition. But, for the club of industrialized OECD countries the evidence suggests that this dynamic versions of traditional trade theory will not give a sufficient explanation. Several authors (FAGERBERG (1997) or WOLFF (1997)) found that for this countries trade is rather driven by innovations than by costs. Even more, on a more disaggregated industry level the pattern of convergence reverses. Within manufacturing industry the different OECD countries tend to produce and export highly specialized (WOLFF (1997), GUSTAVSON, HANSSON and LUNDBERG (1997)). The pattern of specialization is stable or even increasing. This result is not covered by the predictions of the above theory. Therefore we would suggest that the above theory is suitable for the process of catching up, but for the industrialized world other theories are more suitable.

2.5 Regional Competition and Human Capital Allocation

The extraordinary role of human capital for the technological capabilities and the general economic performance leads to an additional directly related question: What determines the allocation of human capital in the world regions? Why are certain regions well endowed with human capital with good opportunities for growth, and other regions do not show significant human capital accumulation? How do accumulation processes take place?

At least two sets of reasons for the relative abundance of human capital in a region must be investigated. 1. Local human capital accumulation determines at least the regional abundance of the immobile components of human capital. Differences of regional accumulation of human capital may change the relative regional human capital intensities. 2. In real world the "regional characteristic endowment" is not exogenous. Components of human capital may migrate (at least to some extend) from one region to another. Even if there are no large scale migrations, the partial mobility of important components of human capital may however be able to affect the aggregate.

Let us begin with the local human capital accumulation: Original human capital accumulation is directly linked to the decision for schooling. Education can be explained by personal investment decisions. See FREEMAN (1986) and WILLIS (1986) for surveys. Human capital theory may serve as a model to identify the determinants of personal skill levels. The individual human capital accumulation is depending on a considerable set of determinants. The most important factors for the decision are the expected earnings, the costs of schooling, the time preference rate, and the risk of the human capital asset in the personal portfolio. All these factors may vary between regions. Clearly, reductions of the private costs of schooling by public subsidies will increase the attractiveness of human capital. Public school systems with low admission fees and high quality supply of schooling, or student grants may be examples for these kind of subsidies. If family aspects for poor regions are considered, family human capital investment decisions can even be linked with the number of children (see BECKER and TOMES (1976), BECKER, MURPHY and TAMURA (1990)). In these family models the skills of children serve as a substitute for the number of unskilled children to assure an optimal income support for the total family. Even if human capital were totally immobile, there would be many elements affecting the accumulation level and structure. The immobile segments of regional human capital endowments can be endogenously influenced by policy activities. Regions that supply positive conditions for efficient human capital accumulation will in a first stage have a good starting point for competing in attracting human capital. At the time of the market entry of a schooled person the location of schooling clearly gives an advantage for regions with schooling institutions. SHAW (1991) came to the conclusion that personal investments in skills needed in local industries will dampen the willingness to move. Especially the more immobile groups will tend to stay in the region of education. For these groups local preference for the home region is a crucial factor. More mobile groups will be attracted from additional aspects and start moving towards more preferred regions.

The second aspect of world regional human capital allocation is the potential mobility of people. As the regional mobility of human capital is directly based on personal migration decisions, the tools to analyze migration in the theory of labor and regional economics can be applied. A detailed comprehensive review is given by ISSERMAN et al. (1986). See also MALKO (1986).

In a standard optimal decision problem for migration the decision is determined by the earnings in the two locations and the vector of local characteristics. BHAGWATI and KRUGMAN (1985) surveyed the empirical findings and found several important aspects for the migration decision. For internal migration the personal and regional income differential, the education level, urbanization and distance are important. International migration, especially of highly educated people is driven by additional motives: professional opportunities and working conditions, and the general political and environmental living conditions must be included. These results also correspond with classes of key-factors identified by WEIDLICH and SANIS (1991). In this study the labor market situation, the living standard and the public sector are found to be important. In order to elaborate the implications for the regional position, we shall study some selected important elements of the migration determining vector in more detail. Two questions arise: What are the motivations for human capital owners to move into a certain region? What are the determinants for the decision to stay in a certain region?

Since the regional earning differential is an important aspect for the migration decision, we have to analyze the determinants of human capital earnings. Neo-classical theory allows at least for two reasons for earning differentials for the same skill level in different locations. First, a relative difference in human capital abundance together with restrictions on labor mobility. Second, differences in technologies. For identical endowments, technologies determine the relative productivities and relative factor earnings.

Neglecting factor market restriction, both reasons will cause migration. But, the determination of the direction of migration and the regional implications is extremely difficult. The relative abundance argument predicts human capital to migrate towards regions with relative scarcity of skilled people. But, this will hold only, if the technologies in the regions are identical or sufficiently similar. Therefore, a necessary condition for this direction of human capital migration is a similar technology. If the technical advantage in the human capital abundant region is sufficiently large, the incentive to move will disappear and a one way incentive for factor mobility towards the opposite direction will take place. Homogenizing regional human capital through migration necessarily needs sufficient similar technological capabilities in the regions.

The second reason for an earning differential focuses on technological differences. The productivity of human capital is depending not only on the skill level, but also on the technology used. A certain skill level combined with an old technology generates less productivity than a new technology elsewhere. Therefore, regions without potential access to the most efficient technology will not be able to employ a certain skill level efficiently and cannot offer corresponding salaries. Human capital attracting regions must be in the top league of technology supplying regions. The experience for fast copying new technologies, and the ability to innovate is crucial for a region. These arguments are exactly in line with the ideas of the "new growth theory" as well as the "technological gap approach". The technological performance of a region might be the better, the larger the existing stock of human capital in that region. The positive externalities in terms of improving technological positions may serve as a reason, why human capital attracts human capital for a given location with relative abundance of human capital. The increasing improvement of technologies caused by human capital will increase human capital productivity and earnings.

This effect reminds to the idea of economies of scope in the discussion of growth and concentration phenomenon of single firms. In fact on the more aggregate level of regions, this process of mutual attraction of human capital and technologies seems very similar. This idea is compatible with the idea of gravity and cluster formation of regional centers as recently suggested by KRUGMAN (1991a,b) or MURPHY, SCHLEIFER and VISHNY (1989a,b). These centers are characterized by vertical integration. The formation of regional clusters well known in regional economics by "positive feed back", including technical and pecuniary externalities and increasing returns to scale does not compete with the ideas suggested here. Both arguments are complements.

Krugman gives an examples for Stanford University and Silicon Valley: "There was a noticeable cumulative process operating through university itself: the revenues from the research park helped to finance Stanfort's ascent to world class status in science and engineering, and the university's rise helped make Silicon Valley an attractive place for high-tech business. [...] Perhaps the most important thing to emphasize in these high-technology stories is the importance of non-high-technology factors in the agglomeration process. Both in Silicon Valley and around route 128 advantage is the existence of a pool of people with certain skills." (KRUGMAN (1991a, pp. 64)).

Apart from earnings, a vector of local characteristics and qualities is determining migration decisions. The empirical controversy about the relative importance of earning differentials versus amenity factors for determining the migration process is discussed by CLARK and COSGRAVE (1991) who found evidence for both. The theory of migration offers a large variety of important non monetary factors (see e.g. ISSERMAN et al. (1986)). Like the supply of public goods and the affinity to the local cultural arrangements, which leads to a "home preference":

The idea of interdependencies between the public sector and migration was brought into the discussion by TIEBOUT (1956). Again, potential increasing returns to scale will tend to polarize regional developments. If human capital concentration leads to scale economies, tax revenues to finance the optimal supply of public goods can be collected at a much smaller tax rate. The chance to attract additional human capital and to keep it in the region by a better supply of public goods will increase. This proposition is also supported empirically by WEIDLICH and SANIS (1991).

The major result can be summarized: Relative abundance of human capital will likely promote general regional technological advantages and therefore attract additional human capital. The process of human capital concentration accelerates. Human capital is a key-factor for the regional characteristics and for the regional allocation process. In reality regions will not develop equally. Human capital migration and differences in the speed of technology diffusion may lead to local agglomerations. Since the major characteristic of a region is the human capital abundance, the regions have to compete for human capital.

The competition of regions will become the competition to accumulate, attract and bind human capital locally. If a region is successful in competing for human capital, the general economic situation will improve and a process of acceleration and catching up will take place. Human capital accumulated today determines the opportunities of the future. Thus, for backward as well as leading regions education is not only important, but a central condition to stand future competition.

3. THEORETICAL AND PRACTICAL ASPECTS

OF

HIGH TECHNOLOGY POLICY

3.1 Endogenous Growth Theory and Theory of High Technology Policies

The theoretical justification for high technology policy stems from the observation by Kenneth Arrow (1962) that economic activity based on new knowledge suffers from an inherent market failure. High technology, by definition, involves the production and commercialization of new economic knowledge. New knowledge is inherently differently from the more traditional factors of production – land, labor and capital. These traditional factor inputs are more or less known and their value added is more or less certain. This is not the case with new economic knowledge.

More than most other economic goods, the production of knowledge generally suffers from all three sources identified by Arrow (1962) as constituting market failure – indivisibilities and monopoly, uncertainty, and externalities and public goods. The first source of market failure emanates from the propensity for new knowledge to be a discrete rather than a continuous commodity. As a result, both economies of scale and scope are often associated with the production of knowledge. The second source of market failure involves the extraordinarily high degree of uncertainty inherent in new economic knowledge. While virtually every economic good is subject to uncertainty, almost none is exposed to the degree of risk involved with introducing new products and technologies. There are two additional elements of uncertainty inherent in innovative activity that are not present in other goods. The first is in the realm of production. How a new good can be produced is typically shrouded in uncertainty. The second level of uncertainty involves demand. To whom the product can be sold and which types of marketing should be utilized is a conjecture at best. Even if the technological knowledge can result in a new product, it is not at all clear that the product can be profitably sold. Technological knowledge can enable a new good to be produced, but there is no guarantee that sufficient demand exists, or that the new technological knowledge can be transformed into economic knowledge.

The third source of market failure stems from the public good characteristics and externalities inherent in much knowledge-generating activity. The production of knowledge does not preclude other economic agents from applying that knowledge for economic gain. It is difficult to delineate and enforce property rights to newly created knowledge. The externalities associated with the production of new knowledge make it difficult for firms undertaking such activities to appropriate all of the economic returns accruing from their investment.

The market failure aspects involved in knowledge-based economic activity provides theoretical justification for government intervention, particularly to support what would otherwise be an under-production of that activity. However, a more practical consideration of technology policy institutions is how to avoid what has become known in the literature as *regulatory capture*. The main goals of creating such institutions are the avoidance of regulatory capture, that is having those policy makers with a mandate to devise and implement technology policy be captured by particular interest groups. A problem that is not particular to technology policy is that the centralized power and interest groups that are actually promoted through coalition structures can influence the political process and restrict or at least impede the entry of new firms. That is, the institutions shaping and implementing technology policies are particularly vulnerable to the special interests represented by a highly concentrated group of large producers. Administrative procedures to diminish the influence of political rent-seeking activities generally fall under the heading of providing *accountability*, *independence*, and *transparency*. The principle of accountability suggests that a greater degree of political scrutiny is required to help compensate for the inevitable imbalance between the concentration of producer interests on the one hand, and the relatively dispersed interests of the general public on the other hand. According to the principle of independence, weakening the link between the control of administrative agencies by elected officials will also tend to reduce the likelihood and extent of regulatory capture. The principle of transparency generally suggests that institutions implementing technology policies should be charged with revealing to the public the maximum amount of information and reasoning upon which technology policies are based.

The traditional or neoclassical approach to growth theory focused on the linkages between the inputs of labour and capital and output in a production model framework (Solow, 1956 and 1957). Economic growth was then explained either by increases in the quantity of the inputs or by the productivity of the inputs. But the neoclassical models could not fully explain variations in growth rates over time for any particular country (time series) and across different countries at any one point in time (cross sectional). The residual, or "unaccounted growth" was attributed to exogenous technological change. This technological change was largely considered to be "manna from heaven".

The concept of *endogenous growth* embraces a diverse body of theoretical and empirical work that emerged in the last decade. This alternative approaches to growth theory differs from neoclassical growth theory in the emphasis that economic growth is an endogenous outcome of an economic system, and not merely the result of forces that impinge from the outside. As Romer (1994, p. 3) points out, the endogenous growth theory, "does not settle for measuring a growth accounting residual that grows at different rates in different countries. It tries instead to uncover the private and public sector choices that cause the rate of growth of the residual to vary across countries." The major contribution of the so-called "new growth theory" has been to endogenize technological change in the process of long-run rate of economic growth. Technological change consists of a number of dimensions, such as research and development (R&D), stock of scientists and engineers, the extent of human capital, labour skills, and learning capacity of firms and individuals. Rather than being purely exogenous, these dimensions of technological change become endogenous in the new growth theory, in that greater rates of growth afford higher levels of R&D investment, superior training of the workforce, better education, etc. (GROSSMAN and HELPMAN, 1991). And the higher levels of these dimensions of technological change lead, in turn, to higher growth rates. Thus, Romer (1986 and 1990) pointed out that there are increasing returns to technological change and endogenous growth.

AUDRETSCH and FELDMAN (1996) and AUDRETSCH and STEPHAN (1996) argue that the mechanism by which these increasing returns to new knowledge take place is through the spillover of knowledge. Knowledge spillovers can be defined as knowledge that is generated in one organization but commercialized in another organization.

According to BAUMOL (1993, pp. 259-260), "...so far as capital investment, education, and the like are concerned, one can best proceed by treating them as endogenous variables in a sequential process – in other words, these variables affect productivity growth, but productivity growth, in turn, itself influences the values of these variables, after some lag. To some degree, the same story can be told about the exercise of entrepreneurship, investment in innovation, and the magnitude of activity directed to the transfer of technology." Thus, BAUMOL (1993, p. 260) concludes that, "productivity growth, and the resulting enhancement in GDP per capital, are, in turn, among the main stimulants serving to enhance the values of those same variables...investment is heavily influenced by output per capita, being systematically higher in countries whose GDP per capita is higher. Similar remarks apply to a country's expenditure on education, its investment in R&D, and a number of other variables usually cited as stimulants of productivity growth".

The implications for government policy in the development of high technology under the endogenous growth theory are strikingly different than those under the traditional neoclassical growth theory. The role of government in the traditional neoclassical growth theory is limited and minimal. The returns from investment in new knowledge are appropriated by those firms and individuals undertaking those investments. Thus, there is no theoretical reason for governments to intervene in high-technology markets.

By contrast, in the new growth models there is a compelling reason for governments to undertake a vigorous and active policy in shaping high technology. This is due to the existence of knowledge externalities in the form of knowledge spillovers. As a result of the externality, the social value of new economic knowledge exceeds the private value, which represents the type of market failure first identified by KENNETH ARROW (1962). By supporting the creation of new knowledge, activities which generate the spillovers of that knowledge, and the commercialization of knowledge, government policy can correct the market failure inherent in knowledge-based economic activity.

3.2 Trends in International Innovations and the Presence of MNCs

Globalization of research and development (R&D) since long is a major topic for academic researchers. The exchange of new ideas during international conferences and the collaboration across boarders in such prestigious projects as in high energy physics, nuclear fusion or space research is reality since several decades. The same is true in areas such as genetic engineering or oceanography but probably there less obvious as no joint large-scale facilities are required. Global R&D for the business community is now considered a major important topic than some twenty or thirty years ago. For decision makers in governments globalization seems to be more a problem than an opportunity as the territorial boundaries and the respective legal systems cannot easily be surpassed (with the exception of the European Union).

A particularly strong trend towards the globalization of R&D began in the 1980s and now, in the mid 1990s, no end of this process is coming in sight (GERYBAZE, REGER, 1997). Multinational companies (MNCs) play a key role both in the generation and in the diffusion of new technology. Certainly, deregulation in the eighties has facilitated this process which is obvious for such markets as telecommunications (GRUPP, MAITAL, 1996), and one should never forget that companies like IBM always had large production and R&D facilities in Europe, what was also true for trusts like ITT before the company disappeared. Yet, the new observation in recent years is that the R&D and international location strategies of transnational cooperation have changed substantially.

At the same time international trends in innovation in terms of technical preferences are changing. If one accepts patent statistics as a proxy for innovative output, one can arrive at the conclusion that since the end of the eighties some areas are the winners of structural change in innovation and some are the loosers. Among the winning areas we mention turbines, telecommunications, optical instruments along with railway technology, medical instrumentation, agro chemistry, and pharmaceuticals (the latter two areas being heavily influenced by the new biotechnology). On the shrinking side we find nuclear energy, armament technology, semi-conductors, and computing (these developments peeked at the end of the eighties) along with textile machines, food processing, photography, and consumer electronics (BMBF, 1997). Environmental concerns have been overplayed by concerns of employment, and, although most environmental problems remain unresolved, the development of environment-friendly or resource saving technology is now in the down-swing.

MNCs, following these structural changes in technology, can combine their priority decision with a location decision and pursue some parts of R&D in one country, other parts in another. Those locations, maybe states or regions within countries, get more or less attractive if competence centers or networks between existing firms and public institutions, and favorable frame conditions in combination offer competitive advantages against others. By favorable frame conditions we mean both hard facts (country or state legislation, availability of skilled labor force etc.) as well as soft factors (such as nice housing opportunities, developed traffic systems for the long distance but also for daily use, touristic and other leisure opportunities, school teaching in several languages, and many more).

This is not to hide that there are several deficits in the economic analysis of globalisation of R&D. Most studies provide us with macro economic or sectoral results of the internationalization of R&D and do not disclose business related strategies with implications for managers. It is also not to deny that many more such investigations on US firms are available than on European or Asian companies. Many more studies deal with transnational enterprises but are silent on their R&D.

One can observe different strategies of MNCs. Recently, GERYBADZE and REGER (1997) published a survey on some twenty MNCs explicitly focusing their R&D. They found two clusters of companies „going international" in different ways. The first group of high-tech corporations has a strong global orientation, invests a relatively large amount in R&D and shows a strong presence abroad. This group performs 50 per cent or more of corporate R&D in other countries than the one where the headquarters is located. To this group belong companies like ABB, IBM, Philips, EISAJ, and chemical-pharmaceutical companies like Ciba-Geigy, Hoechst, Roche and Sandoz.

The second cluster consists of a group of enterprises mainly active in the area of medium-to-high tech. They have divisions classified as high-tech but their overall R&D intensity is lower than for the first group at least on average. This group does not transfer more than half of the R&D function to countries foreign to the headquarters location. A typical value would be 20 to 30 per cent of R&D which is internationalized, indeed. This group of countries includes companies like Siemens, Sulzer, BASF, Sony, Sharp, Bosch and others in the sample studied.

Thus, the presence of MNCs with distributed R&D facilities is a matter of fact. Globalized R&D is increasing from a low level in most countries. The net outflow of R&D is a concern for some countries but whether it is better to make „national" companies work abroad and participate in foreign national systems or to invite foreign companies to the own territory remains largely open. Technology spill-overs and knowledge flows certainly accrue in both cases and the debate of the net R&D flows and their benefits is largely a question of employment within the national territory and also tax revenues from local R&D, production and services.

3.3 International Trends in Service Industries

Most industrialized countries are in the process of becoming a service economy. Most obvious is the structural change in employment: Even those economies suffering from dramatic unemployment in manufacturing can have at the same time monotonously increasing jobs in the service sector. But this restructuring does not mean that manufacturing industry will soon seize to exist. As a rule of thumb one may assume that most of the new service firms use capital goods to provide their services. To give some examples we just mention credit card machines, computers, coin change machines, cafeteria appliances, cleaning machines, service robots and so forth. Inventions for the special market of „service machinery" show above average growth-rates (GEHRKE et al., 1994). The structural change towards a service society will always result in demand for capital goods from the manufacturing sector (GRUPP et al., 1996, p. 55). The challenge for machinery industry is, then, whether or not it provides the „right" machinery for the service society of the future, which will enhance its competitiveness in the manufacturing sector.

In the near future, it can hardly be expected that a rapid expansion of R&D-intensive sectors will be enough to solve the unemployment problems of highly developed industrialized nations. But, still, the technology-intensive sectors may also benefit from the shift towards service industries. Know-how-intensive service providers in particular are rapidly gaining ground and already now provide jobs for many. Their success is increasingly dependent upon innovation and the use of new technologies. This in turn generates new markets for technology producers, particularly for information and communication technologies, infrastructure facilities for the transport and communication sectors and medical technology. Technological advances are geared increasingly to the service sectors needs.

Parallel to this, the service sector is expanding its own research and innovation activity. In the USA, for instance, service enterprises already generate one third of their technical know-how through their own R&D efforts. In the United Kingdom, this figure is one forth. As a rule, company-oriented services expand fastest is areas where there is a demand for their products among innovating industries. Conversely, know-how-intensive service enterprises are still able to contribute to maintaining and enhancing the respective countries' attractiveness as a site for industry even when the service sector has undergone dramatic internationalization, such as in the past several years (BMBF, 1997).

The globalization of industry has, in turn, sharply stimulated the demand for services (transportation, finance, distribution, research and engineering) and accelerated the trend towards tertiarisation. The „service society" generates also new demands on technology policy. In general, this should result in a continued shift away from promoting the production of new technologies and towards promoting their use and dissemination. Ties to the technology supply should remain intact.

Let us consider one country in detail. In Germany's manufacturing sector nearly all jobs created after 1985 have since been lost in a net balance, whereas the service sector is characterized by a steady growth of employment. After 1991, and certainly after 1992, the growth rates became modest, but still there is no loss. If one examines the functional specifications of all business positions, then one finds

Tab. 12: Change in employment in industry and services in the five large OECD countries 1981/83 to 1991/93

	Germany (West)	France	UK	USA	Japan
	in 1000 employees				
Industry	118	-805	-1,040	-821	1,642
R&D-intensive branches	374	-287	-456	-542	1,127
Other branches	-257	-518	-584	-279	516
Services	3,007	2,128	1,306	18,540	5,804
Distributive services	633	74	489	4,917	622
Services for firms	164	651	817	5,597	562
Government services	305	879	na	2,027	6
Services for private persons	1,906	525	na	5,998	4,614

Source: OECD, calculations of DIW; in some cases the distinction between services for private persons and services for firms is not exact

that up until 1985 more than 37 per cent of the employees worked in production, maintenance, or repair of machines whereas this share in 1993 reduced to 32 per cent. Job function specifications in office work, planning, research, managing, educating and information in the same period of time expanded from 37.2 per cent to 42.4 per cent in the entire German economy.

What is reported here for Germany, can be observed in more or less the same way in the other large OECD countries. Tab. 12 shows the increase or decrease of employment between 1981/83 and 1991/93 for the United States, Japan, West Germany, France and the United Kingdom. With the only exception of Japan and R&D-intensive branches in manufacturing in Germany, all other branches in the countries considered suffered from a net loss in industrial employment. On the other hand, there is not one case of decreasing employment in the service industries be it services of distribution, services for firms, government services or services for private persons.

According to the table the increase in service industries was largest in the United States (nearly 30 per cent). One objection consists in the argument, that this increasing employment is problematic as it is low income jobs with low skill requirements. It is true, indeed, that 20 per cent of the increase in service jobs are in the area of retail and transportation and about 40 per cent is in services for households which includes the large restaurant and pub sector, yet, a similarly large share of service employment takes place between service providers and firms as users. In this case we speak of banks, insurances and so forth and this is a service sub-sector with relatively high skill requirements. It is exactly the United States where this share of service employment is largest so that the overall observation, that increasing service jobs are connected to low wages, maybe true, but it is less true for the United States than for other countries.

Let us now consider skill requirements and technology dynamics and elaborate the last argument further.

3.4 Skill Requirements and Technology Dynamics

The trends towards a „service economy" also has consequences for the demands on technical performance: Business-directed services continually need impulses from innovative areas in the industrial sector in order to develop an ongoing basis. Advanced services are needed if research and development, marketing, financing, production, and the like are pursued. This sector reinforces the growth impulses coming from industry and strengthens the industrial base within its service products. On the other hand, innovative contributions within the value added change are shifting from hardware production to software and services. There are expensive areas in the service sector that are not dependent upon technology production locations but require advanced technological solutions to fulfill their primary role. In this regard, it is also essential, that greater attention be paid to potential applications for, and the optimal combination of technology in the expanding service sector.

If not the functional specification but the qualification of the employees serves at a benchmarking criterion for the human-capital intensification, then for major OECD countries one arrives at the following assessment. In the first half of the nineties one has to confirm a trend claimed already earlier that the share of employees with a higher education degree (university, polytechnical or related schools) and the share of academic staff (university degrees only) is increasing in the manufacturing sector and in the service industries. This means that there is tendency to employ relatively more highly qualified persons both in the service sector, which is expanding, and in the manufacturing sector with a loss of jobs.

More interesting is another tendency. The structural change towards a service society is also accompanied by an increasing share of highly qualified employees there. In most years and in most countries the share of highly qualified employees in the service sector (except government employees) is about one per cent point above that in industry. For the immediate future one may assume that an intensification of human capital is ongoing in all sectors of the industry and any structural change towards more employment in the service sector gives an additional relative growth of higher qualified jobs (GRUPP et al., 1996, p. 56).

If we now, in summing up, consider the economies as a whole, that is, if we judge on both the manufacturing and the non-manufacturing sector, then the significance of human capital for economic growth can be diagnosed without doubt. Roughly speaking about half of the manufacturing and the service sectors are human-capital or knowledge-intensive; both figures increase in recent years. Therein the service sector is more and more dominating from year to year and thus, the sectoral change towards a knowledge intensive economy is spurred by the sectoral change towards a service economy in addition to the increases within each of the sectors. These seem to be two sides of the same coin.

If it is right, that there is more growth in overlapping, transdisciplinary fields of technology as compared with the core of the traditional technological areas, then it becomes apparent that the future challenges for education and re-education and also vocational training cannot be mastered within the classical schools, faculties, disciplines and circles alone. Future skill requirements go in the direction of interdisciplinary knowledge and life-long learning. This brings the question onto the agenda, whether our traditional institutions for education are sufficiently fit to train the next generation of employees.

As an example for the significance of multidisciplinary requirements and technology dynamics, we point to the example of German industry which - according to a questionnaire survey - has proven the multiplicity of technologies required. Even traditional industries are increasingly using several technologies at a time and thus staff originating from diverse schools and with diverse grades. There is no observation that tells us that in other countries this situation is much different. Thus, the close connection of technology dynamics and skill requirements can no more be denied.

Being educated themselves earlier, not only the young people, but also their teachers have to be retrained in particular in countries where for various reasons the educational staff is over-aged and cannot be replenished quickly enough because of low fluctuations.

3.5 Technology Dynamics, Skills, and Unemployment

One of the main objections to the inferential material in section 1.5.1 was that biased technological change was in the nature of a residual, exactly that in regression analyses, giving rise to a labeling problem. In the present section, we peer inside the technological change black box, examining US and UK studies that include technology proxies. In addition, we review an interesting German study that addresses the relative importance of trade and technology factors in explaining relative unskilled worker employment. We also briefly consider skill upgrading at the level of the firm. Such changes and policy implications are further discussed in section 2.7.

Our starting point will again be the two studies cited in Tab. A1. We begin with the US study. Having earlier decomposed the increase in the nonproduction worker share of the wage bill and total employment into their between-and within-industry components, BERMAN et al. (1994) regress within-industry shifts in the wage bill share (results for employment shares are not reported) on changes in output and changes in either capital or equipment and plant intensities. Dummies for the 1970s and 1980s are also included, given the finding that the change in the wage bill share is increasing through time. (A simple cost function is used to derive a share of nonproduction wages in total wages, from which evidence on the elasticity of substitution between production and nonproduction labor can (theoretically) be derived as well as the presence of capital-skill complementarity. This share equation is then first differenced to yield the basic estimating equation.)

The authors' estimates point to capital-skill complementarity and equipment skill complementarity, although capital accumulation does not contribute materially to the explanation of skill upgrading. Altogether, the independent variables explain around 12 percent of the variance in changes in the wage share of nonproduction workers. Adding in technology variables - specifically, the fraction of investments devoted to computers, and R&D intensity (the ratio of R&D expenditures to sales) - substantially improves the fit. The two proxies for technological change account for almost three-quarters of the observed shift away from production labor.

Similar results are reported by MACHIN (1996) for 16 two-digit UK manufacturing industries, using almost identical procedures but this time also presenting regressions for within-industry changes in the employment share of nonproduction workers. MACHIN provides separate regressions for his two technological change indicators: annual R&D intensities, and the number of innovations introduced/used. He finds that a one percentage point increase in R&D relative to sales increases the nonproduction worker wage bill share by 0.07 percentage points, and the employment share by .05 percentage points, although his results for innovations are only weakly statistically significant. Machin also provides disaggregative regressions using Workplace Industrial Relations Survey (WIRS) establishment data that allow him to evaluate the impact of increased computer usage. He finds among other things that increased computer usage is associated with increased employment shares of nonproduction workers and reduced employment shares at the lower end of the occupational employment range.

Another well-known piece of evidence consistent with the biased technological change argument is KRUEGER'S (1993) analysis of computer usage and occupational earnings. He finds that working with computers (versus not working with them) is associated with a cet. par. increase in wages of between 15 and 20 percent. Moreover, his estimates imply that the expansion in computer use during the 1980s can explain up to 50.5 percent of the observed increase in the return to education. (See also ALLEN, 1993.) Unlike the two preceding studies KRUEGER's analysis is not restricted to manufacturing industry.

A very recent study by STEINER and WAGNER (1997) is of particular interest because of its attempt to address the relative contribution of trade and technology factors in the decline in unskilled worker employment in German manufacturing, 1975-90. The authors' fixed effects, partial equilibrium model relates the relative demand for unskilled workers to relative wages, a trend variable, and a vector of (other) demand variables (e.g. the capital-output ratio) affecting the relative demand for the unskilled.[5] The coefficient estimate for the trend variable is supposed to capture factors common to all industries; in particular, skill-biased technological change and the overall decline in the supply of unskilled labor. The coefficient estimate for the relative wage variable captures the substitution elasticity between unskilled and skilled labor. For the authors' preferred specification the substitution elasticity is around -0.32, much lower than reported in other extant German estimates, while the secular decline in unskilled worker relative employment is in the order of 3 percent a year.

To gauge the effects of trade and technological change, the authors split their 31-industry sample according to quartiles of import penetration and productivity growth, respectively. For the former, the trend decline is modestly higher in industries with relatively high import shares (3.7 vs. 3.0 percent). For the latter, the trend decline is considerably higher in industries with high productivity growth rates (4 vs. 2.2-2.9 percent), suggesting a larger role for skill-biased technological change than for international trade - although the authors themselves consider the two forces to be interrelated. Interestingly, as was noted earlier, the substitution of unskilled by skilled workers due to the high relative earnings of the unskilled in Germany appears to have been small relative to the trend decline in the relative employment of unskilled workers.

In section 1.5.1 we noted that, despite its appeal in the US, the technology story has not gone unchallenged. This is also true at the empirical level, even if there has been little disagreement about the long-run course of events. That is, the complementarity between capital and skill is well established (e.g. GRILICHES, 1969) and the role of capital accumulation and technology in shifting demand in favor of higher order skills accepted. The main bone of empirical contention is whether technology's impact accelerated in the 1980s and 1990s.

In particular, MISHEL and BERNSTEIN (1996) have argued that the technological change story must proceed beyond its typical focus upon broad employment and education differentials to examine the entire skill and wage distributions (i.e. the demand for workers at various education and wage levels, where the latter are also assumed to proxy skill). The basic motivation here is the need to disaggregate.

MISHEL and BERNSTEIN's decomposition of within-industry wage inequality proceeds as follows. Their dependent variables reflect two measures of wage inequality, namely, between group inequality (or "education quantities," defined as the share of workers in a given education category) and overall wage inequality (or "wage quantities," defined as an industry's utilization of low, middle, or high-wage workers). Six education categories and five wage quantities are distinguished, and separate regressions run for each. The independent variables comprise a technology vector and a control for industry employment growth. Three technology indicators are deployed: the gross real equipment stock and the gross computer stock per full time equivalent, and the share of scientists and engineers in each industry. (All variables are measured as first differences.)

Because the effects of technological change can take the form of changes in skill bias as well as changes in the pace of technological change, the empirical model allows a distinction to be drawn between changes in complementarities and changes in the overall impact of technology through time. This is achieved by also interacting the technology covariates with time. (Three time intervals are recognized: the 1970s, which provide the reference period, and the 1980s, and the 1990s.) Changing complementarities are thus directly revealed by the (two) interaction terms. The overall impact of technology is obtained by multiplying the complementarities specific to each period by the average within-industry change in the relevant technology indicator over that period. Comparing these per period effects then establishes whether or not the impact of technology has accelerated through time. The reduced-form model is estimated over just 34 manufacturing and nonmanufacturing private sector industries over the three time periods (i.e. n=102), and estimates are provided for two specifications, namely, with and without the computerization covariate.

The authors' estimates are not favorable to the accelerated technological change argument, even if it is generally the case that greater levels of technology are associated with proportionately fewer high school equivalent workers and fewer middle and lower paid workers (namely, the bottom three-quarters of the wage structure). Specifically, as far as the educational quantity (i.e. education upgrading) regressions are concerned, the large majority of interaction terms between the relevant technology indicator and the time period are statistically insignificant. That is, there are no real signs of the complementarities shifting through time. Disregarding statistical significance, the estimates do not suggest a more profound effect for technology than for other factors, such as industry shifts. These results pertain to males. For females, on the other hand, there are some signs of acceleration in the technology effect but these are quantitatively very modest.

For wage quantities much the same negative conclusions hold, but in this case the result follows from technological change being less biased in the 1980s than in the 1970s for men in the bottom half of the distribution; correspondingly for the more skilled groups (the top 25 percent) technological change was less favorable. The pattern for women is again different, but once more there is no support for an accelerated technology effect adversely impacting the bottom half or three-quarters of the distribution and favorably impacting the top half.

The very directness of this study vis-à-vis its precursors may mean that the biased technological change explanation may have to share somewhat more equal billing with other explanations of wage and employment developments in the 1980s and 1990s (e.g. institutional changes), even if the long-term impact of technology on skill upgrading is not controversial. In other words, attributions of biased technological change on the basis of the predominance of within-industry movements may still be subject to a labeling problem. That being said, worrying features of the study concern its level of industry aggregation, lingering ambiguity over the reduced forms, and conflict with KRUEGER's (1993) results since MISHEL and BERNSTEIN's computerization variable fails to indicate stronger complementarities through time where these might be expected.

It might useful be pointed out at this stage that, KRUEGER'S study has been critiqued by DINARDO and PISCHKE (1997), who report that use of his methodology with German data produces the result that working with pencils yields a wage premium no less than working with computers! Using the German Qualification and Career Survey, which contains information on a variety of tools used on the job, one of the authors' specifications suggests a return to computers of 18.6 percent in 1991 and to pencils of 13.5 percent. Since everyone can use pencils, the inference might be that the return to computers is a selection effect - increased computer use picks up some unobserved skill whose return has also increased through time - albeit one that is not easily identified with standard statistical procedures. But, in the final analysis, DINARDO and PISCHKE are more critical of the use of the computer variable as a direct indicator of technological change than they are of the notion that accelerating technological change underpins observed changes in wages.

There are of course many factors behind changing pay inequality observed in Anglo-Saxon countries. For his part, MACHIN (1996), whom as we have seen reports fairly strong evidence of skill bias at the upper reaches of the occupational spectrum, is concerned to point out that these occurred at a time of radical transformation of the UK labor market (i.e. the Thatcher reforms). In particular, he alludes to the "shift in the balance of power" between management and labor during the 1980s. MACHIN recommends that such factors need to be modeled to obtain a fuller understanding of the determinants of changes in the employment structure.[6] He might also have emphasized the need to examine skill upgrading at the level of the firm, not least because of the breadth of the technological change concept.

In fact, MACHIN does present some findings pertaining to skill upgrading, 1984-90, using establishment data from the British Workplace Industrial Relations Survey(s). He reports that at the higher end of the nonproduction worker occupational distribution (middle/senior managers and senior technical/professional workers) most of the observed changes in employment shares are within industry while they are predominantly between industry at the tail (clerical workers). Furthermore, his regression analysis of changes in employment shares on the introduction of microcomputers in the workplace points to a positive association at the top end of the wage structure and a negative relation at the bottom, unskilled manual worker level. He interprets this evidence as indicating that computers provide an important means of upgrading the workforce.

Here again we have evidence of a direct indicator of technological change explaining some part of the observed change in the structure of employment, even if the process may be considerably more noisy than is indicated in this study.[7]

3.6 New Firms and Small Firms: Role for Innovation and Structural Change

The traditional view about the role of new and small firms is that they do not have a lot to do with the process of change, let alone structural change. This is because the most prevalent theory in economics focusing on change, the model of the knowledge production function (Griliches, 1979), links knowledge-generating inputs to innovative output. The most important source of new knowledge is generally considered to be R&D. But most of the R&D expenditures in Europe, as throughout the OECD countries tend to be made in large firms (COHEN and KLEPPER, 1992). New firms, which are particularly small, and have around an average 8 employees in manufacturing in various OECD countries (AUDRETSCH, 1995; MATA, 1994; WAGNER, 1994) and an even fewer number of employees in the services (CAREE and THURIK, 1996), simply do not seem to possess the resources to provide much in the way of change, or innovative activity. While new firms can and do have employees with very high degrees of human capital, the number of such employees is typically trivial compared to large corporations, such as Phillips, Thompson, or Siemens. The convention wisdom suggests, then, that due to possessing only a negligible amount of the crucial knowledge-producing inputs, principally R&D and human capital, the capacity for innovation and change in new firms is quite limited.

Towards the end of the 1980s, studies started being undertaken to identify the relative innovative activity contributed by small and large firms. These studies spanned most European countries, including the United Kingdom (ROTHWELL, 1989), Italy (SANTARELLI and STERLACCHINI, 1990; and AUDRETSCH and VIVARELLI, 1996), Germany (HARHOFF and LICHT, 1996), and the Netherlands (KLEINKNECHT, 1989), as well as the United States (ACS and AUDRETSCH, 1988 and 1990) and Canada (BALDWIN, 1995). The results were surprising and did not at all confirm the conventional wisdom that innovative activity is largely the domain of the largest enterprises. Rather, the evidence from a wide spectrum of European and OECD countries clearly documented that small firms as well as large enterprises play an important role in generating innovative activity.

One attempt to reconcile the new evidence that small firms as well as large enterprises generate innovative activity was to suggest that perhaps the innovative activity of small firms was less consequential than that contributed by large enterprises. This interpretation argued that, due to a lack of knowledge-generating resources, small firms and especially new startups simply did not posses the resources required to generate innovations, especially the kind that contribute to structural change (HARRISON, 1995). While the significance of innovative activity is difficult to measure, what little evidence there is suggested that the innovative activity of small firms is no less than that of their larger counterparts (ACS and AUDRETSCH, 1990; AUDRETSCH, 1995).

The conventional wisdom that expected innovation and structural change to come from largely large enterprises erred because the implicit model underlying that review miscast the process of innovation and ultimately structural change. In this conventional view the firms are exogenous. They then invest in knowledge-generating activity, such as R&D and human capital, in order to obtain the output of innovative activity. Thus, the firms are exogenous and the knowledge leading to innovative activity is endogenous. In this conventional model the disadvantage confronting small enterprises, and especially new enterprises, which tend to be the smallest firms of all is clear. They simply lack the resources required to generate change. From the vantage point of the conventional model of the knowledge production function, one wonders why any rationale person would ever start a new firm, especially in an environment where innovative activity plays an important role.

The flaw in this conventional view provided by the model of the knowledge production function is the implicit unit of analysis at the level of the firm, which leads to what appears to be the logical assumption that the firms are given or exogenous. But when the lens is shifted to the unit of analysis of people, or the individual, a very different result emerges. While firms are no doubt receptacles creating and storing knowledge (DOSI, 1988; TEECE et al., 1994; and NELSON and WINTER, 1982), at least some knowledge is embodied in people, either as individuals or collectively.

A rather large literature has emerged focusing on what has become known as the appropriability problem (BALDWIN and SCOTT, 1987). The focus of this literature has again been focused on the unit of analysis of the firm. The underlying issue revolves around how firms which invest in the creation of new knowledge can best appropriate the economic returns from that knowledge (ARROW, 1962). What has been almost completely overlooked in the literature is that individuals are also confronted with an analogous appropriability problem. When the lens is shifted away from the firm to the individual as the relevant unit of analysis, the issue of appropriability remains, but the relevant question becomes, *How can people with a given endowment of ideas and capabilities best appropriate the returns from that knowledge?*

If a person can pursue his ideas within an existing firm for roughly what he thinks they are worth, he will have no reason to start a new firm. But if he cannot pursue those ideas, or at least be rewarded for them, he has an incentive to start a new firm, either alone or in a team, in order to appropriate what he considers to be the value of his knowledge. Under what conditions is someone likely to remain in an incumbent firm or alternatively become involved in a new start-up? If the ideas and competence of a person, or his knowledge, is compatible with that of the incumbent firm, or what has become known as the firm's core competence and technological trajectory (DOSI, 1988; and DOSI et al., 1995), the person is more likely to be able to remain in an incumbent firm in order to appropriate the value of his knowledge. This is because there is more likely to be a convergence between the individual and the decision-making hierarchy in the evaluation of the ideas. Colleagues in the decision-making hierarchy are more likely to assign a roughly similar value to the ideas and be willing to implement them. Such (potential) innovations can be considered to be incremental in that they are compatible with the core competence and technological trajectory of the firm. The implementation of such incremental innovations do not require significant change in the firm or its personnel.

By contrast, a radical innovation can be defined as beyond the boundaries of the core competence and technological trajectory of the firm. Implementation of a radical innovation would require significant changes in the firm and its personnel. If the knowledge embodied in an individual involves a potentially radical innovation, there is more likely to be a disparity in the evaluation of that potential innovation between the individual and his colleagues in the decision-making hierarchy. The incumbent firm is less likely to agree to pursue changes that involve activities outside of its core competence and technological trajectory. This means that for the individual to appropriate the value of his knowledge he must start a new firm.

An implication of shifting the lens of the appropriability problem from the firm to the individual is that, in an effort to appropriate the value of their knowledge, people are more likely to start new firms when a radical innovation is involved but less likely to start a new firm when the innovative activity is incremental. This suggests that structural change, which involves change and innovative activity that is fundamentally different and beyond the technological trajectories and core competencies of the incumbent firms, is more likely to come from new firms than from incumbent firms.

Shifting the lens of the appropriability question to the individual suggests that the traditional model of the knowledge production function is less likely to hold in the case of innovative activity inducing structuring change, or radical innovation, but more likely to hold in the case of incremental innovation, which does not typically induce structural change. In the case of incremental innovation, the knowledge generated in a firm through its R&D and human capital investments tends to be pursued and appropriated within the boundaries of that firm. Thus, the firm can rightly be viewed as being exogenous and the generation of knowledge and innovative activity endogenous.

However, in the case of innovative activity inducing structural change, or what could be termed as radical innovation, the traditional model of the knowledge production function is less likely to be valid. In this case, the effort by individuals and teams of people to appropriate the value of their knowledge through innovative activity leads to the creation of a new firm. This actually leads to a reversal of the traditional view of the knowledge production function, where the knowledge can be considered to be exogenous and a new firm is endogenously created.

There is considerable anecdotal evidence and case studies documenting the importance of new firms in structural change, along with the resistance and inability of large incumbent enterprises to undertake structural change inducing innovative activity (AUDRETSCH, 1995). IBM resisted the development of the personal computer and later the microprocessor for years. The personal computer ended up being developed and introduced in a new startup, Apple Computer, and the microprocessor was developed and introduced by Intel. Siemens decided not to pursue the ideas of an employee to develop a work station, which led to his decision to leave Siemens and start a new firm in California, Sun. The biotechnology industry has its origins from scientists who were unable to commercialize their knowledge in large incumbent pharmaceutical companies and university laboratories and resorted instead to starting their own companies (AUDRETSCH and STEPHAN, 1996). Based on their studies on the emergence of the biotechnology industry, AUDRETSCH and STEPHAN (forthcoming) conclude that structural change in the form of new industries appears to come from knowledge created with perhaps one purpose in mind, but which is valuable in a very different context.

3.7 Labor Reallocation in Dynamic Markets

A conventional measure of quantitative flexibility in labor markets is the Index of Structural Change.[8] This index has often been used to address the ability of the labor market to adjust to shocks. Thus, for example, ALLEN and FREEMAN (1995) have assembled data on industry ISCs, inter al., to suggest that there has been no increase in flexibility in the US labor market in recent years, from which they infer that quantitative flexibility is unlikely to explain the different performance of the US and European economies in recent years.[9]

Part of the ISC data they provide for US one-digit occupations, 1956-93, is reproduced in Tab. A1. This points if anything to a decline in occupational shifts in the US over the last two decades as compared with the 1950s, '60s, and '70s. Abstracting from the issue of the usefulness of the SIC construct, one interpretation of this result is of course that there has been no acceleration in technological change. Another possibility, also noted by the authors, is that the decline in relative wages for the less skilled in the US has necessarily reduced the scale of employment shifts, perhaps because of a reduction in institutional rigidities (e.g. the decline in unionization). Yet another is that supply has reacted too slowly to shocks, thus requiring increased wage flexibility.

In comparing SICs for European countries with those for the US, ALLEN and FREEMAN emphasize the lack of major disparity in respective flexibilities, as measured by ISCs. They ultimately conclude from the different unemployment and real wage records of the US and Europe that the US has paid for its good employment performance via a weak wage performance. Flexibility, on this view, transcends overt restrictions on freedom of contract.

While accepting the latter point, it remains moot how far one can proceed in analyzing labor market reallocation on the basis of occupational ISCs, not least because the evidence also points to considerable shifts within occupations. A better approach to labor reallocation is to examine what happens at the level of the firm. First, and more generally, examination of the process of labor reallocation at the plant level within US manufacturing rather tends to confirm what we have learned from more aggregative analysis but with one important qualification. Thus, it has been found that job reallocation (the sum of job creation and job destruction) in the US is not widely different from that in many other nations. Vulgo: job churning is a normal state of affairs. Also, across all sectors there is excess job reallocation, that is, the sum of job creation and destruction often considerably exceeds that quantity required to meet net employment changes. Decomposition of this index of simultaneous job creation and destruction into its between-industry and within-industry constituents shows that the latter dominate the former, the interpretation now being that the process of job reallocation is driven by plant-level heterogeneity. (This is the important qualification.) Relatedly, there is little overall indication that greater exposure to international trade - as measured by import penetration or export share - impacts gross job flows or net job growth. Additionally, job creation is higher in industries with greater total factor productivity growth. Because job destruction is not higher in these sectors, the implication is that industries with higher productivity experience greater within-industry reallocation as well as net employment growth. (For an amplification of these points, see DAVIS and HALTIWANGER, 1992; DAVIS et al., 1996.)

Second, and more specifically, analyses of skill upgrading within plants also reveal evidence of considerable plant heterogeneity. Although BELLMANN et al. (1996) are able to discern patterns in German establishment data - for example, a decline in the demand for workers without professional/vocational training that is monotonic in firm size, and major differences in the skill composition of the workforce in growing versus declining and closing firms in favor of the former - other analyses point to greater heterogeneity. Thus, in a personnel rather than employment based survey of 1,000 manufacturing firms in the German province of Lower Saxony, ADDISON and WAGNER (1997) report considerable heterogeneity in levels of and changes in skill composition within firm size classes, age cohorts, and industries. They find no support for the notion of "creative destruction," nor do they find that the skill composition of exiting firms is in any observational sense inferior to that of survivors. They do find that the employment share of those with a university or polytechnic degree is positively associated with output and trade competitiveness but this result does not extend to skilled workers more generally.

The bottom line of establishment studies is therefore one of plant heterogeneity. As DAVIS et al. (1996, 158) note: "employment growth outcomes exhibit enormous heterogeneity among plants and firms that operate in the same classifiable sectors." The problem of heterogeneity is twofold. In the first place, it reminds us that technology encompasses many kinds of change that extend well beyond machines or computer programming or technical processes (e.g. management ability). Second, it manifestly complicates the design of labor policy.

Turning in conclusion therefore to policy, the main implications were rehearsed in WELFENS et al. (1997) and are only briefly noted here. These were that policy initiatives should seek to build on the notion of "universal complementarity" (MINCER, 1993) - namely, the strong empirical association between formal schooling and postschool training investments and returns - while safeguarding the position of the disadvantaged worker. The precise mix of policies for the latter is admittedly opaque in the absence of programs that have applied fully (as opposed to quasi) experimental procedures (BLOOM et al., 1997; ORR et al., 1996), and must anyway proceed on an incremental basis. As for the generality of the non-disadvantaged, the question of "what works best for whom" is we would argue best left to the market given the historical record (see, for example, GOLDIN and KATZ, 1995) and pending much more refined empirical analysis of alleged training shortfalls in private-sector training (on the theory of which, see BOOTH and SNOWER, 1996).

3.8 Firms from Eastern Europe and the NICs as Newcomers in Europe

The emergence of firms from Eastern Europe and the NICs is having a profound impact on Europe. The most immediate impact is in terms of new competition. On the one hand, firms from Eastern and Central Europe, as well as the NICs have access to considerably less expensive labor. The 1992 daily earning of labor have been estimated to be $78.34 in the European union, but only $6.14 in Poland, $6.45 in the Czech Republic, $9.25 in Hungary, and $8.98 in Romania (data adopted from JENSEN, 1993). The wage gap is even greater in Asia. The 1992 daily average wage was $1.53 in China, $2.46 in India, $3.12 in Pakistan, $1.25 in Sri Lanka, and $1.49 in Vietnam. Firms from these countries also have access to enormous populations willing to work at these low wages.

On the other hand, the skill and human capital levels in at least some of these countries are quite high. Certainly countries such as Hungary and Poland have a long tradition of worker discipline. Taken together, firms from Eastern Europe and the NICs are able to combine low costs with quite high skill levels. This has upset the patterns of comparative advantage that the post-war Western Europe was built upon.

GIERSCH, PAQUE and SCHMIEDING (1993) point out that the German Wirtschaftswunder, or economic growth miracle, was fueled to a considerable extent by relatively low labor unit costs and an undervalued currency. Technology developed in the United States could simply be adopted in Germany, as was also the case elsewhere in Europe, with the end result of lower unit costs of production and international competitiveness in Europe. But as the European countries caught up to the United States, and the unit cost of labor began to even surpass that of the United States in countries such as Germany, the comparative advantage of high-cost Western Europe is shifting away from traditional moderate-technology industries and towards newer high-technology industries. Firms from Eastern Europe and the NICs are increasingly able to produce in moderate-technology industries at a substantially lower cost.

The three largest countries in Central and Eastern Europe, what was at that time Czechoslovakia, Hungary and Poland, signed treaties with the European Community in 1990. At the heart of those treaties was a declaration of cooperation concerning trade, commercial and economic relationships. These agreements anticipated the set of Association Agreements involving those countries, and the European Union, which were signed in December 1991, and became ratified by the fifteen national parliaments. In the preamble of what became known as the *Europe Agreements,* a commitment was made to the "development of trade and investment, instruments which are indispensable for economic restructuring and technological modernization" (CEPR, 1992). The Europe Agreements are not without problems, particularly with respect to conflicts and implementation. According to Winters (CEPR, 1992, p. 1), "The agreements are disappointing in the degree of support and encouragement they guarantee to Czechoslovakia, Hungary and Poland)...Indeed they sometimes appear to be designed as much to minimize the adjustment that the revolutions of 1989 cause in the EC than to maximize the benefits that accrue to Czechoslovakia, Hungary and Poland."

The timing of the association process was divided into two stages, each lasting five years. A key condition upon passage into the second stage is the "progress to a market economy" (CEPR, 1992, p. 14). The first condition for making progress to a market economy is the free movement of goods. This involves the abolition of customs duties on "most industrial goods originating in the three countries" as well as all quantitative restrictions" (MAYHEW, 1992, p. 14). In addition, an "anti-dumping" clause was included for protection of domestic industries against serious injury. Finally, under the European Agreements the Association Countries are held responsible for adhering to the competition laws of the European Union, as mandated under the "Treaty of Rome". Similarly, all international trade agreements under the GATT must be adhered to (MAYHEW, 1992, p. 16).

As WINTERS (1992, p. 20) points out, despite the promised trade liberalization inherent in the European Agreements, iron and steel producers in the European Union were threatening antidumping actions against competitors in the Czech and Slovak Republics, Poland and Hungary: "As previously positioned, Czechoslovakian, Hungarian and Polish producers suffer a potential double-jeopardy – if Eastern and Central Europe must converge towards that practiced in the European Union. Similarly, practices involving customs law, company law, banking law, company accounts and taxes, intellectual property, protection of workers at the workplace, financial services, rules on competition, protection of health and life of humans, animals and plants, consumer protection, indirect taxation, technical rules and standards, transport and the environment all need to conform to the analogous practices currently found in the European Union.

In view of the large number of institutional adjustments that must be rapidly implemented in Eastern and Central Europe, Winters (1992, pp. 25-26) called for, "It is clear that (Czech and Slovak Republics, Poland and Hungary) need the legal framework – the soft infrastructure – to establish a market economy, and that they need it quickly; off-the shelf institutions seem to make sense in these circumstances and in many cases the EC model is as good as any other. Moreover, given their aspirations to join the EC it seems better to adopt the necessary institutions *ab initio*. The difficulties, however, are two fold. First, (Eastern European countries) have no discretion about the final goal – harmonization – and no influence on the ways in which the EC might move the goal posts either through new legislation or the interpretation of existing legislation. Second, the timetable for approximation looks unduly quick...In particular, it appears to be intended that approximation precede the (Eastern European)-EC free trade, which is not due for ten years. This reverses the normal order of integration and leaves a distinct impression that the EC is willing to trade freely only on its own terms. By requiring (Eastern Europe) to adopt the same legal restrictions on economic activity as it has itself, the EC undermines many of the advantages of mutual trade. If (Eastern Europe) feels happy, with, say, lower worker protection, it makes sense for the EC to buy from them those goods for which this offers significant cost reductions. It is far from clear that the EC conventions, developed for countries such as France and Germany, are ideally suited to the needs of the poorer transitional economies, and yet the Europe Agreements appear to offer the latter no alternative, even temporary."

The challenge to Europe posed by the new competition from Eastern Europe and the NICs is whether to resist that new competition in traditional moderate technology industries in the form of barriers and protection, or whether simply to acknowledge that the events of 1989 have shifted the comparative advantage of the high-cost Western Europe to knowledge-based economic activity.

3.9 Globalization and the Rising Importance of Diffusion

Product and process innovations clearly are crucial for productivity increases and economic growth. However, the rapid diffusion of new technologies and an optimum use of best-practice technologies are also important. With respect to the latter Germany suffered from a critical backwardness vis-à-vis the US, namely about 1/3 according to a recent study by McKINSEY (1996). Moreover, application of such technologies often is in sectors different from the innovative sector. Technology diffusion as a percentage of total embodied technology clearly was dominated by the service sector in the G-7 group in 1993 (OECD, 1997, p. 7). While the US, the UK, Japan and Italy recorded shares of more than 50%, France, Canada and Germany achieved only 44%, 42% and 43%, respectively. In particular Germany as a country with an underdeveloped service sector thus foregoes opportunities for higher economic growth and employment creation. In the mid-1990s the share of services in GDP was about 10 percentage points lower in Germany than in the US; the differences in the respective shares of employment in private sector services was of a similar magnitude. This apparent gap in the service sector is a major structural deficit in Germany, and overcoming obstacles to the expansion of this sector is a major policy challenge. This, however, could be difficult to meet since the high percentage of long-term unemployed - often former workers and employees from industrial firms - will rarely have the matching skills required for new jobs in service companies. Moreover, workers from the manufacturing sector which, being a high capital intensity / high productivity sector, used to pay rather high wages, will often find it unacceptable to voluntarily switch to a new job in the less capital intensive service sector which often will pay lower wages but offer greater job security.

3.10 Challenges for Achieving Efficient R&D Policies in the EU

The post-war view of R&D policy, not just in Europe, but also in all the OECD countries was based on an implicit routinized model of innovation in an economy where the most important inputs were land, labor and capital. R&D and technological change itself were viewed as being simply supplemental to these main factors of production. This was also an economy of relative certainty and stability, in that it was known what was to be produced, how it was to be produced, and who was to produce it. The international competitive advantage was generally achieved through cost reduction resulting from large-scale mass production to exploit scale economies.

The supplemental role of R&D in the post-war economy was designed to reduce costs through process innovation and to generate incremental innovations. The routinized role of R&D was perhaps first articulated by Schumpeter (1942, p. 132) who observed that, "Innovation itself is being reduced to routine. Technological progress is increasingly becoming the business of teams of trained specialists who turn out what is required and make it work in predictable ways."

Because of the relative certainty regarding markets and products, the appropriate policy response was to target outputs. That is, specific industries along with particular firms could be targeted for R&D through government programs. The targeting of specific firms in selected industries was clearly a successful policy for Japan in the post-war period and helped the Japanese achieve the competitive advantage in industries such as automobiles and electronics (AUDRETSCH, 1995).

The routinized model of innovation in an economy based on relatively high certainty and large-scale production also shaped R&D policy in Europe. The prevailing view in Europe was that its competitive disadvantage in high-technology industries was the result of a deficiency in firm size, which in turn was attributable to small and restricted domestic markets. As a response to "The American Challenge," in the form of the dynamism, organization, innovation, and boldness that characterize the giant American corporations," J.-J. SERVAN SCHREIBER (1968, p. 153) prescribed an R&D policy that would undertake "the creation of large industrial units which are able both in size and management to compete with the American giants" (p. 159). Because giant corporations were thought to be needed to amass the requisite R&D resources for innovation, SERVAN-SCHREIBER (1968, p. 159) argued that "The first problem of an industrial policy for Europe consists in choosing 50 to 100 firms which, once they are large enough, would be the most likely to become world leaders of modern technology in their fields. At the moment we are simply letting industry be gradually destroyed by the superior power of American corporations." This R&D policy prescription of targeting outputs is echoed in the 1988 Cecchini Report to the Commission of the European Union, where the anticipated gains from European integration are measured in terms of reduced costs achieved through increases in scale economies when firms are no longer limited to domestic markets and can instead operate on a larger European market.

How relevant is this traditional approach to R&D policy which targets outputs and outcomes today? One has to wonder what would have happened to the United States computer semiconductor industry had IBM been selected as "a national interest" around 1980 and promoted through favorable treatment as well as protected from threats like Apple Computer, Microsoft, and Intel. Would the United States be as strong in the computer, semiconductor, and software industries? While the proclamation, "What is good for General Motors is good for America" may have been sensible during the post-war period, it no longer holds in the 1990s. The reason is the routinized model of R&D no longer holds. First, as described in Section 3, globalization has resulted in the comparative advantage of high-cost locations, as is the case throughout most parts of Europe, is no longer compatible with economic activity in mature, traditional industries. The shift in the comparative advantage of high-cost locations in Europe to new and emerging industries means that economic activity is characterized by a high degree of uncertainty. Along with this shift in the comparative advantage of Europe has also come a shift in economic activity that is less based on the traditional inputs of land labor and capital and more based on the input of knowledge. It is no longer relatively certain what products should be produced, how they should be produced, and by whom. This increased degree of uncertainty increases the difficulty of selecting the correct outcomes and increases the likelihood that the wrong firm and industry will be targeted. Rather, the appropriate R&D policies in what Paul KRUGMAN (1994) terms as *The Age of Uncertainty* is to target inputs, and in particular those inputs involved in the creation and commercialization of knowledge. Such R&D policies involve basic and applied research at universities and research institutes, investments in the general level of education as well as advanced technical specialties, and the training and upgrading of the skill levels of workers.

Perhaps a newer aspect of R&D policy involves not just the basic and applied research but also the commercialization of the knowledge resulting from that research. The main conclusion from Section 2.6 is that new firms are especially crucial in the innovative process because they embody the attempt to commercialize knowledge in a manner that would otherwise would not be commercialized, particularly where structural change is involved. The efficiency of R&D policy can therefore be enhanced in an environment where the barriers to starting a new firm are at a minimum.

There is a broad range of institutions that are complementary to R&D and therefore enhance or impede the efficiency of R&D. Nelson (1995) argues that such institutions combine to constitute what he terms as a *National System of Innovation*. For example, the system of finance seems to be an institution that is complementary to and determines the efficacy of R&D. Many of the financial systems found throughout Europe, especially on the continent, were designed to enhance R&D and technological change under the model of routinized R&D (see CRESSY and OLOFSSON, 1997). For example, something of a paradox has emerged with respect to the system of financing for the German *Mittelstand*, or small- and medium-sized enterprises in Germany. On the one hand, there is reason to believe that through the development of a finely layered system of institutions linking together financial institutions, governments, and private firms, that the system of finance in Germany serves as a model for providing funds to small- and medium-sized enterprises. Not only was the *Mittelstand* the backbone of the German *Wirtschaftswunder*, or economic miracle, and subsequent rise to global economic power, but it also appears to have played a more important role in German economic development than in most other countries.

On the other hand, while the German Mittelstand has provided the backbone for Germany's economic success, one aspect has been noticeably lacking in recent years – the emergence of small high-technology companies in the emerging industries, such as software, biotechnology, and computers. And it may be that the lack of entrepreneurial activity in high-technology industries is directly attributable to rigidities and constraints in providing liquidity to new firms in new industries imposed by the German system of finance (AUDRETSCH and ELSTON, 1997). There are two institutional features of the German financial system that sharply contrast with that found in the United Kingdom which may influence the efficiency of R&D. First, companies in Germany typically rely almost exclusively upon banks for external finance. The external capital market remains relatively undeveloped in Germany. Second, not only do the banks represent the major financial intermediary supplying capital to firms, but they are also extensively represented on the supervisory boards of companies. Cable (1985, p. 119) refers to this peculiarity of the German financial system which links finance to supervision as a "quasi-internal capital market."

Perhaps the most striking feature of the Germany system of finance is the overwhelming importance of internal finance. During the 1980s about 90 percent of finance of physical and financial capital formation of large quoted German companies came from internal funds. By contrast, in Britain, only about 58 percent of such finance came from internal funds. There is at best only a limited market for corporate control in Germany. The negligible role played by the market for corporate control is evidenced by the small number of public corporations. In 1989, only 2,682 publicly limited companies, what are known as

Aktiengesellschaften, or Ags, existed in Germany. And of these only 501 were listed companies (DEUTSCHE BUNDESBANK, 1991). Still, as EDWARDS and FISCHER (1994) point out, the bulk of the largest German companies are, in fact, *Aktiengesellschaften*. Of the one hundred largest German companies, 88 are *Aktiengesellschaften*.

Financial and non-financial enterprises exert a high degree of ownership and influence on German firms. In 1988, non-financial enterprises accounted for 39.1 percent of the total nominal value of *Aktiengesellschaften*, and banks accounted for another 11.6 percent (DEUTSCHE BUNDESBANK, 1991). EDWARDS and GORDON (1994) observe that a network of institutions, including intercompany holdings and the proxy voting system (*Depotstimmrecht*), company law, code-termination law, stock exchange regulation, and the system of regulation has evolved providing a system of corporate control in Germany where the largest industrial enterprises exert a key influence.

The system of proxy voting, or *Depotstimmrecht*, enables banks to vote on the shares which are owned by customers of banks. When the indirect control is accounted for, the control of the leading Germany companies by banks is considerable. For example, in 1992, banks controlled 95.5 percent of the voting rights of Siemens, 44.1 percent of the voting rights of Volkswagen, 98.5 percent of the voting rights of Hoechst, 94.7 percent of the voting rights of BASF, 91.3 percent of the voting rights at BAYER, 45.4 percent of the voting rights at These, and 98.1 percent of the voting rights at Mannesmann (THE ECONOMIST, 1995).

While considerable attention has been placed on the role that the *Grossbanken* play in terms of financing the largest manufacturing corporations of Germany, substantially less emphasis has been placed o the other institutions comprising the German financial system. AUDRETSCH and ELSTON (1997) point out that, in fact, the Big Three Banks – the Deutsche Bank, the Dresdner Bank, and the Commerzbank – account for slightly less than one-tenth of all banking assets. The bulk of credit from the Big Three private banks is channeled into the largest firms.

The largest financial institutions are the Sparkassen, which are essentially public savings banks, and the *Genossenschaftsbanken*, which essentially are co-operative banks. While the *Sparkassen* account for around forty percent of all banking assets, the *Genossenschaftsbanken* account for about 15 percent of total banking assets. These financial institutions are generally oriented towards financing the German *Mittelstand*.

One of the major concerns about the German system of finance is that it provides efficient finance for investments where it is well understood what is to be produced, who is to produce it, and how the product is to be produced. Thus, the German system of finance may have excelled at providing finance efficiently for the largest companies in the traditional industries, as well as the traditional mittelstaendische firms producing traditional types of products.

However, the German system of finance is not well equipped for providing finance outside of the traditional industries, that is in high-technology and newly emerging industries. And it is in these emerging high-technology industries that Germany is straggling behind North America and Southeast Asia. Thus, a recent cover story of *Newsweek* is devoted to, "Why Europe is Losing the Technology Race"(NEWSWEEK, 1994). As the lead article of this issue points out,, "The problems at Siemens are far from unique. They are, instead, spread throughout much of Europe's high-tech landscape, and in particular in what the Germans like to call "telematik": the rapidly converging fields of computers, telecommunications and television. With only a handful of exceptions, in nearly every segment of the so-called information-technology industry, there is a rout underway."

Similar sentiment can be found in Germany, where *Der Spiegel* observes that, "Global structural change has had an impact on the German economy that only a short time ago would have been unimaginable: Many of the products, such as automobiles, machinery, chemicals, and steel are no longer competitive in global markets. And in the industries of the future, like biotechnology and electronics, the German companies are barely participating." (DER SPIEGEL, 1994). And the *Wall Street Journal* warns that in Germany, "If you look at the chip industry, it's a disaster. And the computer industry has been for many years. Energy technology as such is a disaster" (THE WALL STREET JOURNAL, 1994).

What does the inability of Germany to shift its economic activity out of traditional industries and into new emerging high-technology and high-information industries have to do with the system of finance? As one of the leaders in the German Bundestag, or parliament, observed, "A company like Microsoft would ever have had a chance in Germany" (THE ECONOMIST, 1995). This is because, "Big German banks and leading industrial companies form a closed cartel that stifles investment in budding entrepreneurs" (THE ECONOMIST, 1995).

The system of finance in Germany consists of a complex of financial intermediaries that may actually have provided more liquidity to firms, even small- and medium-sized firms, than their counterparts obtain in other countries both within Europe and in other OECD countries. Certainly the evidence is that during the *Wirtschaftswunder* and post-war period, the system of finance provided a key complementary role to promoting the R&D policies of Germany, The challenge currently confronting the German system of finance is even more urgent – how to modify the financial system in order to facilitate finance for new firms in new industries. That is, while the incumbent system of finance may have been highly efficient in channeling funds to *mittelstaendische* and large firms alike in traditional industries, it is not at all conducive to financing new ideas that lay beyond the boundaries of traditional industries and enterprises.

In the United States venture capitalists hire scouts to travel around Silicon Valley and other high-technology clusters to identify good targets for venture capital. Venture capital firms are then prepared to back promising start-ups with around $4-$5 million. By contrast, considerably more caution is shown by their European counterparts. For example, Dutch venture capitalists are more focused on later-stage financing, "They like to avoid risks, but they really should be more prepared to give money to people with good ideas" (THE NETHERLANDER, 1997). At the same time there is also evidence that the software companies themselves are not receptive to venture capital: "A number of venture capital companies are willing to supply money to software companies, so much so that they are investing in Israeli and French software companies...But many Dutch software companies are not looking for finance. The software industry itself exhibits a cautious approach to financing."

The United Kingdom has been more successful at implementing structural change than has Germany. One reason has been the existence of what is known as *Business Angel Networks*, which provide a channel of communication between private venture capital investors, commonly known as business angels, and entrepreneurs seeking risk capital (MASON and HARRISON, 1997). These business angel networks typically operate locally on a non-profit basis and their costs are underwritten by the government. Even with the recent emergence of private business angel networks, there still seems to be an important role for support from the public sector, since the evidence suggests that private sector business angel networks are primarily involved with larger, alter stage deals, whereas investments made through non-profit business angel networks generally involve smaller startups at an earlier stage of development. The emergence of private sector business angel networks has not eliminated the need for public sector support of locally-oriented business angel networks.

4. EUROPEAN R&D POLICY FROM A GLOBAL PERSPECTIVE

4.1 R&D Policies in the EU, the US and Far East Asia

European R&D policy needs to be evaluated and formulated within the context of a global perspective. Part of the reason for the importance of a global perspective is the opportunity to learn from the experience of other countries. But the biggest reason is that globalization has shaped the types of R&D policies that tend to be successful in Europe.

There are two driving aspects of globalization. The first involves the telecommunications revolution which has drastically reduced the cost of transmitting information across geographic space. The second aspect involves the emergence of competition from a broad spectrum of countries that were not competing with European nations only a few years, spanning from low-cost countries such as Indonesia and Malaysia, to countries with formidable stocks of knowledge and technological competence, such as Singapore and Taiwan. Taken together, these two forces have altered the way in which R&D policy can be effective in Europe.

Much of the R&D policy in Europe has been targeted towards the established European industries which have historically been the engines of European growth and competitiveness. Such traditional industries include automobile production, metalworking industries and machine tools. The industry life-cycle theory introduced by RAYMOND VERNON (1966) is typically considered to link trade and foreign direct investment to the stage of the life-cycle. There do not appear to be direct implications for R&D policy. But a more thoughtful examination of the framework of the industry life-cycle suggests that the role of R&D policy is shaped by the industry life cycle.

There have been various renditions of what actually constitutes the industry life cycle. For example, OLIVER WILLIAMSON (1975, pp. 215-216) has depicted the industry life cycle as, "Three stages in an industry's development are commonly recognized: an early exploratory stage, an intermediate development stage, and a mature stage. The first or early formative stage involves the supply of a new product of relatively primitive design, manufactured on comparatively unspecialized machinery, and marketed through a variety of exploratory techniques. Volume is typically low. A high degree of uncertainty characterizes business experience at this stage. The second stage is the intermediate development state in which manufacturing techniques are more refined and market definition is sharpened, output grows rapidly in response to newly recognized applications and unsatisfied market demands. A high but somewhat lesser degree of uncertainty characterizes market outcomes at this stage. The third stage is that of a mature industry. Management, manufacturing, and marketing techniques all reach a relatively advanced degree of refinement. Markets may continue to grow, but do so at a more regular and predictable rate...established connections, with customers and suppliers (including capital market access) all operate to buffer changes and thereby to limit large shifts in market shares. Significant innovations tend to be fewer and are mainly of an improvement variety."

While not explicitly stated by VERNON (1966) or WILLIAMSON (1975), the role of R&D does not stay constant over the industry life cycle. In the early stages of the life cycle, R&D tends to be highly productive, so that there increasing returns to R&D. In addition, the costs of (radical) innovation tend to be relatively low while the cost of incremental innovation and imitation tend to be relatively low. Because innovation in newly emerging industries tends to be more radical and less incremental, it is more costly to diffuse across geographic space for economic application in lower-cost locations.

By contrast, as an industry evolves over the life-cycle, the cost of radical innovation tends to increase relative to the cost of incremental innovation and imitation. That is, strong diminishing returns to innovative activity set in relative to incremental innovation and especially imitation. An implication is that it requires an increasingly amount of R&D effort to generate a given amount of innovative activity as an industry matures over the life cycle. At the same time, it requires a decreasing amount of expenditures to transfer new technology to lower cost locations, because innovation activity tends to become less radical and more incremental.

An important implication of the life cycle model is that as an industry matures, the cost of limiting falls relative to the cost of innovating, so that it becomes increasingly economical to transfer that technological knowledge to less costly locations of production, either through trade or foreign direct investment.

GIERSCH, PAQUE and SCHMIEDING (1992) point out that the German *Wirtschaftswunder*, or economic growth miracle, was fueled to a considerable extent by relatively low labor unit costs and an undervalued currency. Thus, technology developed in the United States could simply be adopted with the end result of lower unit costs of production and international competitiveness. But as the European countries caught up to the United States, and the unit cost of labor began to even surpass that of the United States in countries such as Germany, simply following a strategy of technology adoption is no longer sufficient to ensure international competitiveness in Europe. The 1994 mean manufacturing employee compensation (including insurance and other employee benefits was the highest in Germany, at $25.71 per hour. By contrast, the mean hourly manufacturing wage was just $19.01 in Japan and $16.73 in the United States.

Many of the industries which have been the traditional strengths in Western Europe have evolved towards the mature and declining stages of the life cycle. This means that the high-cost *Standort* in European countries become increasingly vulnerable, since the production of rather standardized technologies can be shifted to locations in central and Eastern Europe, or in Asia, with lower production costs.

While labor cost disadvantages can be offset through productivity increases and the substitution of technology for labor, innovative activity itself tends to become more incremental in nature as the industry evolves over the life cycle. Therefore, in mature industries it becomes increasingly difficult for European firms in mature industries to maintain their international competitiveness through innovative activity.

The divergence of real living standards between the developed and developing countries combined with the maturation of traditional industries in the developed countries dictates that either domestic firms lose market shares to foreign companies which are increasingly able to clone existing technologies and apply them to cheaper location-specific costs, such as wages, or else they maintain their competitiveness through foreign direct investment and shifting to production to lower-cost foreign locations.

The consequences of the maturation of traditional industries in high-cost locations is downsizing -- as a result of either a loss in market share or a shift in production out of the high-cost *Standort* to lower-cost locations -- is what has been termed in the press as corporate downsizing. The United States Labor Department recently reported that as a result of corporate downsizing "more than 43 million jobs have been erased in the United States since 1979" (NEW YORK TIMES, 1996). This includes 24.8 million blue collar jobs and 18.7 million white collar jobs. Between 1980 and 1993, the 500 largest US manufacturing corporations cut 4.7 million jobs, or one quarter of their work force (AUDRETSCH, 1995). Recent downsizing announcements by US corporations include 123,000 job cuts by AT&T, 122,000 by IBM, and 99,400 by Boeing. Since 1986 IBM has reduced employment by about 45 percent (BUSINESS WEEK, 1995), Perhaps most disconcerting, the rate of corporate downsizing has apparently increased over time. During most of the 1980s, about one in 25 workers lost a job. In the 1990s this has risen to one in 20 workers (BUSINESS WEEK, 1996).

Such downsizing has not been at all unique to the United States but has become increasingly rampant throughout Europe. Consider the case of Sweden. Some 70 percent of Sweden's manufacturing employees work for large companies, most of them multinationals, such as Volvo, which have been constantly shifting production out of the high-cost location, Sweden, and into lower cost countries, through outward foreign direct investment. Between 1970 and 1993 Sweden lost 500,000 private sector jobs, and unemployment is currently 13 percent of the workforce. And Sweden is not an exceptional case. For example, every third car that is manufactured by a German company is actually produced outside of Germany (HANDELSBLATT, 1994). Similar corporate downsizing has taken place in Germany (DER SPIEGEL, 1995). For example, employment by the ten largest companies has generally fallen within Germany between 1984 and 1995. At the same time, employment by these companies outside of Germany has risen, drastically in some cases. Thus, there is considerable evidence that the largest German companies are shifting jobs outside of Germany, resulting in a wave of corporate downsizing within Germany.

As *Die Zeit* points out in a front page article, "When Profits Lead to Ruin -- More Profits and More Unemployment: Where is the Social Responsibility of the Firms?" the German public has generally responded to this corporate downsizing with accusations that corporate Germany is no longer fulfilling its share of the social contract (DIE ZEIT, 1996).

What is to become of the dislocated resources, in particular labor? The answer is nothing, unless either the price of those inputs, i.e. wages, fall sufficiently to compete internationally, or they are redeployed in new economic activity that cannot be so costlessly diffused across geographic space.

Combined with the telecommunications revolution, this means that information generated by R&D in mature industries can be transferred to lower-cost locations for economic commercialization. By contrast, the knowledge resulting from R&D in newly emerging industries cannot be easily transferred to lower-cost locations for economic commercialization. Thus, globalization changes the nature of the comparative advantage of the particular quality of R&D activity in Europe away from modifications along existing technological trajectories and towards new products and the creation of new technological trajectories. The importance of geographic location to knowledge spillovers and innovative activity in a world increasingly dominated by E-mail, fax machines and electronic communications superhighways may seem surprising and even paradoxical. After all, the new telecommunications technologies have triggered a virtual spatial revolution in terms of the geography of production. According to *The Economist*, "The death of distance as a determinant of the cost of communications will probably be the single most important economic force shaping society in the first half of the next century. It will alter, in ways that are only dimly imaginable, decisions about where people live and work; concepts of national borders; patterns of international trade (THE ECONOMIST, 1995).

The resolution to the paradox posed by the localization of knowledge spillovers in an era where telecommunications has dramatically reduced the cost of communication lies in a distinction between knowledge and information. While the marginal cost of transmitting *information* may be invariant to distance, presumably the marginal cost of transmitting *knowledge*, and especially *tacit knowledge*, rises with distance. VON HIPPLE (1994) persuasively demonstrates that high context, uncertain knowledge, or what he terms as sticky knowledge, is best transmitted via face-to-face interaction and through frequent contact. Proximity matters in transmitting knowledge because as Kenneth Arrow (1962) pointed out some three decades ago, such tacit knowledge is inherently non-rival in nature, and knowledge developed for any particular application can easily spill over and be applied for different purposes. Similarly, ZVI GRILICHES (1992, pp. 29-47) has defined knowledge spillovers as "working on similar things and hence benefiting much from each others research." GLAESER et al. (1992, pp. 1126-1152) have observed that " intellectual breakthroughs must cross hallways and streets more easily than oceans and continents."

That knowledge spillovers tend to be geographically localized is consistent with frequent observations made by the popular press, business community, as well as by policy makers. For example, *Fortune* magazine points out that, "business is a social activity, and you have to be where important work is taking place" (FORTUNE, 1993). A survey of nearly one thousand executives located in America's sixty largest metropolitan areas ranked Raleigh/Durham as the best city for knowledge workers and for innovative activity (the survey was carried out in 1993 by the management consulting firm of Moran, Stahl & Boyer of New York City). *Fortune* magazine reports, "A lot of brainy types who made their way to Raleigh/Durham were drawn by three top research universities. US businesses, especially those whose success depends on staying atop new technologies and processes, increasingly want to be where hot new ideas are percolating. A presence in brain-power centers like Raleigh/Durham pays off in new products and new ways of doing business...Dozens of small biotechnology and software operations are starting up each year and growing like *kudzu* in the fertile business climate" (FORTUNE).

And *Business Week* reports a cluster of innovative activity located in the Seattle region, "These startups clustered in and around Seattle are determined to strike it big in multimedia, a new category of software combining video, sound, and graphics. Why Seattle? First and foremost, there's Microsoft Corp. The $4.5 billion software giant has brought an abundance of programming whiz kids to the area, along with scores of software startups. But these young companies also draw on Seattle's right-brain side: its renowned music scene, acclaimed theater, and a surprising array of creative talent including filmmakers, animators, writers, producers, and artists" (BUSINESS WEEK, 1994).

Considerable evidence has been found suggesting that location and proximity clearly matter in exploiting knowledge spillovers. Not only have JAFFE, TRAJTENBERG and HENDERSON (1993) found that patent citations tend to occur more frequently within the state in which they were patented than outside of that state, but AUDRETSCH and FELDMAN (1996) found that the propensity of innovative activity to cluster geographically tends to be greater in industries where new economic knowledge plays a more important role.

As ARCHIBUIGI and PIANTI show, along with the country studies in Richard Nelson's exploration of *national systems of innovation*, R&D policies in Europe are typically oriented towards mature and traditional industries. R&D in these mature and traditional industries do not tend to transmit into employment growth in the domestic country. Rather, the low-cost of diffusing the information tends to result in the transfer of the economic activity out of the high-cost location and into lower-cost locations around the globe.

Thus, the forces of globalization dictate that European R&D policy needs to shift away from the mature industries and towards new and emerging industries. Why has it proven so difficult to shift R&D out of traditional mature industries and into newly emerging industries? At least some insight is provided by the literature identifying the role that specific technological paradigms play in shaping the nature of innovative activity. This literature, which spans organizational theory and business history suggests that firm behavior and organizations are shaped by the specific technological environment in which firms are operating (Chandler, 1990). In particular, this literature has generally identified that firm behavior is closely linked to core firm competence. That is, firms are organizations with a specific set of competencies within a bounded set of activities. As Nelson and Winter (1982) emphasize, firm core competencies typically have a tacit nature and are stored and organized in the routines which guide decision-making. The learning process through which capabilities and routines are developed and shaped is to a large extent local and path dependent.

The concept of *technological paradigms* links the technological environment within which the firm has operated to the core competence of that firm. Innovations that enhance the existing capabilities and routines are generally viewed as falling within the technological paradigm of the core competence of the firm. By contrast, innovations that detract and destroy the existing capabilities and routines of the firm are generally viewed as falling outside of the boundaries of the core competence of the firm.

Whether or not any given firm adopts a new technology will very much depend upon whether that new technology falls within the core competence of the firm or outside of the core technological competence. This is because the cost of adoption to the organization is considerably lower for competence enhancing innovations than for competence destroying innovations. As DOSI, PAVITT and SOETE (1990, p. 45) point out, "Leadership in an old technological paradigm may be an obstacle to a swift diffusion of the new one, especially owing to the interplay between the constraint posed by the capital stock to readjustment of productive activities and the behavioral trends in 'old' companies which may embody differential expertise and enjoy high market shares in 'old' technologies."

ARCHIBUGI and PIANTA (1992) have analyzed patterns of patenting for specific industries over a broad spectrum of countries and concluded that, even when considered over a long period of time, the technological capabilities of most countries remain remarkably specialized. Most countries, especially smaller ones, tend to specialize in technology in just several industries. Within the technological paradigms associated with these industries new technological developments apparently tend to diffuse fairly rapidly. However, there has been little tendency for countries, and especially European countries, to broaden their technological bases, suggesting that diffusion across technological paradigms is considerably more complicated and costly.

COHEN and LEVINTHAL (1989) argue that firms can influence their ability to adopt new technologies by expanding the boundaries of core competence, or what they term absorptive capacity. While R&D is generally considered to generate new technological knowledge, COHEN and LEVINTHAL argue that it also serves a dual purpose -- to assimilate and exploit existing knowledge, or to facilitate the adoption of existing technology. That is, economists (Arrow, 1962) have long observed that firms invest in R&D in order to internalize knowledge which is external to the firm. COHEN and LEVINTHAL (1989, p. 569) similarly argue that, "While R&D obviously generates innovations, it also develops the firm's ability to identify, assimilate, and exploit knowledge from the environment."

COHEN and LEVINTHAL refer to the two faces of R&D, but there is perhaps also a third face. The nature and direction of R&D activities undertaken, while serving to expand the absorptive capabilities of the firm, may also contribute to defining the boundaries and entrenching those boundaries of the firm's capabilities. Thus, COHEN and LEVINTHAL make explicit reference to the numerous studies identifying that many of the important innovations in new industries come from outside of the emerging industry. For example, most of the computer industry's main innovations originated with developments outside of the industry, particularly in semiconductors. Similar evidence has been found for the aluminum industry. And an important study found that of the twenty-five major discoveries introduced into the United States by DuPont, despite the company's reputation for pathbreaking research, fifteen originated with work done outside of the company. Why weren't these innovations pursued by the firms creating the initial technological knowledge? Presumably because their (restricted) core competencies did not easily permit adopting new technologies beyond the boundaries of the firm's technological paradigm.

It used to be that the literature identified the most obvious difference between R&D policies in the European Union, the United States and East Asia is that technology policies have been targeted towards accomplishing specific projects in countries such as France, the United Kingdom and the United States, while they have been more oriented towards the diffusion of technology in countries such as Germany and Japan (AUDRETSCH, 1989; ; ERGAS, 1987; AUDRETSCH, 1997). This dichotomy between *mission-oriented* and *diffusion-oriented* technology policies, which seemed important for the post-war period, seems less compelling today.

What seems more compelling in the contemporary world is a framework that focuses on R&D policy in terms of the production of new knowledge, the commercialization of that knowledge, and the diffusion of existing knowledge. This framework is better articulated by Richard Nelson (1993) in his *National Systems of Innovation*.

R&D policy has generally shifted in East Asia from targeting selected outputs and incomes, which was more typical during the post-war period, to targeting selected outputs and outcomes. An example of the more traditional R&D policy of targeting outputs and outcomes was prevalent in Japan during the post-war period, starting with automobiles and electronics and later spreading to consumer electronics and computers (AUDRETSCH, 1989). The Very Large Scale Integration (VLSI) project targeted R&D in semiconductors, which was formed in 1976 and operated until 1979 may be one of the last examples of successful targeting of outputs and outcomes in Japan. The goal of the VLSI project was to develop large-scale integration and high-speed semiconductors for use in domestically manufactured computers. Five firms were targeted in the VLSI project – Fujitsu, Hitachi, Mitsubishi Electric, NC and Toshiba. The VLSI Technical Research Association consisted of these firms and was formed to help advance basic research in fields such as micro-processing, crystallization, design and device technology, all of which were essential for development and competitiveness of the Japanese semiconductor industry (IFO, 1997).

R&D policies in the Netherlands have been particularly effective in recent years. The Dutch high-technology industry has been booming. The number of personnel engaged in information technology in the Netherlands increased from about 760,000 in 1990 to around 835,000 by 1991. But then high-technology entered a slump, with employment falling to around 725,000 by 1994. However, as a result of government policies the sector has revived, so that by 1996 there were around 760,000 employed in information technology. One of the policies pursued has been to establish the high-tech company in Silicon Valley. This provides access to the most prominent knowledge source and also gives the company an edge in building a reputation. On the basis of the reputation built in Silicon Valley, the company then moves back to the Netherlands by persuading Dutch investors of the future viability of the start-up.

Still, start-up companies suffer from a lack of venture capital; there is a shortage of qualified people. And the best firms tend to be taken over rapidly by American high-tech companies. For every information technology worker seeking a job in the Netherlands there are an average of five vacancies. In addition, many of the highly-qualified people leave for the United States (THE NETHERLANDER, 1997).*The Netherlander* warns that, "The paradox is that while the IT industry is the biggest economic sector in the world, interest is waning in the Netherlands." One of the pioneers of the Dutch software industry, BODO DOUQUE, who founded the software company Inside Automation in 1984 warns that the high-technology sector "is a disaster. Software is a fantastic product and there are far too few women working in IT. But the politicians are too busy listening to old pre-war companies." In particular, the one billion Dutch guilders pumped into Fokker prior to its bankruptcy would have been better spent on giving one million guilders each to 1,000 start-up companies.

In order to promote investment in Dutch high-technology, two new indices have been introduced which track technology companies – the Microelectronics, Information Services and Telecommunications (MIT) and the MIT Smallcap. Both indices include all the bourse-listed companies in these sectors, with the exception of Philips and KPN, which are excluded from the MITS. The index is the result of a government-private partnership combining the Statistics Netherlands (CBS) and the technology broker Wessilus. The idea behind the index was to increase the visibility of the Dutch high-technology sector. These indexes have contributed to the prediction of a 40 percent growth in the Dutch high-technology sector over the next three to four years.

One of the most promising fields in high-technology in the Netherlands is micromechanics. The industry is centered around the Delft Institute of

Microelectronics and Sub-micro technology (Dimes). Dimes consists of around 300 researchers and is the largest microelectronics university institute in the Netherlands. In addition to a number of contracts with Philips, Dimes is also conducting studies for about 50 smaller companies.

Since the 1980s all OECD countries have established technology policies which are aimed at increasing through the development of scientific and technical resources. Most of this technology policy is undertaken at the national level and is predominantly concerned with levels of funding. Such national levels of R&D funding and national technology policies are problematic, because much of the innovative activity in high-technology is of a regional nature and is overlooked by national technology policies.

4.2 Basic Research in an International Comparative Perspective

The term „science" is understood to cover the creation, discovery, examination, classification, reorganization and dissemination of knowledge on physical, biological or social subjects. „Technology" is science application know-how. As such, it belongs to a large group of like activities which embrace the creation and use of artifacts, crafts and items of knowledge as well as various forms of social organizations. Technology does not only signify the application of scientific results, but any purposive treatment, method, working method and skill in the exploitation of scientific knowledge together with the products of so doing.

The significance of the „research" process in the materialization of the innovations nowadays is uncontested. According to the rules of present day research statistics, a distinction must be made between fundamental research, applied research and experimental development (OECD, 1993). The three subsequent differentiated concepts are often combined under the heading „research and development (R&D)".

„Basic research" refers to experimental or theoretical work geared primarily to the acquisition of new knowledge about the basic original phenomena and observable events without targeting a particular application or use. „Pure basic" or „fundamental research" is not initiated primarily, but exclusively with the aim of advancing knowledge without in so doing raising expectations of an economic or social increase of prosperity, not even as a long-term prospect, nor is it dedicated to solving practical problems. The term „application-oriented basic research" is used in situations where basic research targets certain areas of general interest like climate, cancer, energy saving research, or is focused in their direction. For this grey area between pure basic research and applied research, other concepts such as „strategic" or „long-term application oriented" concepts have also been formulated. These are however, not component parts of the set of conventions specified by national and supra-national organizations.

Science and technology are often distinguished from research and development by by institutional demarcations and then designate the place at which R&D occurs. However, this is a problematic concept. The term science includes college instruction, while R&D activity adds to the general availability state of the art knowledge. It represents knowledge production. Unlike college instruction, i.e. caring for the knowledge base and its dissemination, knowledge production has the status of an economic activity, as it was obvious since long what impact research processes could have an economic growth. Thus, the concept science and technology should be kept separate from R&D and not be demarcated by the institutional approach. For is it not science for which an industrial researcher is awarded the Nobel price? And surely virtually everything that a college does is therefore already science? Basic research is not identical to science and experimental development is not identical to technology.

Therefore, owing to the partial overlaps between the science and technology systems, these are only clearly distinguishable in archetype. Also, R&D activities can only be subdivided into various types analytically but not always in practice.

With these reservations let us have a look at the breakdown of government budget appropriations of European countries first. Some of these funds are used for definite areas of oriented research like the ones mentioned above, another part is dedicated for defense research. We have put all these application-oriented objectives of research under the term „oriented research" and kept separate the non-oriented part and general university funds.

Thus, in comparative perspective, it becomes clear that a series of smaller European countries is strongly oriented towards general universities and other non-oriented research and does spend comparatively little money on oriented research. The Netherlands, Italy, Sweden and Germany also belong to this group with a share of less than 50 per cent dedicated for oriented research. The other EU countries and notably the United Kingdom and France spent relatively little on general basic research and put more emphasis on oriented research (in case of the two last-mentioned countries, for armament also). Thus, we have to conclude, country-specific patterns of spending in basic research persist even within the European Union.

Reportedly the United States government with its large share of defense research spends least on general basic research, whereas Japan with a small defense R&D budget resembles the pattern of Germany. As these two major countries are not covered by EUROSTAT statistics in a comparable way, the data may not correspond precisely and are for 1992.

Most striking is the difference in national and European spending in this respect. The average of the EU 15 countries is included in the figure according to which between 40 and 50 per cent of government R&D appropriation is dedicated towards non-oriented research, whereas the European Commission nearly exclusively is engaged in oriented research. What we observe here is a clear distribution of labor between national European governments and the Commission which hardly contributes to non-oriented basic research. What this means for future R&D policy is discussed in the sections below.

4.3 Links between Research and Industry

Basically, the relationship between non-industrial research institutions and industry should be described as „interaction" in contrast to the older concept of „transfer" (SCHMOCH et al., 1996, p. 57). Knowledge is not only transferred one way, from research institution to industry, but there exists a flow of know-how in the opposite direction. Our arguments that follow are based on a respective investigation of SCHMOCH et al. (1996).

As older studies have shown, basic science contributes to the progress of technology in a decisive way. However, it is difficult to trace the ways and to measure this impact precisely. As difficult as a definition of science vs. technology is the specification of knowledge-flows between academia and industry. As in many cases there is a large time-lag between scientific discoveries and their introduction into technology, there is furthermore the necessity to provide a sufficiently long observation period, a requirement which is often overlooked in questionnaire surveys.

The respective literature points to observations that the scientific input into innovation heavily depends on the industrial sector concerned and the technical area considered. Therefore, what maybe found in case studies maybe „stained" by the industrial sector of the case study. Some of the discrepancies which are reported on the subject are likely to disappear if account is taken for all these complex influence factors.

As scientific activities are performed in non-industrial research institutions as well as in industry, the notion of science-linkage (see next section) does not necessarily imply that an intensive flow of knowledge from academic circles exist. For example, in the case of the British industry, PAVITT (1984, pp. 346-348) reveals that the public research infrastructure heavily supports the development and manufacturing of electronic components, computers and electronic capital goods. In contrast to this, the public contribution to the area of chemicals is quite low, what reflects the fact that firms in this area rely more on their own scientific in-house research.

In Germany, however, GRUPP and SCHMOCH (1992, pp. 96-97) observe a high contribution of universities to chemistry and a much weaker reliance on the public research infrastructure in electronics. Obviously, the actual patterns of knowledge transfer largely depends on the national academic and industrial traditions that have occurred over time and shape the different systems of innovation. From the number of patents universities take out, one can even determine the share universities hold in direct technology production which resembles industrial R&D. Again, this share various between sectors and between countries.

Another important contribution to the linkage between research and industry is the existence of spill-overs. Knowledge created within an institution spills over for use by other institutions. This is so among enterprises and among academic institutions but also between the research and industrial sector.

Enterprises and also individuals have access to knowledge external to them without any institutional transfer mechanisms. The empirical evidence clearly suggests that R&D and other sources of knowledge not only generates these externalities, but studies also suggest that such linkages tend to be geographically bounded within the region where the new economic knowledge was created (AUDRETSCH and FELDMAN, 1996). That is, the new knowledge may spill over across firms and economic agents but the geographic extend of such knowledge linkages tends to be bounded and, thus, the specific national structures come as no surprise.

Coming back to the relevance of the linkage problems for globalization we have to repeat that the importance of location to innovative activity in a world increasingly dominated by e-mail, fax machines, electronic communication and super highways, may seem surprising and even paradoxical at first glance (WELFENS et al., 1997). The resolution of this paradox comes into sight if we consider the distinction between knowledge and information. If we believe in the classic economic idea that the marginal costs of transmitting information may be invariant to distance, we presumably have to admit that the marginal costs of transmitting knowledge, and especially tacit knowledge, raises with distance, country, language, culture, and sector. What VON HIPPEL (1988), terms as sticky knowledge in our context, is knowledge best transmitted via face-to-face interaction and frequent contact. This limits the extent and the main distance of global R&D and reinforces that proximity matters in transmitting knowledge.

Despite the general consensus that knowledge linkages within the given locations stimulates innovative activity, there is little consensus as to exactly how this occurs if we think of the difficulties in establishing links between research and industry per sector and per nation. From this the desire of MNC headquarters to participate simultaneously in several national innovation systems, is perfectly understandable, even if the maintenance of several R&D labs in various countries is costly.

4.4 Position of EU Science-Based Industries

The notion of „science-based industries" is usually discussed on the basis of a typology by PAVITT (1984). He presented an analysis based on an earlier study of TOWNSEND et al. (1981) on industrial sectors. Therein PAVITT identified four main types of firms: Supplier-dominated firms, scale-intensive firms, specialised equipment suppliers and science-based firms.

Science-based firms, the most interesting type in the context of globalisation, are located in the sectors of chemical, electrical and electronic engineering following PAVITT (LOC. CIT.). These science-based industries rely heavily on the R&D activities of firms which largely profit from the rapid development of the underlying sciences in universities and elsewhere. The science-based firms develop a high percentage of process technology in their own laboratories. From this the share of large companies is relatively high as there are minimum levels or thresholds for a size to be relevant for performance in-house R&D. On the other hand a number of high technology start-up companies fall into the science-based sector.

Industrial sectors are not homogenous in their structure. They include companies which produce a broad variety of products, each of them rely more or less on science (SCHMOCH et al., 1996, p. 63). Thus, the sectoral approach which is the basis of PAVITTs approach only gives a rough idea of the underlying patterns. That is why GRUPP and SCHMOCH (1992) have provided an attempt to define the area of science-based products in distinction to the one based on industries. They analyzed 28 areas of technology by means of patent indicators and used the average number of references to non-patent literature in patent search reports as a measure for science intensity. This implicit definition of science, based on scientific publications, is not limited to the academic sector, but encompasses scientific activities in industry as well, because scientists and industry also publish articles in scientific journals.

Following this approach, the most science-based areas, genetic engineering and lasers are located in chemistry and electronics as already PAVITT has concluded in a coarser typology. Across-country comparison shows that Japan and the United States are more active than European countries in science-intensive technology. Within the European Union one can differentiate the continental and the Anglo-Saxon cluster of countries whereby the latter are relatively more active in science-dependent area (United Kingdom, Ireland, the Netherlands).

If one brakes down the overall picture it is obvious that in the seventies and eighties, public research centers and universities concentrated a large part of their activities on the nuclear sector. Prior to this, for instance in Britain, public research centers made enormous contributions to the areas of iron and steel or coal mining. These national topics of public research are often linked to large prestige projects or the requirements of sectoral of local pressure groups and are, therefore, not necessarily science-intensive in the long-run. On the other hand, with laser technology, genetic engineering and other areas, new scientific opportunities are coming up from time to time which then undergo an intensive exchange of ideas with private industry.

Generally, science-dependent areas are international areas and there is little distinction between countries. The science dependence of technology is an intrinsic feature of technology. Yet, the difference between the countries lies in the fact that some national innovation systems are more active in some of the science-based sectors than others and thus – without considering the discipline specific breakdown – look in a macro perspective as if they were more or less science-dependent. So we have to differentiate between the intrinsic properties in science and technology and the extent of activities which may differ between the countries.

Coming back to the position of the EU, we have to express clearly that in Europe the same areas are science-dependent as elsewhere in the world. However, the weaker performance of some (continental) EU countries in science-dependent sectors originates from the fact that they are less active there in comparison with non-science-dependent sectors. Thus, we may reduce the issue to a matter of profiling activities and not to any basic inefficiency in Europe.

4.5 Requirements for Future R&D Policies

Our arguments on the future requirements for R&D policies follow basically WELFENS et al. (1997). Thus, contemporary R&D policy has moved away from the inappropriate idea that the state could direct basic research over technological developments right down to individual national innovations. Equally outmoded is the idea that the State could be satisfied with the role of a subsidiary supporter of basic research and leave the control of technology to anonymous market processes. R&D policy for the start of the 21st century requires a middle way. An active role for the government as an intermediary between social players (companies, associations, interest groups, science communities, consumers, media, employers, and employees, etc.).

For the European R&D policy, this intermediary role must also take into account the fact that it is restricted in its scope from below. The activities of the European Communities must always be seen in contexts with the efforts of national policies and, in addition in some member countries, with below-national policies in federal states that promote research on a regional basis.

The new role of European R&D policy necessitates a policy process which is co-ordinated with industry, science and society. Cooperation does not, however, occur of itself since there are too many divergent interest in the foreground (and more of them in the background). If there is to be agreement over the possibly selective support of basic research with implications for technology at the start of the 21st century, dialogue with other social players must be initiated and pursued on a permanent basis. It cannot otherwise be expected that lasting cooperation can be achieved and that the platforms to be created for a subject-specific understanding will become more than simply forums for the exchange for information. The European R&D policy needs to organize knowledge flows in the sense above and not nearly flows of information.

4.6 Special Role of Small MNCs

As FUJITA (1995) documents, there is considerable evidence that the transnational activities of SMEs have been increasing over time. As he point out, there are two major features that have been shaping the trends in foreign direct investment engaged in by SMEs over time. The first of these trends is that, overall, the share of total foreign direct investment activity accounted for by SMEs remains small in value but large in terms of the number of affiliates.

The second major trend exhibited in the foreign direct investment activities of SMEs is that they have a greater propensity to choose a host county among the developed countries than do large enterprises. FUJITA (1995) reports that while large transnational corporations from the most developed countries had well over one-fifth of their affiliates located in host countries that are still developing, only about one-tenth of the multinational activity made by SMEs (from the developed countries) were located in the developing countries (MITI, 1991). Similarly, small and medium-sized transnational corporations based in developed countries accounted for a mean of 3.2 foreign affiliates between 1986 and 1987. By contrast, large transnational corporations accounted for a mean number of over 60 affiliates (UNTCMD, 1993).

There is at least some evidence that, not only has the absolute value of FDI activities by SMEs been increasing over time, but also their share of the total FDI, at least in several countries. For example, in Italy about one-fifth of the outward flow of FDI in the 1950s and 1960s was accounted for by SMEs (with fewer than 500 employees), but by the 1980s SMEs accounted for around one-third of all Italian FDI (European Network for SME Research, 1993). The number of foreign subsidiaries is 1.6 for SMEs, 2.0 for enterprises with between 500 and 1,000 employees, and 12 for enterprises with more than 2,000 employees.

About one-half of the Italian subsidiaries of SMEs in foreign countries are located in less developed countries. By contrast, the FDI activities of enterprises with between 500 and 2,000 employees tend to be more oriented towards the developed industrialized countries. But the very largest enterprises, with more than 2,000 employees, also orient their FDI activities towards the developing countries (European Network for SME Research, 1993).

Similarly, the Dutch National Bank has reported that the outgoing FDI has more than doubled between the 1984-1987 and the 1988-1990 periods. While Dutch FDI remains dominated by the largest transnational corporations, as evidenced by the fact that the ten largest multinational corporations are responsible for 40 percent of the total outgoing foreign direct investment, the growth rate of foreign direct investment is actually greater for smaller enterprises than for the largest enterprises. That is, the growth rate of foreign direct investment by the largest ten multinational corporations is 110 percent, while the growth rate for outward foreign direct investment undertaken by SMEs is 163 percent (European Network for SME Research, 1993).

A report published by the MITI shows that foreign investment by SMEs in Japan (FUJITA, 1995) has generally followed the trend of their larger counterparts (MITI, 1991). While outward foreign direct investment activity reached a peak in 1988, the upward trend over time has been positive. Perhaps most striking is that the share of outward Japanese foreign direct investment accounted for by SMEs fell during the first half of the 1980s but then proceeded to rise during the second half o the 1980s. At its peak in 1988, SMEs accounted for around 60 percent of the number of Japanese foreign direct investment projects. At the same time, the share of the value of outward foreign direct investment accounted for by Japanese SMEs remained less than one-fifth of the total in the mid-1980s.

The UNCTAD (1993) study of technology transfer found that small multinational corporations use transnational relationships to transfer technology across national borders. The transfer of technology by small multinational enterprises tends to be less formalized than in their larger counterparts. As BUCKLEY (1997, p. 75) reports, this is related to their management style and the crucial constraints. The channel of written instructions is used much less partly because of lack of personnel to codify the technology and partly because many of the skills are acquired through learning on the job. This suggests that policies emphasizing on-the-job training along with the supply of machinery and parts which embody the technology is the crucial transfer mechanism in small MNCs. In any case, manuals and technical handbooks are used only by a minority of small MNCs, and even blueprints and drawings are utilized in only 51 percent of the cases.

The UNCTAD study also identified three major types of technology which tend to be targeted for transfer by small MNCs – small-scale technologies, labor-intensive technologies, and specialized high-technology know-how.

As GOMES-CASSERES (1997, p. 33) points out that "Students of international business have traditionally believed that success in foreign markets required large size. Small firms were thought to be at a disadvantage compared to larger firms, because of the fixed costs of learning about foreign environments, communicating at long distances, and negotiating with national governments." These costs "constitute an important reason for expecting that foreign investment will be mainly an activity of large firms," CAVES (1982) concluded in his exhaustive review of the literature on the multinational enterprise. (HORST, 1972; VERNON, 1970; CHANDLER 1990)

GOMES-CASSERES (1997) finds that small firms can overcome inherent disadvantages in engaging in multinational activities through forming strategic alliances. In particular, small firms typically follow one of two different approaches to forming strategic alliances to engage in multinational activities. Which of these two approaches are pursued depends upon the relative size of the firm. Firms that are small relative to competitors and to the requirements of the market tend to engage in strategic alliances to attain scale and scope. By contrast, firms that are large relative to the same benchmarks tend to rely on internal capabilities. This suggests that the importance of alliances in the strategy of a small firms will tend to rise with the importance of scale economies in its market and decline with the size of the firm relative to its competitors. That is, small firms seek to attain scale economies through alliances if that is a requisite for competitive success in their market. However, they are less likely to resort to such an alliance if they occupy a niche in which they are large relative to their competitors. In addition, the benefits that a small firm can derive from a constellation of partners will increase with the sum of the capabilities assembled in the constellation as well as with the capabilities of the firm relative to those of its partners in the alliance. That is, small firms will benefit from the total value created in an alliance network. At the same time, the share of those benefits enjoyed by any given firm depends upon the firms bargaining power within the network.

As FUJITA (1995) points out, small- and medium-sized transnational corporations tend to achieve greater productivity and are more export-oriented than SMEs in general. As enterprises, especially SMEs, become increasingly specialized, pursuing a strategy of niche development plays an important role. This can be observed in the strategies employed by a sector of the German *Mittelstand*. Many of these SMEs, such as Krones, Koerber/Hauni, Weinig, Webasto, and Tetra Werke are virtually unheard of by the public, in contrast to such household names as Mercedes-Benz, Siemens, Bosch, and Bayer. At the same time, the global market share of these companies typically far exceeds that of the giant companies of Germany. When calculated in terms of the specialized products they manufacture, these *Mittelstand* companies have global market shares ranging between 70 percent to 90 percent. What ranks among one of the biggest secrets of Germany, these enterprises account for the bulk of the trade surplus in Germany.

One of the major strategic instruments deployed by these Mittelstand companies in Germany is to combine product specialization with geographic diversity. The focus is typically upon a particular market niche, usually one that requires technical expertise. Mot of the companies resources are then devoted towards maintaining the market leadership in that niche. Diversification is generally considered to be an anathema to focusing upon the core product. Because of their degree of specialization and relatively small size, *Mittelstand* companies are often at a disadvantage in terms of economies of scale. This is where the second part of the strategy comes in – globalization. The product-market specialization is leveraged across broad geographic markets. Such globalization of marketing and sales provides sufficient scale to recover R&D expenses and to maintain costs at a reasonable level. An executive of a company that makes laboratory equipment explained that the typical *Mittelstand* strategy is, "If you are small, your front of attack has to be narrow. You'd better focus your business. And if you are focused, you have to find customers for your specialty all over the world in order to recoup your R&D investment." (SIMON, 1992)

SIMON (1992) examined what he terms as the 39 *hidden champions* of the German *Mittelstand*. These companies accounted for an average of 22.6 percent of the global market share in the relevant product market, and 31.7 percent of the European market share. They had a total of 354 foreign manufacturing subsidiaries (not including agents, importers, and other forms of company representation). Each company has, on average, 9.6 foreign subsidiaries – certainly an extraordinarily high number of foreign subsidiaries given the rather modest size of the parent companies. By contrast, FUJITA (1995) reports that, on average, small- and medium-sized transnational corporations based in the developed countries had 3.2 foreign affiliates between 1986 and 1987. The evidence from Germany does suggest that, in order to achieve a globalization strategy for SMEs, foreign direct investment plays a central role.

One of the keys to the success of the German *Mittelstand* in FDI activities has been the strong commitment to global expansion. This commitment generally takes two forms: investment in plant, equipment and technology, and investment in human capital. Even when a high initial investment may not be justified in terms of short-term returns, the SMEs consider it important to undertake such global investments because of the demonstration effect – to show potential customers and business partners that they are committed and intend to participate.

A central element of the transnational strategies deployed by Mittelstand companies has been to set the same high standards in the host market as they do in the home market. In particular, this refers to the servicing of the production through the creation of strong reliable service networks. For example, the service network of Heidelberger Druckmaschinen, the world leader in offset printing, is as comprehensive in Japan, where there are a number of subsidiary establishments, as it is in the German home market. Another example of the presence of a strong service network created in a host country is provided by Weinig, which is the world leader in automatic molders, which are specialized woodworking machines. Weinig is closer to its customers in Japan than in Germany. This may be attributable to the fact that Weinig Japan has a service branch office on each of the four main Japanese islands. By contrast, in Germany, the service operation is centralized at the headquarters in Tauberbischofsheim. All of Weinig's Japanese service engineers have been trained in Germany for an average of one year. In addition, they receive additional training at the Germany headquarters each year.

By pursuing an aggressive strategy of expansion in foreign markets the German Mittelstand companies have been able to overcome the inherent size disadvantage that would otherwise confront them if they restricted their sales solely to the domestic market. Due to the limited size of the domestic market, these SMEs would not have been able to attain sufficient scale economies necessary to maintain their product niche at such a profitable level. This has enables the Mittelstand of Germany to overcome the risk inherent in a high degree of product specialization. The greater the degree to which an enterprise is specialized, the higher is the exposure to risk, especially in terms of its vulnerability to market fluctuations.

The German Mittelstand companies do not pursue a strategy of blindly searching for the technological frontier. Rather, the Mittelstand companies are much more focused on combining technology with customer orientation. This takes numerous forms. One example of this closeness to customers is customer training. As the complexity of products increases, the customer requires a greater degree in operating and maintaining the products. Such training is one of the strengths of the German Mittelstand. It is well known throughout the world, and certainly in Asia, that German technicians are superbly educated. In fact, some of the SMEs of Germany actually establish foreign subsidiaries mandated with providing training. For example, Festo, a leading manufacturer of hydraulic equipment, established Festo Didactic, which has become an important company devoted to training engineers in hydraulics and industrial automation. Through training of customers and engineers in host countries, the technological know-how developed in Germany is transferred to firms and employees in the host country. It is the combination of being oriented to both a specialized product niche, typically combining both sophisticated technology with careful devotion to consumer needs, that makes a strategy of foreign direct investment so crucial to the German *Mittelstand*. In order to perceive and understand the peculiarities of each host market, the company benefits by producing at the location of the host market. Apparently the knowledge that is transmitted, which involves a large tacit element, can best be obtained through close geographic proximity, but not over a longer geographic distance. A second reason why presence is important in the foreign market is to provide services, such as training to he customers. While such services could be contracted out, the asset specificity of the product, combined with the high technological sophistication, virtually bundles the service component with the manufactured product. The value of the manufactured product to the customer goes down unless he has access to high-quality service.

As described elsewhere in this report, innovative activity plays a central role in why many small and medium-sized enterprises come into existence in the first place. Entrepreneurs start new businesses in an effort to appropriate the potential economic value of their ideas. Not only do such innovative niches exist in the home country, but increasingly they also exist in foreign markets as well. As *Business Week* points out, "US niche players actually create new markets." (BUSINESS WEEK, 1989) As to the type of firms that are involved in creating new markets through strategic niches, "They are companies you never heard of. They produce car-wash systems in Europe and the Middle East, doughnut-making machines in Canada, and agriculture equipment in the Philippines. On the high-tech front, they make parallel-processing computers for Japan and satellite receivers for Germany." (BUSINESS WEEK, 1989)

For example, while the tradition in Japan has been to rest and sleep on floor mats, continual development and exposure to tastes in Europe and North America has resulted in the emergence of a demand for reclining chairs. A small company producing such reclining chairs experienced an explosion in orders after a trade show in Osaka. Another example of such an innovative niche that has resulted in outward foreign direct investment activity is provided by Aeration Industries, International Inc., which is a privately held company with $15 million in annual sales. The company produces motors set on floating platforms that send tiny bubbles of air down about eleven feet, aerating the water and rapidly cleaning up organic waste. While the company has its headquarters in Minnesota, it sells products in more than forty countries and has expanded specialized production to a number of other countries. The President of the company explains the success of its foreign direct investment, "We don't really have any direct competition." (BUSINESS WEEK, 1989)

Another important way that inward foreign direct investment can promote the competitiveness of host-country firms is through providing finance. A number of high-technology industries, particularly from Europe, serve as an important source of finance for SMEs in other countries. One example is the biotechnology industry. It should be emphasized that the entire biotechnology industry in the United States has been developed by SMEs (AUDRETSCH and STEPHAN, 1996). While a few of these new start-ups, such as Genetech, have grown to become large enterprises, virtually all of the biotechnology companies remain SMEs. The reasons from the inability of the large pharmaceutical companies to successfully engage in biotechnology and the relative success of SMEs in biotechnology are presumably based on the competitive advantages of SMEs in newly emerging industries discussed elsewhere in this report.

While the biotechnology industry has been largely developed in the United States, which partially reflects a concentration of scientific and technological knowledge as well as finance capital, at the same time outward foreign direct investment by European companies is providing an important source of capital. As *Business Week* observes, "The US biotech industry is perpetually searching for money. And more and more of it is coming from Europe." (BUSINESS WEEK, 1994)

Outward foreign direct investment also can provide a mechanism for gaining access to knowledge sources that would otherwise be inaccessible. An example of an industry where knowledge transfers only within a geographically bounded region is biotechnology. Biotechnology is a new industry that is knowledge based and is predominately produced by new enterprises. The relative small scale of most biotechnology firms may be attributable to the diseconomies of scale inherent in the "bureaucratic process which inhibits both innovative activity and the speed with which new inventions move through the corporate system towards the market" (LINK and REES, 1990). ZUCHER, DARBY and BREWER (1994) have provided considerable evidence suggesting that the timing and location of new biotechnology firms is "primarily explained by the presence at a particular time and place of scientists who are actively contributing to the basic science." More specifically, they find that firms are likely to locate in geographic areas where scientists who have published leading articles on gene sequencing are located. Studies have indicated that biotechnology firms are likely to be founded in close proximity to a research center (AUDRETSCH and STEPHAN, 1996). For example, a region such as the San Francisco Bay Area, which produces a disproportionate amount of research in biotechnology, is also the home to a disproportionate number of new biotechnology firms.

Biotechnology companies are defined by their scientists. Many of these scientists, particularly senior scientists with strong reputations, do not work for the company full time, but instead are members of university faculties. These university-based scientists fulfill a variety of roles within biotechnology companies. Some are founders, others serve as members of scientific advisory boards, while still others serve as directors. The degree of knowledge provided by university-based scientists varies according to the role played by the scientist (AUDRETSCH and STEPHAN, 1996). Certain roles, such as being a founder of a biotechnology firm, are more likely to dictate geographic proximity between the firm and the scientist than are other roles that the scientist play. This is because the transmission of the knowledge specific to the scientist and firm dictates proximity.

In order to gain access to these knowledge resources foreign enterprises interested in biotechnology rely upon a strategy of outward foreign direct investment in the geographic areas where the technical knowledge is most heavily located. For example, on 14 November, 1994 Rohne-Poulenc-Rorer (RPR) announced that it would invest $100 million in the first year alone in US biotechnology companies in order to promote research and bring promising products to the market. (BUSINESS WEEK, 1994) On the following day, a rival European drug manufacturer, Ciba-Geigy Ltd., with the home country of Switzerland, responded by announcing that it was entering into a significant minority investment in an American-based biotechnology company, Chiron Corporation, located in Emeryville, California. As *Business Week* observes, "Europe's drug giants, with few local biotech innovators, are hungry for bigger pieces of the action." (BUSINESS WEEK, 1994) The specialized tacit knowledge in the biotechnology industry which is concentrated in just a few location is best accessed through outward foreign direct investment in small biotechnology companies at that location.

Similarly, there are numerous examples of European computer companies which have established affiliates in Silicon Valley in California. (THE ECONOMIST, 1994) This new knowledge can often be transferred back to the home country. Much of this transfer is in the form of human capital, as individuals move from one location to another. When employees of the SMEs have accumulated enough experience and knowledge in the knowledge cluster, such as Silicon Valley, they may in some cases return to the home country. They bring with them technological know-how, organizational capabilities, and established contacts that facilitate knowledge-based economic activity in the home country.

The examples of these high-technology European SMEs engaging in outward foreign direct investment in the United States illustrate two important points. The first point involves the location of the foreign direct investment. What is important is not access to the United States *per se*, but rather access to the knowledge embodied in the individuals and network of firms located in a tiny geographic area – in this case, Silicon Valley. The second point is that the outward foreign direct investment was undertaken by these SMEs not with the aim of penetrating the market in the host country, but rather with the goal of accessing valuable scarce economic knowledge and then transferring it back to the home country in order to increase market share in the home country. The knowledge can then be applied in the home country which will subsequently enhance the competitiveness of that country.

As the competitive advantage of the OECD countries becomes increasingly shaped by new economic knowledge, for reasons explained elsewhere in this report, it is likely that SMEs will become more aggressive in undertaking foreign direct investment as a mechanism for gaining access to new economic knowledge.

5. The Future Role of R&D Policy: Policy Options and Recommendations

5.1 Innovation and Innovation Policy

With economic globalization it is clear that national R&D subsidies are likely to have strong positive external effects for various reasons: There will be spillovers from innovative domestic companies to subsidiaries of foreign companies; foreign competitors could acquire the firm which benefited from an R&D subsidy but has not yet brought the innovation to the market. As one may assume that uncertain future profits from such an innovation are not fully taken into account in the price for the respective merger or acquisition it is clear that there will be international external effects. There will be a technology transfer effect and positive growth and tax revenue effects abroad. All this could imply that government funded R&D will decline as the expected positive income, employment and tax revenue effects of subsidizing innovation becomes more uncertain in a world of high capital mobility. A falling R&D-GDP ratio is, however, not what is needed to improve EU competitiveness and the prospects for employment and income growth. On the contrary, EU governments could agree on a minimum R&D-GDP ratio in order to stimulate economic growth. Such a European Innovation Pact would aim to internalize some of the positive external benefits of national R&D. At the same time there is no need to strongly increase supranational R&D expenditures, except possibly for some key areas in basic research and in R&D projects deemed important for progress in the global warming problem. Establishing trans-European R&D networks and intranets/internets could be another expanding domain of EU innovation policy which certainly requires a critical minimum effort.

Policy options of higher supranational R&D expenditures largely will depend on the ability of the Community to shift the emphasis in the EU budget from agriculture to high technology. To illustrate the benefits of major policy shifts one might commission a study to analyze which economic benefits are to be expected if the R&D budget had the size of the agricultural budget.

Improved monitoring and evaluation of R&D programs at the national and supranational level help achieve higher efficiency in the public funding of innovation projects. More important, however, would be that governments launch an EU wide initiative to foster the role of venture capital markets. This would have to include adequate tax reforms.

Given the many political resistances against FDI liberalization in many countries there might be no immediate need in the South to accept foreign majority ownership in all sectors but EU diplomacy should be firm in pushing for full gradual liberalization in the field of foreign investment. From this perspective the WTO needs a partner organization which explicitly deals with the problem of international restrictions on foreign investment and problems in patent protection. One might consider assigning this task to the World Intellectual Property Organization (WIPO) in Geneva. This would lead to four organizations active in maintaining free trade and foreign investment in the world economy: WTO for trade, IMF for capital flows except foreign direct investment, WIPO for intellectual property rights and foreign direct investment and a reformed ITU (International Telecommunications Union) as a basis for free flow in information.

High R&D expenditures of innovative sectors is only one of the keys to high productivity growth, the other is rapid diffusion - i.e. application - of new technologies. While most new technologies are developed in high technology manufacturing industries (information technology, pharmaceuticals, aerospace) the most important user is the service sector whose role in international technology trade increased in the 1980s.

Innovations and Technology Diffusion

Innovation together with technology diffusion are two keys for international competitiveness and employment creation in western Europe. Fundamentals of innovativeness are shown in Fig. 1. The basis for innovation and diffusion is a modern education system which allows to raise the number of skilled workers, engineers and managers to be raised. Education in school and universities is only one important aspect of "upskilling", retraining and training on the job are also crucial. Expenditures on education in a broader sense reached lower levels in most EU countries than in the US in the early 1990s. In a period of intensified global technological and economic competition EU countries that reduce the quantity and quality of education and training are bound to suffer in the long term. Compared to the US and even to some Asian NICs most EU countries have assigned a low priority to upgrading education. With more intense competition in goods markets and falling relative prices of labor intensive products - produced increasingly in Asian countries and Eastern Europe - high wages of unskilled labor in continental EU countries are bound to contribute to unemployment. While it is not true that wage increases generally were too high in the 1980s and early 1990s it is obvious that wage dispersion should have increased at the expense of unskilled labor in Europe. Though wage dispersion increased in the US and the UK it remained flat and temporarily even reduced in Germany and other continental EU countries. This will not only stimulate rising foreign direct investment outflows from high wage EU countries, it will also reduce the incentive for higher education and thereby weaken the future ability of EU countries to successfully compete in the global technology race.

Competition is needed to ensure innovativeness where anticipated profits will play a major role for incumbent firms and newcomers. Only if market exit barriers are low will market entry barriers be rather small. High and rising subsidies for smoke-stack industries impair market entry in the EU. Moreover, the EU suffers from a lack of venture capital firms so that EU newcomer dynamics are relatively poor compared to the US. This partly explains why EU firms are underrepresented in new growth fields (biotechnology, laser, robotics). R&D expenditures are crucial for innovation. EU countries reached only about half the R&D-GDP ratio of Japan, and half a percentage point less than the US in the early 1990s. Germany recorded a marked fall in this ratio after 1989 when it declined from 2.9% to 2.2 % in 1996. While one may anticipate a recovery of this ratio in the long term this steep fall is a serious problem since the advances of NICs and east European newcomers capturing increasingly medium and high technology shares in world markets should have been a starting point for Germany to raise R&D expenditures relative to GDP in the 1990s. Moreover, a stronger focus on high technology also would have been appropriate. Since the end of the cold war Germany has lost its historical advantage of a low military R&D-GDP ratio and both Germany and Japan will face much stronger high technology competition from the US, the UK and France in the long term. Finally, since high technology markets are rather narrow worldwide, the renewed civilian R&D dynamics of these countries will encourage US, British and French high technology firms to aggressively move into medium technology markets in which many German firms used to enjoy a rather strong and uncontested position. This position generated Schumpeterian rents which in turn were the financial basis for continuous innovations. About ½ of OECD R&D expenditures in the private sector, 2/3 of R&D investment is performed in the business sector. EU countries compare rather well with the US in this respect. However, the system of public R&D support of many EU countries overemphasizes subsidies (40% of all public R&D support in Germany) instead of tax credits which represented almost 90% of public support in the US in the early 1990s. Subsidies are an easy prey for established big firms, while small and medium sized firms as well as newcomers - with poor political connections - are at a disadvantage. Tax credits are more neutral in this respect.

The information system of a society is crucial for innovation as well as the diffusion process. With advanced communication networks and widespread computer use there are new global opportunities to learn about new technologies and products, store knowledge and disseminate know-how; one may even create virtual firms. Therefore, innovation cycles are shortening and Schumpeterian rents from first mover advantages and innovations, respectively, are declining for firms acting in regional markets. Since privatization and liberalization of the telecoms sector in Europe and Asian countries will be fully achieved only at the turn of the century this tendency will be reinforced after 2000. Continental EU countries still suffer from rather high telecoms prices reflecting monopolized markets for public voice telephony (until 1998 the liberalization date set by the European Commission) and barriers to entry for newcomers in many countries. The internet host rate of the US which has competitive long distance networks since 1984 is twice that of Germany, that of Finland which introduced full competition in the 1990s is four times as high as that of Germany. There are many opportunities to improve the EU information system but key member countries such as Germany and France are moving rather hesitantly in this field.

Patent protection is important for innovators. The system of international patent protection has been strengthened in the context of the GATT Uruguay round so that incentives for innovators have increased worldwide. However, the new digitized information highways that are being built in the US, Europe, Asia and elsewhere improve prospects for imitators. Hence effective protection of innovators might be reduced in the long term. Innovative firms might react to this tendency with an even stronger tendency to serve markets by foreign subsidiaries which allows the flow of know-how to be controlled in contrast to (external) licensing and patent trade. For EU countries aiming to raise employment it will be crucial to offer locational advantages that stimulate foreign direct investment inflows. Germany and France recorded massive outflows but rather poor inflows in the 1980s and early 1990s. Germany's per capita inflows from the US in 1995 were only 1/10 of those in the Netherlands. Small foreign investment inflows and high outflows explain the low ratio of investment in machinery and equipment relative to GDP in 1995 (only some 8%).

Venture capital financing is extremely important for technology-oriented newcomers in manufacturing and services. In continental EU countries traditional banking systems dominate, while specialized venture capital firms - a key ingredient to US innovativeness and employment growth - are a rare exception in most EU countries. As many big firms in OECD countries embraced downsizing as the dominant strategy for the 1990s it would have been quite important to make sure that the growth rate of newcomers is rather high. This is a major deficiency in continental EU countries.

5.2 Policy Options

In summing-up the policy options in the age of globalization we shall structure our arguments along four cases of transnational R&D which have been worked out by GERYBADZE and REGER (1997). Type A company is dependent on excellence in R&D and is located in a large highly advanced home country with strong R&D capabilities in the particular field. Type B corporation is dependent on excellence in R&D but is located in a small country or in a country with a lesser developed R&D capability in the particular field. Type C firm can benefit from proximity to a world class lead market and can establish an effective coupling to lead markets, R&D and innovation. Most of these activities can be performed close to the corporate headquarters at least within the same nation state. And finally type D corporation is strongly dependent on access to an foreign lead market. Due to the small size of its home country or the small size of the markets, the firm is forced to perform critical functions abroad. Demand and corporate resource allocation will be geographically and often functionally separated.

In case of the EU, cases A and C apply to companies from large countries and cases B and C applies for companies from small countries. From this, the first option for policy would be to differentiate between MNCs with headquarters in either large or small EU countries. It seems not to be possible to device a common European policy in this respect. On the other hand, types A and B relate to companies being active in an area of strong science-based and research-oriented innovation, whereas type C and D relates more to an efficient coupling to lead markets, demand articulation and innovation. The second option thus, would be that, again, a new policy in the science-based sectors and in the demand triggered areas should look different.

If we add to this the necessity to couple European level R&D policy with national (and region or state specific) actions it becomes entirely clear that a simple approach in R&D policy is not recommended. As many degrees of flexibility as possible should be allowed for.

To the extend that a supply side R&D policy prevailed in the European Union we have to emphasis that science-based innovation is important in many cases but not in all. In global innovation, down-stream related processes such as effective national lead-markets and demand stimulation and articulation are also important. In this sense, it is recommended that R&D policy should try to warrant that those lead-markets be in the European Union where strong global players are active in. In so far as by non-R&D measures the rapid and stable development of those markets can be facilitated, R&D policy should join in with other European policies in order to achieve the maximum benefit.

Avoiding naive policy planning which was sometimes pursued in the seventies, also means not to set up large planning bodies and to abstain from mechanical shaping and controlling of science and technology institutions. Instead, the characteristics of an advanced science and technology policy on the European level should be based on the assumption that decision making occurs through negotiations of many diverse actors on various hierarchical levels. The top down approach is not useful at the turn of the century: players have to seek alignment and consensus. The European Commission and the governments of member states should jointly behave as facilitators in offering two-way information channels and forums for the debates. If required the Commission should provide strategic information inputs using technology foresight, technology assessment and strategic policy evaluation in science and technology. In so doing, it should not rely on EC bodies and agencies but on - from the perspective of member states - unbiased organizations or multi-national groups of think tanks. It is always helpful to organize strategic information in terms of alternative scenarios that strategic choices become visible.

5.3 Adjusting Guidelines, Promoting Cooperation and Increasing Transparency

Facing increasing international competition EU countries should implement clear guidelines for innovation policy and encourage benchmarking studies on innovation policy. Future guidelines should put more emphasis on the information society and the creation of virtual technology-oriented firms, but one might also want to encourage „overlapping projects" where the combining of different science fields in an innovative meaningful way finally leads to profitable innovation projects.

In a globalized world economy potential partners might be found in many more countries than previously. In practice the number of international R&D joint ventures will always be rather limited and certainly be guided by positive experiences. However, with the economic opening up of eastern Europe and newly developed R&D capabilities in Asia there are new options and opportunities for firms and government research centers. Encouraging international research cooperation on the basis of selected demonstration projects - with positive international external effects - could be an important policy area. Projects especially in the field of health, the environment and international traffic safety could be useful.

With rising public R&D spending adequate reporting on the basis of a standardized indicator system becomes important. At present it is unclear which indicators are useful for which areas and to which extent one could monetize economic costs and benefits for all major R&D projects in which public subsidies are involved. It is clear that the EU requires much better data collection and data analysis in the field of patents, innovations and diffusion. Historically, most national statistics have developed without a strong focus on economic application or usefulness. For a modern Europe one of the guiding principles for public statistics should also be its usefulness for economic policy and innovation policy in particular.

5.4 Environmental Problems and Growth: Some Policy Conclusions

Taking into account the problem of global sustainable growth is crucial if there is to be a coherent international and national policy approach to growth. For OECD countries reducing adjustment costs by higher flexibility in technologies and in factor markets is important from a global perspective. In the words of BRETSCHGER (1997c, p.31/32): „To conclude, it should be remembered that the increase in prices of natural resources has to be effectuated by political measures if negative externalities of natural resource use are present. This has to be accomplished first. Also, and even more importantly, the sectoral change that is required for sustainable development has to take place at low economic costs. If adjustment costs are high, there is a drag in the growth process and the development path may become non-sustainable. The lower costs of the reallocation in the direction of sectors that generate a lot of spillovers and do not use natural resources intensively, the better the chances for sustainable development. The political aim to lower adjustment costs is a better measure to achieve sustainable development than the general promotion of savings. This holds true because higher savings are not unambiguous in favor of sustainability, as long as some investments have a pollutant effect. In the international context, efficient prices of environmental services also lead to an income transfer from developed to less developed countries that increases the chances for LDCs to achieve a sustainable development of their own.“

Resource-saving technological progress in the North leaves a larger pool of nonrenewable resources for low income-low technology countries which therefore face reduced pressure to embark upon costly substitution technologies. With higher sustainable growth rates in the South higher growth rates in the North can be expected through trade-led growth. More recent technologies will become available in the South if the economic and political regime create an open environment for foreign investors, if patent protection is fully enforced and foreign majority ownership accepted.

5.5 Facilitating Network Building

Before we recommend some instruments of support for network building in more detail, it is necessary to emphasis the scope of already existing knowledge exchange systems managed by the partners involved without policy assistance. Above all, large companies with huge R&D resources at their own disposal are capable of establishing and keeping up relations with non-industrial research institutions and even competitive firms without any public support. Nevertheless, we think that the contacts between large enterprises and academic institutions can still be intensified, whereas the contacts among large enterprises themselves is probably less so a subject of EU policy. But small and medium size companies have problems establishing research linkages which they control themselves and which are not defined via partnership with a big MNC. Against this background a variety of facilitating options for the promotion of knowledge exchange has emerged over the last several years. We mention institutional arrangements, financial support, transfer agencies and also the exchange of personnel here.

During the first few years, many industrial countries have introduced new media of science and technology information in order to improve accessibility and transparency (see, for instance SCHMOCH et al., 1996). Further in this direction would be an improvement in European linkage of public library systems, for example, which is the case within countries but is not easily established across national borders. Special information services and data bases on science and technology related issues which are maintained in Europe can also be helpful here. Translation services would open access to non-native European innovation systems.

As to institutional arrangements, the establishment of contract research institutions in general outside of universities plays the major role. This sort of research is developed in some EU countries, but not so well established in others. Their research interests are medium in character and focus on the application of knowledge and thus can serve in network building.

The establishment of R&D networks by participation at conferences, the initiation of specific R&D corporations or other instruments is a quite difficult and time-consuming task. A decisive precondition would be a well developed private and public R&D base so that every partner can profit from joining the network; a win-to-win situation is always required. This calls for more coherence in national R&D systems.

The promotion of inter-European trans-border co-operation is permanently considered a challenge. It should also include the exchange of persons by special subsidies. Because of different career structures in universities and firms and the social problems of mobility, the transfer of personnel will always be limited compared to other measures. It is thus an area of high impact elasticities if policy can trigger of more exchange.

5.6 Exploiting Communication Opportunities

Innovative telecommunication technologies provide new opportunities for learning about market developments, research projects and for creating virtual research networks. After the full liberalization of telecommunications in 1998 one may expect rapidly falling international telecom prices and thus an endogenous incentive for greater intra-EU cooperation as well as for global competition and cooperation. Finland with its very competitive market - similar to the situation in US - shows very encouraging results. The number of internet hosts in the mid-1990s was more than twice that in Germany and higher than in the US.

System integration will be a big technological topic of the future. It is unclear whether telecom operators or software companies will be better suited to shape and determine future developments in this field. The advance of mobile telephone and wireless local loop technology plus developments in the satellite business will open up new options to create international networks.

The main challenge for the Internet is that present pricing schemes will not allow the establishment of a broader information society in a commercial sense. The Internet is overflowing with information but most providers have neither a clear-cut profile nor are they able to generate business by selling specific sets of information. Flat rates are typical for the large internet providers and this points to inability to apply price differentiation and problems in selling information as a good in its own right. Since quality competition barely exists in the internet and price competition dominates, providers increasingly use advertisements to keep prices down. The Internet platform, therefore, degenerates almost to a white noise phenomenon of limited economic value.

It is well known that markets for information are rather imperfect because the supply side has to reveal part of its information in order to get business going at all. It is, therefore, practically impossible to recover costs on the same basis as in normal markets. One possible way of obtaining value-added from the Internet on a solid and broad scale is to encourage the build-up of reputations by competing top providers. A high reputation should allow internet users with a specific communication profile to create a club of users, which would rely on a fixed contribution and differentiated prices for specific bundles of information.

If EU countries were to simply follow US patterns, the commercial value of the internet would remain rather limited. One may recommend that the EU commission establishes a certification process which assigns quality labels to internet providers. European internet providers could become leading players only if they first develop a thriving European information market. Government certainly has a role to play in the nurturing the information markets.

5.7 New Role for the EU in Education Policies

At first glance there is no economic justification for EU policies in the area of education. However, this assumes that there are neither international external effects nor opportunities for positive network effects in EU information markets and in learning and research. There is a role for the EU to play in the co-financing of basic research but also in helping with the establishment of special universities. Military academies in EU countries could become European military academies once common EU defense policies have been rooted more firmly than the present overlap between WEU and the Community.

The European Commission should also have the right to establish special European universities considered to have strong positive external effects: European internet university programs and Continuous Civil Service Academies with a curriculum designed specifically for updating and upgrading the human capital of civil servants working on EU matters.

In order to stimulate innovation the European Commission could obtain the right to allocate more than the present 1% of EU structural funds to innovative projects. This share could be increased to at least 15%. One might also consider the redesign of regional policies in the EU, in a way that would emphasize less investment in capital equipment and instead have a twin focus on innovation and investment.

EU competences in other fields of education should remain mute since the principle of subsidiarity - and efficiency gains at a lower level of political governance - assigns competences to the nation state, the region or the municipality.

5.8 Improving Patent Protection

One of the most important topics in the area of intellectual property rights protection is the extent to which the private rate of return from investment in the production of new economic knowledge diverges from the social rate of return. As Mansfield (1988, p. 6) observes, "To economists, the social rate of return from such investments is important, because it is a measure of the payoff to society from these investments. A high social rate of return indicates that society's resources are being used effectively and that more should be devoted to such investments, if the rate of return remains high."

The theory of legal protection for intellectual property is built around the assumption that the process of innovation is to some extent deterministic and to some extent stochastic (COHEN and KLEPPER, 1991 and 1992). The deterministic aspect of technological change stems from purposeful activities undertaken by economic agents to produce new knowledge that can be commercially exploited. Such a commercially viable outcome from the application of such new knowledge, which results in either new products or new processes, constitutes an innovation. Probably the most important and certainly the most visible activity undertaken to generate new knowledge is research and development (SCHERER, 1991 and 1992).

The stochastic aspect of innovative activity is the result of considerable uncertainty inherent in the process of technological change. According to SCHERER and ROSS (1990, p. 615), "Technical innovations do not fall like manna from heaven. They require effort – the creative labor of invention, development, testing, and introduction into the stream of economic life. To some extent innovative effort is a haphazard thing..."

The relatively large weight of the stochastic component in the process of innovation gives rise to what has been termed in the industrial organization literature is a the *appropriability problem* (COHEN and LEVIN, 1989), which refers to the ability of firms to reap the economic returns accruing from their investment in knowledge-generating activities, such as R&D. The theoretical justification for the protection of intellectual property is to prevent such erosions of the return accruing to firms investing in new economic knowledge. If the costs of imitation are sufficiently low relative to the costs of innovating, it is conceivable that the innovating firm will no longer be able to recover the costs incurred in generating the new product.

The patent system has been shrouded with controversy longer than most other economic institutions have been in existence. Ever since the Republic of Venice began granting patents in 1474, the relative merits of patents have been hotly contested. At the heart of the debate has been the virtues of disrupting the competitive process by awarding what in some cases amounts to a virtual monopoly. Exclusive patent rights to inventions are generally granted for three main reasons:

- To promote inventive activity,

- To To foster the development and commercial utilization of those inventions, that is innovative activity, and

- To facilitate the disclosure of inventions to the public, thereby ultimately promoting their diffusion.

Whether, in fact, the patent system actually is conducive to these three aspects of technological change remains controversial, however, because the central mechanism for spurring innovative activity is through granting some degree of monopoly power. On the one hand, disrupting the competitive process might not only result in higher prices but also in less subsequent technological change. On the other hand, as SCHUMPETER (1942, pp. 89-90) argued, monopoly power is an important incentive to undertaking innovative activity. Anticipated market power in new products may provide essential incentives to innovate, since, "enterprise would in most cases be impossible if it were not known from the outset that exceptionally favorable situations are likely to arise." SCHUMPETER (1942, p. 83) saw little contradiction in the patent system, because "A system that at every given point of time fully utilizes its possibilities to the best advantage may yet in the long run be inferior to a system that does so at no given point of time, because the latter's failure to do so may be a condition for the level of speed of long-run performance."

By contrast, SCHERER and ROSS (1990, p. 624) acknowledge a clear dilemma involved in the granting of lengthy monopoly power through exclusive patent rights, "The patent system makes a deliberate trade-off, accepting during the patent grants life dead-weight surplus losses in order to ensure that new products and processes, along with the surpluses they create, will not be discouraged by fear of rapid imitation. Only after the patent expires, when competitive imitation can run its full course, are consumers able to have their new product along with the extra surplus competitive pricing brings."

It should be emphasized that the impact of the patent system on actual competition and technological change is much more complicated than has been captured in theoretical models. Such complications moved SCHERER and ROSS (1990, p. 624) to conclude that, "Although devised to solve an important incentive problem, the patent system is a crude and imperfect instrument. Because of diverse real-world complications, the patent protection given an innovator may be too little, too much, or of the wrong kind."

One of the major challenges confronting the effectiveness of the patent system is the propensity for competitors to *invent around* a patented invention. The patent that can totally pre-empt access to an entire class of products or processes technologies is by far the exception. In addition, MANSFIELD (1983, p. 138) points out, "In some fields, reverse engineering – which crudely speaking, involves analyzing and tearing a product apart to see what it consists of and how it is made – is a well developed art. Even if a new product or process is not subject to reverse engineering, it may be possible to invent around the patents on which it is based (if it is patented)." To the extent that the relevant technology can be transferred at a relatively low cost, the cost incurred by imitating an innovation made by a competitor can frequently be substantially lower than the cost of developing and introducing the innovation itself. The advantage of being among the first adapters may actually be superior to the well-publicized advantage of being the first mover.

The link between the protection of intellectual property rights and global competition revolves around the question, *How can the institutions protecting intellectual property be developed in order to enhance the competitive advantage of a particular country's firms?* and *How can the institutions protecting intellectual property be developed in order to enhance economic activity undertaken within that country?* Although these two questions sound deceptively similar, in fact they are not. This is because of the increased degree to which companies are engaged in multinational activities. Policies that enhance the competitiveness of firms may not enhance the level and type of economic activity within the country in which the firm declares as its home base.

But more than anything, these two questions suggest that an answer can only be provided by comparing the regimes of intellectual property protection across countries and, perhaps, over time. In fact, such analyses have been virtually non-existent. There have been very few studies explicitly linking the regimes of intellectual property protection to the international competitiveness of firms and industries over countries.

One line of research has attempted to identify the manner in which perhaps the most obvious aspect of intellectual property protection – the number of registered patents – varies from country to country. In an exhaustive study based on the number of patents registered in the United States, ARCHIBUGI and PIANTA (1992) compare the patent activities of the major OECD countries over the decade of the 1980s. They find that the growth rate of patents within the domestic country (that is, patents awarded to residents of the country) grew fastest in Japan. Similarly, the growth rate of external patents (that is, patents awarded to residents within the country by other countries) has also been greater in Japan than in any other country. Japan has registered almost as many patents in the United States as has all of the (twelve) member countries of the European union combined. In fact, all countries exhibit a rapidly growing involvement in foreign patents, with the presumed goal of appropriating the returns from their inventions in global markets.

But what are the implications of these trends in patent activity for international competitiveness? The Royal Swedish Academy of Engineering Sciences has linked patent activity to international competitiveness in comparing Japan and Sweden. One of the major conclusions is that, "It may be due to a lack of patent culture in Swedish companies, while Japanese companies have consciously built up a patent culture…Differences in patent positions may indicate more substantial difficulties in the ability to generate and capture the returns on innovation. The failure to compete with companies at the frontier of development depends more on a lack of technical competence rather than legal or informational barriers" (Royal Swedish Academy of Engineering Sciences, 1993, p. 41).

On the basis of a more detailed comparison of Swedish and Japanese multinationals, the Royal Swedish Academy of Engineering Sciences (1993) determined that the Japanese companies value the importance of patents much more highly than do their Swedish counterparts. The Swedish companies tend to emphasize the importance of superior marketing and production cost reductions. In addition, the Japanese companies value the advantages of patents in protecting both product and process technology much more highly than the Swedish companies. The advantages bestowed by patents include protecting proprietary product technology, protecting proprietary process technology, creating retaliatory product technology, enhancing the possibilities for selling licenses, and increasing the possibilities of accessing technology through cross-licensing. Japanese companies also clearly indicate an increased strategic role for patents than do their Swedish counterparts.

This increased strategic role extends not just to patents, but also to licenses, standard setting, and cross-licensing. It is not surprising that companies in Japan report a much greater degree of attention by top management to patent matters than do their counterparts in Sweden.

In reviewing the patent system of Japan, ORDOVER (1991, p. 48) has concluded that, "The Japanese patent system is a complex web of policy choices more or less consciously structured to affect R&D diffusion while maintaining overall incentives for R&D investment. The Japanese patent system subordinates the short-term interests of the innovator in the creation of exclusionary rights to the broader policy goals of diffusion of technology. Because the scope of the patent is narrow under the Japanese patent law and the novelty requirement is quite weak, it rewards those who reverse engineer and modify, often in minor ways, the existing inventions and penalizes those who wish to protect their major technological breakthroughs."

The Japanese patent system, which, combined with weak trade secret law, serves to induce innovators to disclose strategic information sooner than does the American system. In particular, "its institutional features encourage diffusion by creating strong incentives for licensing and cross-licensing of patents" (ORDOVER, 1991, p. 45). For example, in Japan a patent is granted to the first filer and not, as is the case in the united States and Canada, the first to invent. By awarding the patent to the first to file, inventors are given a clear incentive to register with the Patent Office as soon as possible. This has the effect of disseminating the information faster than it would be otherwise.

Under the Japanese patent system an application must *lay open* for 18 months subsequent to being filed. This speeds up the diffusion of the knowledge contained in the patent. The patent system in Japan also permits third parties to oppose the granting of a patent. By contrast, in the United States and in Germany the patent examiner makes the initial determination of where the statutory requirement have been in granting a patent. Intervention by third parties is only possible after the patent has been granted. Allowing pre-grant opposition enhances the incentives for firms to license the innovation for several reasons. First, licensing the invention is a pre-emptive tactic which decreases the incentives for competing firms to oppose the patent application. The opposition phase creates strategic incentives for early bargaining between the innovator and those potential rivals who would be disadvantaged if the patent is granted. In addition, during the opposition phase the applicant can be opposed by a large number of filings which have been prepared by expert staffs over a long time period. The applicant has only a limited time period of several months to respond.

Under Japanese patent law, an inventor is entitled to royalties only from those who utilized the potentially patentable invention knowingly after the application has been made. This provides a strong incentive for an inventor to notify all likely users of the contents of a patent. In addition, the Ministry of International Trade and Industry (MITI) can compel a patent-holder to cross-license the invention if it is deemed that the patent comprises a technology of national importance.

Both GILBERT and SHAPIRO (1990) and KLEMPERER (1990) have pointed out that the scope of patent claim is distinctly different between Japan and the united States. Prior to 1988, Japanese patent law limited each application to a single independent claim, which was referred to as a head claim. KLEMPERER (1990, p. 114) provides the example of an invention for a bicycle, which would not only have to patent the bicycle, but also the separate bicycle parts that comprise the bicycle. As ORDOVER (1991, p. 48) points out, "It is not clear how the restriction to a single independent head claim affects R&D incentives of dissemination. It clearly leads to a multitude of patents, with all the negative costs that this imposes on the innovator and the society." The second dimension of the scope of the patent claim is a delimitation of the scope of the coverage of the patent. Scope is defined as the portion of an abstract product or technology space covered by the patent. The rather narrow scope of coverage granted by patents tends to reduce the exclusionary value of the patent right (SCOTCHMER and GREEN, 1990). This again enhances the incentive to engage in cross-licensing among firms.

The regime of intellectual property protection in Japan tends to bias technological development towards externally acquired technologies. MANSFIELD (1988) compares the composition of R&D expenditures between 50 matched pairs of Japanese and American firms. He finds that the Japanese tend to have cost and time advantages over their American counterparts in making innovations based on external technology. However, for innovations based on internal technology there is no significant difference in the average cost or time required to develop the innovation between Japanese and American firms. The ratio of innovation cost or time for a new product based on external technology to that for a new product based on internal technology tends to be much lower in Japan than in the United States. In particular, Japanese firms take about 25 percent less time, and spend about 50 percent less, in developing an innovation based on external technology than one based on internal technology. By contrast, in the united States the commercialization of an innovation based on external technology requires about the same expenditure of effort as does the commercialization of an innovation based on internal technology.

Whether the Japanese system of protecting intellectual property has found an optimal way in which to offset the conflicting tensions posed by the need for appropriability, exclusion and diffusion is certainly debatable. It must be remembered that the system of protecting intellectual property rights in Japan evolved in an economy that was focused on imported technology (AUDRETSCH, 1997). Consistent with that is the well-known capability of Japanese firms to adapt, to modify and commercialize imported technology. It may be that the system of protection for intellectual property in Japan could be more effective in meeting the needs of a technological follower rather than those of an intellectual leader. As ORDOVER and WILLIG (1990) point out, a technological leader is more likely to value the aspects of appropriability and exclusion rather than diffusion. As they show, this is even more the case when the market power of an innovative firm can be dissipated by competition from foreign firms.

The production and application of intellectual property deserves special attention in economics, because as Arrow (1962, p. 616) emphasized some three decades ago, new economic knowledge is decidedly distinct from other economic goods: "The central fact about the processes of invention and research is that they are devoted to the reproduction of information. By the very definition of information, invention must be a risky process, in that the output (information obtained) can never be predicted perfectly from the inputs." Arrow (1962, p. 619), in fact, provided for an economic rationale for government intervention in the form of protection of intellectual property, "We expect a free enterprise economy to under invest in invention and research (as compared with an ideal), because it is risky, because the product can be appropriated only to a limited extent, and because of increasing returns in use."

The need to balance appropriability on the one hand against competition and diffusion on the other has been the subject of a fairly large literature. However, when it comes to the five basic regimes of intellectual property protection – patents, copyright, trademarks, trade secrets, and misappropriation, there has been considerably less analysis undertaken. The main issues involved in what research has been done involves the scope and the duration of protection. These elements are generally viewed as shaping the appropriability conditions as well as the ease of diffusion. Generally it is thought that a broader scope and longer duration correspond with greater appropriability and therefore a greater incentive to innovate. However, the degree to which competitors are excluded reduces the degree of competition and presumably static efficiency and the extent to which diffusion of new knowledge is impeded reduces dynamic efficiency. Most of the knowledge in the economics literature involves the relationships between patent protection, exclusion and diffusion. Considerably less is known concerning the links between the other regimes of intellectual property protection and the appropriability conditions, as well as exclusivity and diffusion.

This is also true for the links between appropriability on the one hand and technological change on the other. This large literature has not been reviewed here, but one of the central conclusions is that patent activity tends to increase where appropriability conditions are greater. (COHEN and LEVIN (1989). But the use of patent activity to measure innovative activity has been challenged in the literature. For example, PAKES and GRILICHES (1980, p. 378) argue that "patents are a flawed measure of innovative output; particularly since not all new innovations are patented and since patents differ greatly in their economic impact." In addressing the question, "Patents as indicators of what?" GRILICHES (1990, p. 1669) concludes that, "Ideally, we might hope that patent statistics would provide a measure of the innovative output...The reality, however, is very far from it. The dream of getting hold of an output indicator of inventive activity is one of the strong motivating forces for the economic research area." In any case, whatever the qualifications in measuring the link between appropriability and patent activity, very little is systematically known concerning the link between technological change and the appropriability conditions afforded by the other regimes of intellectual property protection. This represents a clear and unfortunate oversight of economic research. This may be particularly so because, as

SCHERER (1983, pp. 107-108) points out, the propensity to utilize any particular regime of intellectual property protection may vary from industry to industry, "…the quantity and quality of industrial patenting may depend upon chance, how readily a technology lends itself to patent protection, and business decision-makers' varying perceptions of how much advantage they will derive from patent rights. Not much of a systematic nature is known about these phenomena, which can be characterized as differences in the propensity to patent."

SCHERER (1983) found a lower propensity to actually rely on patent protection as a mode for protection of intellectual property in the office equipment industry. (SCHERER, 1983) Such a disparity in the propensity to patent across industries is explained by Mansfield (1984, p. 462), "The value and cost of individual patents vary enormously within and across industries…many inventions are not patented. And in some industries, like electronics, there is considerable speculation that the patent system is being bypassed to a greater extent than in the past. Some types of technologies are more likely to be patented than others." In any case, neither SCHERER nor MANSFIELD, nor virtually anyone else for that matter, has even attempted to systematically identify which regime of protection of intellectual property protection is being substituted for patent protection or how the reliance upon specific regimes of intellectual property protection varies from industry to industry.

5.9 Mobilizing Entrepreneurship in Universities

Universities in the EU offer a rich pool of students and academics. Universities could play a more positive role for entrepreneurship - thus also creating new jobs - if universities were encouraged to incorporate in some curricula complementary modules on business and entrepreneurship. While it is true that the typical time lag between final examinations and creation of an own business is rather long for academic entrepreneurs (e.g. some 10-15 years in Germany) optional courses on business creation for all students could turn out to be a useful investment for society. Such reforms would widen the long term entrepreneurial basis and it would create a generally more receptive climate for entrepreneurs in Europe. The European Commission could stimulate adequate reforms in EU member countries.

The present university system in most EU countries is dominated by state universities which have insufficient incentives to nurture entrepreneurial talents. More private universities which face pressure to find external research funds will consider a strong track record of alumni which are entrepreneurs as important. Therefore the European Commission could support – e.g. via an endowment for a chair – creation of private universities in countries in which such universities are quite rare.

5.10 Perspectives: Globalization and Political Innovation in a Democracy

The globalization of the economy in the sense of a growing international trade network - with more products and more countries covered - and a rapid rise in foreign direct investment implies both rising trade in differentiated products and more complex internationalized production networks of multinational companies. With the advance of Asian NICs - disregarding transitory problems in their financial markets in 1997 - in medium technology fields Schumpeter rents of EU countries are melting away. Moreover, as innovation cycles are shortening EU firms face the problem of how to appropriate an adequate rate of return on investment plus innovation expenditures within a shorter period, so that on the one hand exploiting economies of scale becomes more important. On the other hand, for innovative firms marketing expenditures are likely to increase because they are an option to reinforce market segmentation across customer groups and countries so that profitable price differentiation remains a valid strategy for improved recovering of innovation costs.

Facing an internet revolution worldwide in the coming years - namely more powerful browsers in combination with advanced hardware plus wider international access to the internet as a consequence of falling PC and telecoms network user prices - it is clear that the EU's firms will face stronger innovation competition around the world. It will become more difficult for firms from OECD countries to recover R&D investment costs by first mover advantages and high prices in a rather long pioneer stage. With the pioneer stage shortening and imitation threats strengthening worldwide innovative firms could pursue more intensive patenting strategies on a global scale. At the same time it holds that with faster worldwide imitation the time span of effective patent protection is shortening. One way for innovative firms to secure an adequate rate of return on innovation will be to pursue international mergers & acquisitions in order to build up market power in the world market. The aircraft industry, pharmaceuticals and electro turbine industry are examples for this development.

Globalization implies that the quest for mobile capital will intensify so that competing locations will have strong incentives to create hospitable economic frameworks and an attractive system design. This development implies a growing role of the economic system worldwide and (transitory) less influence for the political system. With more mobile production factors and trade in more diversified products and intermediate inputs governments in European welfare states typically face problems in maintaining a broad tax basis - corporate tax revenues relative to GDP are declining across Europe. At the same time governments face pressure for privatization because state-owned companies are poorly positioned for becoming a fully accepted partner in international business cooperation and M&A ventures.

Free trade is considered to be the natural way for expanding prosperity across the globe. While there is no doubt that free trade supports economic catching-up processes it could be more doubtful whether there will be full convergence in the long run as the new growth theory and the new trade theory point to core-periphery developments. Moreover, with scale economies gains from trade will be rather asymmetric depending on international specialization patterns of country I and II. Facing rather large gains in industries with scale economies one cannot rule out that nations' competing R&D efforts could lead to excessive national expenditures for such sectors. Too much R&D support indeed can be expected if large gains in the market plus major employment effects in state-owned firms are at stake. A first step towards more rationality in the R&D policies therefore is partial (or full) privatization by an initial public offering in the stock market. Discretionary power of both managers and bureaucrats typically will be restricted by the critical eye of analysts in the stock market.

Due to the revolution in telecommunications and the internet technology which bring unprecetented transparency across countries and regions mobile investors are fully aware of advantages and disadvantages of alternative locations for investment projects. This in turn raises pressure on governments to adopt policy innovations from abroad. At the same time governments in EU countries could decide to adopt more cooperative policies in order to avoid the pressure for reform. It should be clear that a certain amount of pressure on governments to adopt reforms is quite useful in democracies in which pressure groups and the bureaucracy are two forces that typically slow down adjustment and innovations.

The presence of foreign multinational companies can be a catalyst for political efficiency in the sense that MNCs from abroad will request and require that internationally competitive solutions be adopted. Multinational companies will increasingly be influential vis-à-vis the political systems in Europe. Their influence could even rise further after the start of the Euro since full transparency in costs and prices will encourage MNCs to largely disregard any traditional preferences in their investment decisions in favor of the headquarters country. If some EU countries would suffer major and sustaining outflows of foreign direct investment along with declining inflows a falling investment output ratio, slower growth and higher unemployment will be unavoidable results. In a world with rising FDI flows each EU country should emphasize steps for raising FDI inflows while not discouraging FDI outflows that are natural and necessary for an efficient international division of labor.

Innovation in Economic Policy

Globalization of the economy requires EU countries to step up their R&D policy and to stimulate the creation of new technology oriented firms. Given the vested interests of incumbent firms the lobby for innovative newcomers certainly is weak. Few countries - like the US and the UK - have established functional venture capital markets. Certainly continental Europe is facing major problems in this field. Even more difficult to achieve could be the necessary increases in government R&D spending. European monetary union and the stability pact, respectively, impose a maximum deficit GDP ratio of 3% on Euro countries after

1999. Disregarding the smaller EU countries, which except for Greece record an almost balanced budget in 1998, the major EU countries - narrowly reaching the 3% margin - have little room to manoeuvre on the expenditure side. With pressure for government expenditure cuts public R&D spending is likely to fall as a ratio of GDP in the future in the Community. Given the high rate of unemployment in most EU countries there are, however, favorable prospects for stepping up programs for the support of new technology-oriented firms. The basic economic rationale to do so lies in the positive external effects of such firms. Given the rising social security contribution rates caused in continental EU countries' pay-as-you-go systems by aging of society there will be political resistance against high income tax rates in the future and this in turn could force governments to reduce R&D expenditures relative to GDP. This would be exactly contrary to what is required in the European information & high technology society. Politicians might consider to shore up support for R&D projects by implementing a new policy field related to innovation policy, namely communication policy. In the information society the creation of fast integrated networks, including access for universities, schools and small and medium-sized firms is important as are new services offered via the internet - possibly including a venture capital market in the internet (launched in the US in 1997).

In the field of economic policy in a democracy innovations are rather difficult to launch. There typically are five reasons for this:

- Market entry in the political market is often difficult since there are minimum voter shares in many countries

- The need to achieve majorities in parliament makes innovations more difficult than in the marketplace where even small minorities of flexible consumers can help to successfully launch a product innovation;

- Coalition governments which often include a small innovative party are often themselves unstable.

- Rent-seeking by vested interest groups helps the incumbent government to survive by supporting existing industries - not the small innovative sectors of the economy which are rarely effective in political lobbying.

- There is a political constitution which can be invoked by conservative forces to defend the status quo. The judicial system has a tendency to interfere in favor of incumbent firms because those have more financial clout and thus can mobilize more expertise than innovative newcomers.

Systemic competition therefore is quite important. From this it follows that economic policy in general and R&D policy in particular must be willing to adopt successful procedures from partner countries and that political interference should be limited in Western Europe in order not to unduly restrict market dynamics. At the same time it holds that government should assume its responsibility at the various government layers and pursue clear-cut policies which must include standardized reporting procedures.

Appendix A: Tables and Figures

Tab. A1: **Changes in the Employment and Wage Bill Shares of Nonproduction Labor and Between- and Within-Industry Decompositions, U.S. and U.K. Manufacturing Industry**

Sample	Employment Share			Wage Bill Share		
	Total Change[a]	Between - industry component	Within - industry component	Total Change[a]	Between - industry component	Within - industry component
U.S., 1959-73	0.069	-0.009	0.078	0.051	-0.018	0.069
U.S., 1973-79	0.299	0.112	0.187	0.293	0.085	0.208
U.S., 1979-87	0.552	0.165	0.387	0.774	0.306	0.468
U.K., 1979-90	0.367	0.066	0.301	0.668	0.114	0.554

Note:[a]Annualized percentage point rate of change in the relevant share.
Sources: U.S. - *Berman, Bound, and Griliches (1994), Table IV, p. 37;*
   U.K. - Machin (1996), Table 7.2, p. 134.

Globalization, Economic Growth and Innovation Dynamics

Tab. A2: Shares of international stock by broad sectors

Percentage shares

		Outward			Inward			GDP shares (1992)		
		Pri-mary	Secon-dary	Ter-tiary	Pri-mary	Secon-dary	Ter-iary	Pri-mary	Secon-dary	Ter-iary
United States	1982-84	30.5	40.3	29.3	17.0	33.7	49.4			
	1991-93	13.0	37.3	49.7	10.2	37.9	51.9	4.0[7]	20.6[7]	75,4[7]
Canada[1]	1982-84	22.4	45.2	28.6	31.4	40.1	24.3			
	1991-93	7.6	43.1	49.3	15.1	51.5	33.4	6.7[7]	20.7[7]	72.6[7]
Japan[2]	1982-84	20.5	30.8	46.3	n.a.	74.7	25.3			
	1991-93	5.5	26.9	65.8	n.a.	57.5	42.5	2.6	29.5	67.9
France	1991-92	6.2	40.7	53.2	5.3	37.4	53.1	4.1	25.6	70.3
Germany[2]	1984	3.8	59.7	30.1	0.2	53.1	46.1			
	1991-93		50.6	44.8	0.1	48.6	51.1	1.9	33.9	64.2
Italy	1982-84	20.7	39.4	39.8	7.5	55.0	37.5			
	1991-93	6.4	31.1	62.5	3.3	39.9	56.8	3.7	24.0	72.3
Nether-lands	1984	0.1[3]	68.6	31.3	0.3[3]	54.0	45.7			
	1991-92	0.1	54.7	45.2	0.1	52.1	47.8	7.8	21.6	70.6
United Kingdom	1984	33.3	31.8	34.8	33.9	40.8	25.3			
	1991-93	17.9	37.2	45.0	25.1	34.0	40.9	4.3	25.5	70.2
Finland[4]	1982-84	n.a.[3]	60.0	41.7	n.a.	n.a.	n.a.			
	1991-93	n.a.	73.2	19.0	n.a.[3]	51.4	36.2	7.0	28.6	64.5
Norway[1]	1991-93	15.1	57.8	25.4	34.8	11.6	53.1	20.9[7]	17.4[7]	61.7[7]
Sweden[5]	1991-93	n.a.	60.9	35.3	n.a.	46.5	48.2	3.4	25.8	70.8
Australia	1982-84	18.2	30.9	51.5	21.2	30.1	48.6			
	1991-93[4]	16.1	28.6	50.9	17.1	25.2	51.4	7.6	15.0	77.5

[1] Unallocated is 2% of outward investment,
[2] Unallocated is 3-6% of outward investment, < ½% of inward investment,
[3] Mining, oil, petroleum included in chemicals
[4] Unallocated fluctuates widelyk,
[5] Unallocated is 2-6% outward investment, fluctuates for inward investment,
[6] 1983-84,
[7] 1991

Source: OECD (1997), Globalisation of Industry, Paris, 35.

Tab. A3: Stock market capitalization in selected OECD countries (End November 1996)

Country	Stock Circulation (Bill. DM)[1]	Stock Market Capitalization Coefficient[2]
USA[3]	13,354	122
Japan[4]	4,881	63
Great Britain	2,544	152
Germany	1,002	27
France	892	38
Canada[5]	756	88
Switzerland	624	135
The Netherlands	555	93
Italy	386	23
Sweden	357	103
Spain[6]	332	39
Belgium	180	44
Denmark	105	40
Finland	90	47
Norway	85	38
Austria	48	14

[1] prices of domestic stocks listed on the stock exchange;
[2] stock circulation in percent of the 1995 nominal GNP;
[3] New York Stock Exchange and NASDAQ;
[4] Tokio Stock Exchange;
[5] Toronto Stock Exchange;
[6] Madrid Stock Exchange

Source: Deutsche Bundesbank (1997), Monatsbericht Januar 1997, Frankfurt/M.

Fig. A1:   Competition and Innovation in Telecommunications

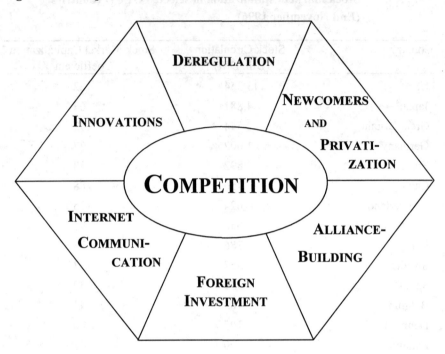

Fig. A2:   **Fundamentals of Innovativeness**

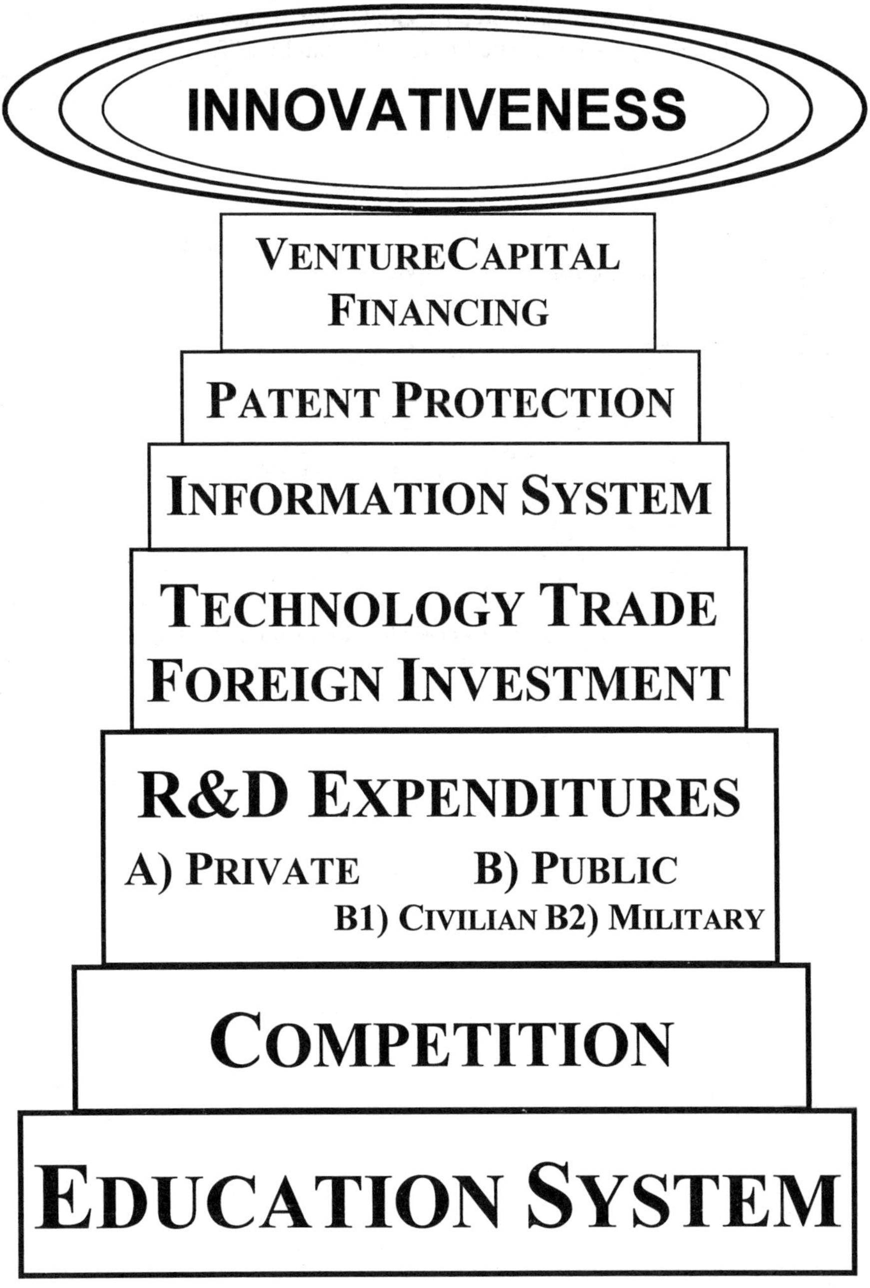

INNOVATIVENESS

VENTURECAPITAL FINANCING

PATENT PROTECTION

INFORMATION SYSTEM

TECHNOLOGY TRADE FOREIGN INVESTMENT

R&D EXPENDITURES
A) PRIVATE   B) PUBLIC
B1) CIVILIAN B2) MILITARY

COMPETITION

EDUCATION SYSTEM

Fig. A3:   **Number of technology areas with significance for German industries and their heterogeneity** (for details see GRUPP, 1997; the survey data originate from BEISE and LICHT, 1996, p. 13)

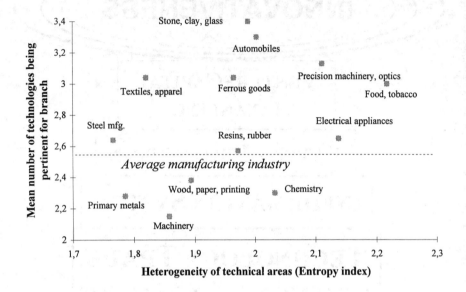

Fig. A4: **Breakdown of government R&D budget appropriations between oriented, non-oriented and general university funds of the EU and overseas countries and the Commission of the European Union 1994**

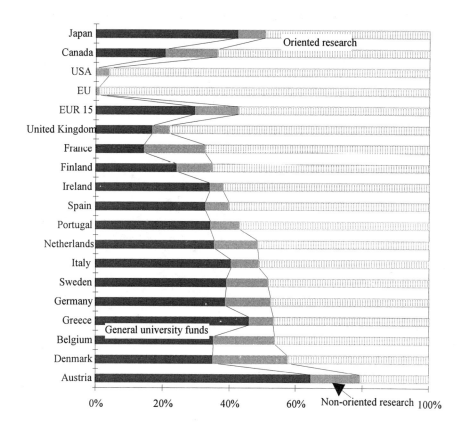

Source: *EUROSTAT, NSF*

Executive Summary

Since the 1980s global competition has intensified as foreign direct investment increased strongly, new countries opened up as host countries (or became influential as source countries) and innovative forms of inter-firm cooperation were established. Rising foreign direct investment could stimulate economic growth worldwide to the extent that it contributes to technology spillovers, international technology trade, improved use of know-how and a higher overall investment output ratio plus a higher marginal product of capital worldwide. The spatial distribution of foreign investment flows is in turn influenced by regional or local clusters of R&D centers and the availability of human capital or other factors which can be profitably combined with firm-specific advantages important for multinational companies (MNCs). Moreover, public support for R&D and the quality of the education system also play a role for attracting MNCs.

In the 1980s and early 1990s international competition intensified in the OECD countries but also worldwide. On the one hand, newcomers from Asian NICs entered medium and advanced technology fields; on the other hand the US, France and the UK as well as Russia reduced their emphasis on military research and development (R&D) after 1990. Hence, the end of the Cold War led to intensified competition in markets for civilian products. The ratio of civilian R&D to GDP has increased in most countries worldwide, and there are prospects for a rapid increase of R&D outlays in some NICs and the People's Republic of China at the turn of the century. Moreover, the internet has reinforced access to new technological knowledge.

The link between globalization and foreign direct investment is important for the EU as is the interdependency between foreign investment and trade in a world of many newcomers from Asia and eastern Europe. Multinational companies contribute to economic development but also impose adjustment pressure on governments in the EU which compete for mobile investment. However, while many MNCs try to shop around for the highest subsidies and tax breaks initially, a given commitment to investing in certain countries can help to establish new standards in the field of social policy and environmental policy. Reputation for products built up in leading markets will not easily allow a watering down in other markets which in principle could be served with products of minor quality. More ambivalent could be the environmental role of MNCs with respect to using different production processes across countries where competition pressure is likely to stimulate MNCs to prefer countries with soft environmental standards.

Theoretical aspects of high technology policy deserve more attention, and a special EU research program on this might be useful. Based on recent theoretical advances it is obvious that the combination of rising product differentiation and technology intensity with scale economies and technological spillover effects are important to consider. Here the single market reinforces scale economies; in this respect the economic opening-up of eastern Europe also is important since there are new dynamic markets emerging and new opportunities for R&D subcontracting and cooperation. Eastern Europe offers an interesting pool of skilled researchers.

It will be important to take into account the links between globalization, employment dynamics and innovations. Product and process innovations clearly are crucial for productivity increases and economic growth. However, the rapid diffusion of new technologies and an optimum use of best-practice technologies are also important. With respect to the latter Germany and other continental EU countries suffered from a critical backwardness vis-à-vis the US, namely about 1/3 according to a recent study by McKINSEY. Moreover, application of such technologies often is in sectors different from the innovative sector. Technology diffusion as a percentage of total embodied technology clearly was dominated by the service sector in the G-7 group in 1993. While the US, the UK, Japan and Italy recorded shares of more than 50%, France, Canada and Germany achieved only 44%, 42% and 43%, respectively. In particular Germany as a country with an underdeveloped service sector thus foregoes opportunities for higher economic growth and employment creation. In the mid-1990s the share of services in GDP was about 10 percentage points lower in Germany than in the US; the differences in the respective shares of employment in private sector services were of a similar magnitude. This apparent gap in the service sector is a major structural deficit in Germany, and overcoming obstacles to the expansion of this sector is a major policy challenge. This, however, could be difficult to meet since the high percentage of long term unemployed – often former workers and employees from industrial firms – will rarely have the matching skills required for new jobs in service companies. Moreover, workers from the manufacturing sector which, being a high capital intensity / high productivity sector, used to pay rather high wages, will often find it unacceptable to voluntarily switch to a new job in the less capital intensive service sector which often will pay lower wages but offer greater job security.

Germany and many other continental EU countries suffer from high unemployment rates which largely reflect an underdeveloped service sector, insufficient R&D expenditures and lack of training and education as well as inadequate diffusion policies. Labor market rigidities and insufficient wage dispersion also impair regaining full employment. Part of the existing productivity gap in continental EU countries vis-à-vis the US is apparently related to underdeveloped stock markets and rather poor capital productivity compared to the US.

The rapid growth in foreign direct investment in the 1980s has accelerated the transfer of international technology since technology trade is mainly intra-company trade (e.g. between parent company and subsidiaries) or license swapping between multinational companies (MNCs). A high rate of product innovation allows firms to charge higher prices in world markets, and a high rate of process innovation facilitates the widening of markets and the exploitation of dynamic scale economies. Innovativeness is, therefore, not only a key to international competitiveness but to firms' ability to pay high real wages in EU countries.

The process of globalisation goes along with observable growth in productivity and income across nations. Economies who participate in world trade are in competition for ideas and techniques. Therefore a countries potential to develop and adopt advanced techniques has turned out to be one of the decisive factors of economic performance. This process is predominately determined by the stock of human capital. Basically countries with sufficient R&D activities are profiting from the process of globalisation. Different technological capabilities of countries induce heterogeneous productivity growth across economies.

The observable heterogeneity of the global growth process let to a large body of empirical and theoretical research. One of the main conclusions from the empirical literature is that the hypothesis of absolute convergence formerly predicted by growth economists does not hold, i.e. not all countries do automatically converge to the same steady state position. However, if countries are clustered, further statements can be made. Six "clubs" with similar developments in terms of income levels and average growth can be identified: the industrialised elite, the industrialized catching up countries, the strongly catching up countries, the slowly catching up countries, the slowly falling behind and the strongly falling behind countries. Overall a process of "conditional convergence" can be observed for the first four convergence clubs while countries of the last two clubs tend to diverge. Conditional convergence implies that an economy will converge to a steady state that is characterised by a set of fundamentals specific to the country. Meanwhile a thousands of regressions have been run to identify those fundamentals. The most important ones are the investment rate, the human capital endowment, the R&D intensity and the countries integration into world markets. The empirical results therefore strongly support the hypothesis that only countries with sufficient abilities to innovate or acquire new technologies are able to converge in terms of their productivity levels and income.

The empirical findings of the variety of growth processes of different countries or country groups need to be explained theoretically. The traditional neo-classical growth theory of the Solow-Swan type regarded the technological growth process as exogenously given. The technologies were equally available without costs in every country. As a result global convergence was predicted. As these predictions of traditional neo-classical growth theory do not correspond with the stylized features of the global growth process, a new interpretation was introduced. If human capital accumulation is included and countries have different saving rates, the models implications cannot be rejected easily by the empirical facts. Nevertheless, the global public good character of the technologies remains a serious problem in this theory. Hence the "new growth theory" appeared. A major result from "new growth theory" is to emphasize on the importance of human capital for any kind of technology related activities. But unlike in the traditional theory human capital is not just accumulated but generates externalities, scale economies and innovations. And this result should be also used to explain diffusion processes of technologies, which will probably give a better understanding of the global growth process. In "new growth theory" technological progress is endogenously generated. With the endogenous "production" of technological progress diverging growth processes in different countries can be explained. The internal accumulation and allocation of resources – especially of human capital – determines the R&D activities, the technological ability and finally the productivity growth rates of a country. Therefore, the countries preferences determine the growth position. This mechanism suggests why convergence cannot be observed for all countries. On the other hand, looking carefully at the now existing literature of the new growth theory, the most innovative contribution is the modeling of innovations on a firm level. The firms profit maximizing behavior leads to R&D activities and technology growth as an endogenous process. Confronting the implications of "new growth theory" with the global growth process, there are again doubts about the explanatory power of this type of models. New growth theory tries to identify differences in productivity growth by different activities of innovations. Technologies are either exclusively developed and used in one country (no international integration) or available without costs from the other country (integrated world). But, the real world is different. At any point in time different countries have different stocks of production related knowledge and technological capabilities. There is little doubt that these differences result from innovation and imitation activities. But the distinction between innovation and imitation is crucial to explain the global process of growth and development. The technologically leading countries, the industrialized elite, are forced to sustained innovation since their comparative advantages as technological leaders would otherwise get lost. Traditional and new growth theory serve well to explain this type of technology and innovation driven process of growth. But these theories fail to explain the development of middle and low income countries. If countries are fare behind, imitation rather than innovation can explain growth opportunities.

Catching up or developing countries will basically not focus on innovations and inventing new technologies. Instead of innovation these countries mainly rely on the adoption and imitation of techniques developed outside their own country. Since imitation is usually associated with lower costs and does not bear the same risks as innovation these countries have "an advantage of backwardness". The less developed countries basically try to get hold of existing knowledge and known technologies by devoting resources to a process of technological catching up. The clusters of country groups which are observable in the world economy however show that a process of technological upgrading is not for free. Instead a set of favorable initial conditions is necessary. Most important the country has to build up capabilities to absorb advanced techniques. These capabilities are essentially human, administrative, and organizational knowledge. A number of empirical and theoretical studies point out that the education of the workforce is especially important and that a process of upgrading cannot occur unless the country meets a critical level of human capital. Otherwise the country is running the risk to be caught in a low growth trap. Once the initial conditions are met a process of technological convergence will set in. At the beginning, this process may be slow but it will become self-preserving or even accelerate, if the country is able to assimilate advances in productivity into additional comparative advantages and growing export shares. Increasing exports are necessary to get hold of sufficient foreign exchange to finance technology intensive imports necessary as inputs in production or reverse engineering. A dynamic process of upgrading may also attract additional capital through foreign direct investments. FDIs will generally tend to speed up the process of technological upgrading, because they raise the rate of capital accumulation and offer additional access to advanced techniques. But, as countries catch up, the advantage of backwardness diminishes and the speed of catching up reduces. The country is likely to converge in an s-shaped manner. The slowdown results from the reduction in techniques suitable for imitation as the technological gap becomes closed. Simultaneously the costs necessary to encode advanced techniques increase. Finally economies tend to converge to a final position and a final gap remains. It seems reasonable that FDIs are less important for the final level of convergence. The final gap will depend on the factors that determine the potential to absorb technologies. Some authors further point out that the country will not be able to fully close the technological gap by imitation alone. Instead a final gap will remain unless the country switches from imitation to innovation. With this switch the country becomes member of the industrialized elite club. Again human capital is most important with this respect. Sufficient human capital will delay the forces that tend to slow down the process of catching up and support the switch from imitation to innovation.

The process of upgrading will also affect comparative advantages and the structure of the economy. The permanent shift in factor endowments described in the open economy version of traditional neo-classical growth theory as well as the permanent improvement of the relative technological position of the country will permanently cause a change in the position of comparative advantages. The change in the relative endowment will change the Heckscher-Ohlin trade position and the technological catching up will change the Ricardian comparative advantage. With a permanent change of comparative advantages the structure of the economies in the process of catching up will also permanently change. The countries will move towards the production of new industries and move out of the production of old industries. Thus, catching up implies continuous structural change until the countries reach their final steady state position. Further, during the process of upgrading Heckscher-Ohlin and Ricardo trade is inter industry trade. When the countries approach their final steady state position the fundamentals might converge. Due to converging fundamentals (factor endowments and technological abilities) comparative advantages of the Heckscher-Ohlin and Ricardo type disappear. The result is a continuous change from inter industry to intra industry trade.

From the discussion of the extraordinary role of human capital for the technological capabilities and the general economic performance, an additional directly related question arises: What determines the allocation of human capital in the world regions? Why are certain regions well endowed with human capital with good opportunities for growth, and other regions do not show significant human capital accumulation? How do accumulation processes take place? At least two sets of reasons for the relative abundance of human capital in a region must be investigated. 1. Local human capital accumulation determines at least the regional abundance of the immobile components of human capital. Differences of regional accumulation of human capital may change the relative regional human capital intensities. 2. In real world the "regional characteristic endowment" is not exogenous. Components of human capital may migrate (at least to some extend) from one region to another. Even if there are no large scale migrations, the partial mobility of important components of human capital may however be able to effect the aggregate. Horizontal integration of catching up countries in world markets is compatible and even goes along with the idea of gravity and cluster formation of regional centers The formation of regional clusters which is well known from regional economics, by "positive feed back" includes technical and pecuniary externalities and increasing returns to scale. Within global regions with unrestricted product and factor markets (including the labor market), national borders disappear and internal regions will be formed as subregions and agglomerations. These internal regions will not develop equally. Human capital migration and differences in the speed of technology diffusion may lead to local agglomerations. Since the major characteristic of a region is the human capital abundance, the regions have to compete for human capital. The competition of regions will become the competition to accumulate, attract and bind human capital locally. If a region is successful in competing for human capital, the general economic situation will improve and a process of acceleration and catching up will take place.

European R&D policy has to be considered in both a national, an EU-wide and a global perspective. Basic evaluation of the EU R&D Framework Programme and the proposed task forces suggests that some progress in European innovation policy has been achieved, but EU firms are – compared to the US – still underrepresented in the new dynamic technology fields. More policy emphasis should be put on the role of small and medium-sized firms on the one hand; on the other hand, the challenges for international organizations are crucial. With more and more members the role of the European Patent Agency is becoming more important, yet more difficult to maintain efficiency. The role of the WTO which has a focus on trade-related intellectual property rights and some aspects of foreign direct investment is also crucial. One may, however, raise the question whether or not the World Intellectual Property Organization should play a stronger role and incorporate full responsibility for foreign direct investment which is almost fully complementary to international technology trade. International cooperation could become increasingly difficult in the era of globalization; however, adequate division of tasks between national governments, supranational institutions and international organizations will be a crucial step towards emerging global network governance.

The role of the stock market could also increase because the age of high technology competition at the turn of the century will reduce the relative importance of banks in financing innovative firms. European monetary union creates new opportunities for reinforcing the role of stock markets on the one hand, and, on the other hand, for more securitization. The hesitant steps on the continent to establish new stock markets for young firms should be encouraged politically, but there is also a need to stimulate the venture capital business in Euro countries and other EU countries. Asymmetric information problems between the innovator and the bank are typical of innovation projects so that insufficient access to (cheap) capital could limit the innovativeness of firms in the EU. The role of equity capital should be strengthened in the late 1990s in Europe. With workers facing a weaker bargaining position in the new environment of economic globalization one may consider tax incentives for workers encouraging them to allocate savings to investment funds (of a certain minimum rating). The role of capital markets could also be reinforced by reforming the social security systems, namely by partly replacing the current pay-as-you-go systems with capital-funded security programs. With monetary union growth-enhancing policy strategies of EU countries could become particularly important as the external value of the Euro can thus be strengthened. Removing impediments to growth and improving conditions for investment and entrepreneurs thus are crucial.

For the EU a high overall attractiveness for outside investors is of prime importance in the future when the quest for increasingly mobile real capital will intensify. This holds not only because high foreign investment inflows raise the overall investment output ratio but also because modernization and network effects from foreign investment contribute to EU competitiveness. Foreign direct investment abroad in turn could strengthen EU competitiveness if a similar complementarity between exports and foreign investment were observed as in the case of US foreign investment. Whether the net employment effect of foreign investment outflows is positive for the source country much depends on whether world demand has to be assumed as given or inelastic, respectively. If both the source and the host country record positive output and employment effects that reinforce the profitability of innovative firms one may expect a positive impact of rising global foreign investment flows on R&D. Globalization can also stimulate R&D by facilitating firms to realize economies of scale over a wider range of international markets. To the extent that globalization means a shortening of innovation cycles technology-oriented firms could face pressure to quickly serve national markets with differentiated customer-tailored products so that the Vernon approach to trade and foreign investment has to be modified; the traditional product cycle model of foreign investment argues that innovations mainly occur in countries with high per capita income that will serve foreign markets by exports first – only later, in the standardization stage, will production be shifted abroad in order to capture cost advantages important for price sensitive standardized products.

Multinational companies play an increasing role in a world in which imperfect markets for information require firms to engage in foreign direct investment as a means of safeguarding technological leads and ensuring adequate ability to appropriate innovation rents in world markets. According to DUNNING and other authors firms will consider foreign investment as a preferable alternative to serving foreign markets via exports and licenses if firm internal transaction costs are relatively low (compared to arm's length transactions) and if such investment is the best way to ensure that the benefits from innovation can profitably be appropriated. Firm-specific advantages, typically based on technological or organizational leadership, are the basis for successfully setting up production abroad – i.e. in a country in which the indigenous firms enjoy natural advantages with respect to knowledge about customers' preferences and locations as well as to access to political support for business projects. Production abroad can be not only a way to exploit technological leadership but also a strategy of product differentiation in markets where consumers have a preference for differentiated home-produced goods. The dynamics of the EC single market have shown an increase in intra-EU corporate mergers and acquisitions which can be understood as both reflecting the need for exploiting economies of scale and the need for stronger product differentiation under local production. Firms often will not establish fully developed subsidiaries abroad; rather the headquarters company will offer certain functions (e.g. R&D, financing) as a pool resource for all subsidiaries. Thus it will be interesting to analyze under which conditions R&D centers are mobile internationally. Indeed, one should distinguish between immobile and mobile Schumpeterian industries, where the latter stands for technology intensive sectors. In some industries R&D indeed can be set up in many countries so that foreign subsidiaries can become a means to tap technologies developed abroad. The presence of US or Asian technology-oriented subsidiaries in the EU in turn could contribute to the technological dynamism of Western Europe. In oligopolistic world markets oligopolistic rivalry could also be a prime motive for foreign investment.

With a global tendency to higher civilian R&D/GDP ratios there are strong incentives for technology-oriented firms to engage in multinationalization. National governments are facing an increasingly multinational world economy characterized by high capital mobility, low barriers to trade and an intensified quest for mobile production factors; with governments often acting in a rather isolated manner national governments face increasing problems in effectively implementing economic policy – including R&D policies.

Technological competition has increased for various reasons, including the rise of the share of civilian R&D in the US, the UK, France, Russia and other countries. Moreover, with new technology fields developing and Asian as well as post-socialist east European economies emerging as new competitors for EU countries in labor intensive and medium technology intensive industries there is a new tendency towards increased high technology competition in OECD countries. Since high technology markets are rather small, the reorientation of US R&D resources is stimulating US firms to aggressively move into medium technology markets so that EU firms face new problems in earning Schumpeterian rents in the world market which are the basis for self-financed innovation projects. With innovation cycles shortening and newcomers from Asia and Eastern Europe moving into established markets of EU firms there is a double problem for European industry. An interesting challenge also lies in the fact that innovation increasingly is linked to the service sector – including network industries – which also was among the leaders of globalization in the 1980s and early 1990s.

The positioning of the EU industry in the global world economy is crucial in the coming years. Most important will be the ability to attract sufficient foreign direct investment inflows from technology intensive source countries and to step up EU foreign direct investment outflows into countries with a dynamic technological background in America, Asia (plus Australia) and eastern Europe.

Improving the links between research and industry on the one hand, and, on the other hand, mobilizing entrepreneurship of universities and specialized research institutions could be important steps for a bigger impact of R&D in terms of commercial success of scientific progress.

Globalization of the economy means strongly increasing international competition. Price transparency is increasing for technological reasons and transportation costs are falling so that EU countries are facing stronger competition in labor-intensive products. However, there is also an increasing EU-external supply of technology-intensive commercial goods since the US and Russia have reoriented military R&D towards civilian industries. Moreover, Asian NICs and some Latin American NICs are catching-up vis-à-vis Europe because of rising ratios of R&D to GDP and improved education systems. The internet has contributed to accelerating the global diffusion of know-how, but the internet also offers new opportunities for EU countries; it allows creation of innovative virtual firms and of electronic commerce. Even more important will be opportunities for firms to internationalize at reduced costs and to rely on powerful intranets for coordination of firms.

It is important for the EU to reconsider the role of R&D policy in the future and better evaluate policy strategies at the national level. Encouraging transeuropean research networks as well as co-financing international benchmark studies for policy evaluation could be important impulses from the EU level. Prudent policy guidelines and improved policy transparency plus special support for technology-oriented start-up companies could also be particularly important in the future. Problems of patent protection and education policies as well as opportunities of mobilizing the innovative potential of universities in the information society will have to be considered, too.

Twelve main policy conclusions emerge:

- Globalization means intensified international interdependence as stronger links via trade, foreign investment – in a broad sense portfolio capital flows plus foreign direct investment – and the internet are increasing among OECD countries and worldwide. Globalization will continue after the turn of the century so that there are important long-term policy issues associated with this new quality of factor mobility. This mobility has strongly increased for real capital and skilled labor; in the future the internet provides a new platform for making semi-skilled labor more mobile worldwide. Financial market integration is likely to proceed faster than the integration of the real sphere of the economy. Instabilities in national and international financial markets could become an impediment to sustained growth in the world economy. Such instabilities and high unemployment in many industrialized countries as well as poverty in LDCs are main areas of long-term policy concerns.

- For EU countries globalization means intensified international technology competition and thus a need for further specialization. Accelerated innovation worldwide implies higher growth and, possibly, major environmental problems. Additional government co-financed R&D programs with an ecological focus and measures to internalize negative external effects of growth therefore are required. As know-how and knowledge become more accessible around the world in the internet era EU foreign commercial policy might on the one hand support internet development initiatives in developing countries but also should emphasize that EU countries will keep their markets open for "outsiders" increasingly offering products with a higher technology content. It will be difficult to maintain such EU promises if full employment in western Europe is not restored and if successful initiatives for high-technology leadership are not launched in the EU. Globalization means a new international division of labor and know-how, where EU countries certainly will have to intensify R&D efforts and improve the diffusion process.

- National governments plus trade unions and employer organizations are primarily responsible for employment developments and high unemployment rates, respectively. High unemployment rates cause resistance of workers against technological progress which is a problem for EU countries eager to improve international competitiveness via technological modernization and innovation. Insufficient wage dispersion in many continental EU countries can be observed where relatively high gross wages for unskilled labor are a major problem in continental EU countries. With reduced income tax rates for low income workers a longer period of underproportionate wage increases for unskilled workers might be easier to accept on the side of trade unions. With more dispersion higher employment and – in the medium term – higher average wage growth would result. This in turn would stimulate aggregate demand and encourage further investment and output growth.

- Expenditures on training and schooling are insufficient in many EU countries given the need to face increasing competition in skill-intensive import goods from eastern Europe and Asia. Given high wages in most EU countries high productivity of labor is required if further increases of the unemployment rate are to be avoided. Continuous retraining and special education programs of firms – partly based on the internet – are options to be strongly considered.

- Capital productivity in EU countries is lower than in the US which points to inefficiencies in European capital markets. The Euro will create more integrated capital markets but it remains doubtful that there will be strong benefits for Europe if national tax legislation is not harmonized to some extent and if the political will to reform social security systems on the continent is not reinforced. Moving at least partly away from the pay-as-you go systems in most continental EU countries to a new capital-funded pension system with strong incentives for workers to invest in investment funds would be an important impulse for higher capital productivity and ultimately more employment.

- R&D spending should be raised in Western Europe and the efficiency of R&D programs be increased.

- One cannot always avoid double spending in major R&D areas if one is to have the benefits of competition in R&D. Within the internal markets international M&As will raise the pressure on member governments to consider bilateral or multilateral joint R&D programs; and to pursue more specialization in R&D support.

- Encouraging diffusion of innovations seems to be quite important for growth and international competitiveness. New internet options should be envisaged for improving dissemination of information about innovations.

- The university system could be reformed, especially in countries with dominant state-funded universities. New private universities with a strong focus on advanced computer, internet and telecom technologies could be created to encourage a stronger orientation of university research towards the needs of the business community and society.

- Universities should be judged not only in terms of the number of students and scientific merit of professors but also with reference to the number of firms launched by alumni. Universities should be encouraged to establish a proven track record in this field.

- Given the small share of newly created firms in the EU which are technology-oriented one might consider special programs to stimulate the creation of new firms in novel technology fields. However, government money is in principle rarely needed if venture capital markets and stock markets could develop a higher profile in most ECU countries. Capital market policies are important as an indirect way to stimulate R&D in the community.

- ECU research is not sufficiently specialized and innovations of ECU firms often not in the most dynamic patent classes. Some informal coordination of national R&D policies could be useful in the future and the creation of ECU-wide R&D networks could be encouraged. However, creating an ECU-wide R&D network should – disregarding specific exceptions – not be considered if there is no alternative competing network within Western Europe. ECU firms could be encouraged to tap the R&D potential in eastern Europe and Russia where skilled personnel often are available at low costs. At the bottom line it is clear that facing globalization of economic relations EU countries have to improve education, training and R&D efforts in order to maintain a global technological leader status. Low equity-capital ratios of firms in many EU countries raise doubts about the EU's ability to successfully exploit new innovation fields where provision of risk capital is important for survival and expansion of newcomers; more international benchmarking studies are necessary in the future, and one may recommend regular benchmarking in all major policy fields. While Europe's established firms are well organized (problem of vested interests) innovative newcomers and young firms are less organized and less supported by the banking system and the political system. Finally, one may note that high unemployment rates not only discourage investment and innovation because record unemployment imposes limited prospects for new income growth and hence opportunities for higher growth; high unemployment rates also reinforce resistance of workers to technological progress. Restoring full employment in EU countries thus would stimulate economic growth and international competitiveness directly and indirectly.

Appendix B: Globalization, the Information Society and Economic Catching-up in the World Economy

Statement of Professor Welfens before the EIIW Annual Meeting, Potsdam, Dec. 5, 1997

Globalization and Economic Catching-up

Economic globalization means that the international network of trade, foreign investment, portfolio investment and information has intensified to such an extent as to create strong worldwide economic interdependence. Trade between OECD countries mainly consists of intra-industry trade and thus has a pro-competitive impact in the tradables sector of these countries. In contrast, trade between the North and South and among developing countries usually constitutes inter-industry trade. Thus pro-competitive impulses from the world market are quite limited, and this often is reinforced by uncompetitive domestic financial markets and a lax domestic competition policy. Consequently allocative inefficiencies – in terms of static efficiency criteria – are a major cause of low per capita income in both eastern Europe's postsocialist economies and in many developing countries. Economic growth and catching-up, therefore, require initiatives that increase competition in both the nontradables and the tradables sector in poorer countries. As the aspiration levels of people in poorer country continues to be raised by the Internet and the modern media, achieving economic growth will become ever more significant in political terms. From a EU perspective it is also important to encourage such economic catching-up, since it reduces political conflicts and slows down international migration pressures. This holds for the EU vis-à-vis eastern Europe and Northern Africa, but also applies to the US and Mexico and Latin America.

From a political economy point of view it is, however, clear that there will be strong resistance within developing countries to a strict competition policy. Such a policy could indeed be phased-in gradually and linked to some form of industrial policy, while being embedded in an outside-oriented policy approach (under a strategy of long term capital inflows). To some extent membership of the WTO, WIPO and other international organizations could be a substitute for a domestic competition policy – mainly in the tradables sector.

According to neoclassical models of free trade economic convergence is to be expected. Moreover, under neoclassical conditions transportation costs will encourage regional convergence processes within a country. However, innovations and differentiated products plus scale economies imply both core-periphery developments within a country and across countries (VENABLES, 1985; KRUGMANN, 1991). In the information society the range of tradable services will increase, with international trade in R&D intensive services being particularly attractive. Thus, firms will be eager to spread R&D costs over many domestic and foreign consumers. As innovative firms appropriate first-mover advantages and Schumpeterian economic rents, they will attempt to reinforce their market position, on the one hand through further investment in innovation and on the other hand through early application of technological innovations developed in other sectors. In the US and the UK the services sectors were the most important users of new technologies in the 1980s – in Germany the industrial sector continued to be the leading user.

In a period of ever more intensive global competition, access to information about new technology and market trends is crucial. As information itself is a useful input for the firms operating in the modern information society, the exchange, storage and processing of information becomes important for prosperity. However, given the monopolistic structure of the telecommunication sector in most non-OECD countries, prospects for faster learning about new international trends and innovations are poor. Under monopoly the scale of the network will be smaller (and repair service less reliable) than under competition so that access will be rather limited and prices higher. Such conditions reduce producers' ability to learn about new market trends and innovations and also impair growth due to lower investment by foreign investors. Since multinational companies typically establish production facilities across several countries and partly rely on intra-company trade, the price of international communication is important to their investment decisions. As multinational companies are typically active in technology intensive sectors, cheap and reliable access to the global information network and the company's intranet as well as extranets are crucial. In a global intensified quest for mobile real capital, countries with modern and cheap telecommunication networks enjoy strategic advantages as host countries for foreign direct investment.

Monopoly prices in telecommunications are like a tax on communication and learning. Telecommunications in general and the use of new technological paradigms are characterized by network effects (WELFENS, 1995). This means that in the network/paradigm expansion stage users A and B will benefit more if there is a rising number of other users C, D,...N which also use the network/paradigm. Hence, a government monopoly has very high social opportunity costs in the sense that the consumer rent would be much higher if network effects were fully developed and the relevant demand curve had shifted outwards.

In the era of globalization the international interdependence is asymmetric, i.e. small countries are less exposed to the international economy than large countries. Large countries with high per capita incomes enjoy the additional benefit of having a big domestic market allowing economies of scale to be exploited swiftly. While foreign exporters might have access to this big market as well, there is little doubt that biased government procurement and the reputation enjoyed by established domestic firms reinforces domestic firms' opportunities to exploit scale economies at home. Trade in scale intensive goods will create uneven benefits for the home and foreign countries. Depending on the significance of scale effects in the respective product the home country or the foreign country will reap the relatively larger benefits. In the case of foreign direct investment (FDI) such scale benefits could be largely appropriated by the major source countries of FDI assuming that foreign direct investment mainly takes place in technology and scale intensive sectors. From this perspective, the ability of a country to catch up crucially depends on competitive domestic firms that finally become successful investors abroad. A country that is only a host country for FDI can appropriate Schumpeterian economic rents abroad only via trade but not via foreign direct investment.

Information Technology, Innovation and Catching-up

The enormous advances made in computer technologies, the fall in computer prices and the recent technical progress in telecommunications facilitate access to information and reduce the price of communication in those countries where deregulation and privatization has taken place. These developments have created new opportunities for international economic convergence: poor countries may tap the pool of knowledge and know-how worldwide more easily, and there are new options for the creation of virtual firms and the realization of electronic commerce via the Internet. However, in terms of using the worldwide pool of knowledge and combining pieces of information for entrepreneurial purposes, the leading economies might actually be better placed than developing countries, namely for four reasons:

Firms producing scarce hardware and software for the information society are mainly located in the OECD countries. Their innovative products will help to appropriate Schumpeterian rents in information technology products worldwide.

Even if information were easily available on the Internet, useful commercial application and exploitation requires basic, sometimes sophisticated computer literacy and other knowledge. As is well known from the innovation literature (COHEN/LEVINTHAL, 1990, and GEROSKI, MACHIN and VAN REENEN, 1993) the absorption capacity of firms is crucial for profitability in the innovation and imitation race.

In order to tap the pool of knowledge abroad and benefit from R&D spillover effects it will be useful to have subsidiaries already established abroad, especially in those countries where proximity to leading research centers and universities promises considerable positive spillover effects. The ability of subsidiaries to learn abroad and route new knowledge to the parent company, which in turn will distribute it to all the subsidiaries, is crucial for positive supply multiplier effects. Outside the OECD group of countries only some countries in eastern Europe, which attracted high FDI inflows and already constitute source countries, are poised to benefit in a similar way to the leading market economies (WELFENS, 1995).

High technology multinational firms will have to send skilled staff over extended periods to subsidiaries abroad. Few experts will volunteer to countries with political instability and unattractive working conditions, prevalent in many developing countries, so that very high wage premia will be needed to make sure that sufficient skilled personnel is moving abroad. Indigenous skilled personnel often is very scarce, though some Asian countries improved their education systems significantly in the 1970s and 1980s. In many cases it will be simply unprofitable to maintain a foreign subsidiary at all. There are few countries in eastern Europe and the developing world where domestic markets are sufficiently large to make unattractive political conditions of minor importance for MNCs and warrant long term FDI inflows.

n a period of rising capital mobility countries which are major sources of FDI will particularly benefit from sustained global economic growth. It is important to understand the dynamics of profits. From a Schumpeterian perspective high differential profit rates are needed to bring about high investment-GDP ratios. Such profit rate differences can be expected in countries with intensive competition. Moreover, experience and simulation studies in OECD countries (on Sweden see BALLOT/TAYMAZ, 1997) have shown that the R&D stock per employee, general training stock per employee and specific training stock per employee are significant variables for growth and the profitability of firms. The fact that stock figures are so important implies that catching-up will always require efficient accumulation processes. According to BALLOT/TAYMAZ, 1997, the timing is important for different types of investment. The optimal sequence for the allocation of a firm's resources is as follows: (1) accumulate of a general human capital stock before the change in the techno-economic paradigm, (2) invest in R&D, and (3) invest in specific human capital. Moreover, innovators fare better than other firms because they are not only innovative but also build a competence base which supports learning from other firms. From this perspective Europe and the US plus parts of Asia and Latin America are well positioned to take advantage of a more intensive global technology race in the era of the information society. Since a valuable general human capital stock has already been accumulated, there exists a high potential for raising the absorption capacity with respect to innovations. However, only in the US and in some EU countries innovative firms face adequate conditions for the financing R&D. This suggests that both within the OECD and between the North and South per capita income differentials could increase in the future. In many east European transition countries and in most developing countries there exists a serious risk that volatile capital inflows will be reversed at some point, making contractionary macroeconomic policies necessary and thereby undermining improved prospects for the financing of investment and innovation.

Since the EU will introduce a common currency in 1999 and become a country group with relatively less foreign trade (external trade relative to GDP), it is likely to take a benign neglect attitude towards the exchange rate development, thus following the US, and the world economy might witness higher global exchange rate volatility than before. New information technologies and the increased global transparency of markets and countries will reinforce the contradictions between slowly adjusting real sectors and increasingly fast reacting financial markets. Higher volatility could impair the prospects for the financing of long term investment and innovation especially in poorer countries.

Future development policy of the EU (and the US) might partly switch to a strategy supporting the use of modern information technology in developing countries. This will not always be welcomed by such countries because access to information could imply a new potential for political unrest. As the move towards the information society and a knowledge based worldwide economy raises international income differentials between the North and South, informational development policies could indeed be an adequate remedy. This is the case provided that developing countries are willing to on the one hand invest in human capital and encourage investment in modern telecommunication networks and services and on the one hand implement strict competition policies.

Endnotes

1. MACHIN also summarizes results from using a finer definition of the skill structure based on education shares. These shares are shown to be strongly correlated with the share of nonmanual employees.

2. Factor content analysis studies suggest that trade can account for between 10 and 20 percent of the fall in demand for unskilled labor.

3. NICKELL and BELL accept the facts of lower wage flexibility in continental Europe but argue that the favorable German record - favorable in the sense that wages are rigid but unemployment no worse than in the UK or the US (sic) - reflects the superior training of bottom-decile German workers. This, we are told, has "enabled the German economy to respond to demand shifts towards the skilled in a far more robust fashion" (NICKELL and BELL, 1996, 308).

4. However, the proportion of the total change in unemployment resulting from changes in occupational structure can vary greatly within these broad occupational categories.

5. The study disaggregates the two skill groups by (5) categories of labor market experience, a crude proxy for differences in human capital. The fixed effect thus captures (other) time-invariant factors that differ between industries and experience groups

6. MACHIN also calls for investigation of within-industry shifts in the female-male employment and in full time-contingent worker employment.

7. But, for a criticism centering on the indirectness of the test procedure, see RICHARDSON (1995).

8. The ISC is defined as the half the sum of the absolute value of the change in the share of employment in the relevant grouping (region/industry/establishment/occupation). It provides the percentage point change in the distribution of workers that would equate the distribution of employment in two periods. Higher values of the index are supposed to indicate that the labor market responds well to substantive shocks.

9. The proviso being that the need for flexibility has not grown in recent years.

List of Tables

List of Figures

References

ABRAMOWITZ, M. A. (1979), Rapid Growth Potential and ist Realisation: The Experience of Capitalist Economies in the Postwar Period, in: E. MALINVEAUD (ed.), Economic Growth and Resources, Vol. 1 The Major Issues, Proceedings of the Fifth World Congress of the International Economic Association, Macmillan, London, 1-51.

ABRAMOWITZ, M. A. (1986), Catching Up, Forging Ahead and Falling Behind, Journal of Economic History, 46, 385-406.

ABRAMOWITZ, M. A. (1989), Thinking about Growth and Other Essays on Economic Growth and Welfare, Cambridge, Cambridge University Press, 187-219.

ABRAMOWITZ, M. A. (1992), Catch-up and Convergence in the Postwar Growth Boom and After. Paper presented at the Workshop on Historical Perspectives on the International Convergence and Productivity, New York, April 23-24. Reprinted in: WILLIAM J. BAUMOL, R. R., NELSON and E. N. WOLFF, Convergence of Productivity: Cross-Country Studies and Historical Evidence, Oxford: Oxford University Press, 86-125.

ABRAMOWITZ, M. A. (1993), The Search for the Sources of Growth: Areas of Ignorance, Old and New, in: Journal of Economic History, 53 (2), 86-125.

ACS, Z.J. and D.B. AUDRETSCH (1988), Innovation in Large and Small Firms: An Empirical Analysis, in: American Economic Review, 78(4), 678-690.

ACS, Z.J. and D.B. AUDRETSCH (1990), Innovation and Small Firms, Cambridge: MIT Press.

ACS, Z.J. and D.B. AUDRETSCH (eds., 1993), Small Firms and Entrepreneurship: An East-West Perspective, Cambridge: Cambridge University Press.

ADDISON, J.T. and P.J.J. WELFENS (1998), Labor Markets and Social Security, New York, Springer.

ADDISON, J.T., and J. WAGNER (1997), The Changing Structure of Employment in German Manufacturing: A Peek Inside the Industry Black Box, Paper presented at the Third Annual Conference of the American Institute for Contemporary German Studies, Globalization, Technological Change and the Welfare State. Washington, D.C.: AICGS, The Johns Hopkins University.

AGEEV, A.I., M.V. GRATCHEV and R.D. HISRICH (1995), Entrepreneurship in the Soviet Union and Post-Socialist Russia, in: Small Business Economics, 7(5), October, 365-376.

AGHION, P. and HOWITT, P. (1992), A Model of Growth through Creative Destruction, in: Econometrica, 60 (2), 323-351.

ALLEN, S.G. (1993), Technology and the Wage Structure, Unpublished paper, North Carolina State University.

ALLEN, S.G. and R.B. FREEMAN (1995), Quantitative Flexibility in the U.S. Labor Market, Unpublished paper, North Carolina State University.

AMABLE, B. (1993), Catch Up and Convergence: A Model of Cumulative Growth, in: International Review of Applied Economics, 7 (1), 1-25.

ANTONELLI, C. (1998), Localized technological change, new information technology and the knowledge based economy: The european evidence. Journal of Evolutionary Economics, 8 177-198.

ARCHIBUGI, D. and M. PIANTA (1992), The Technological Specialization of Advanced Countries, Boston: Kluwer Academic Publishers.

ARROW, K. J. (1962), The Economic Implications of Learning by Doing, in: Review of Economic Studies, 24, 155-173.

ARROW, K.J. (1962), Economic Welfare and the Allocation of Resources for Invention, in: R.R. Nelson (ed.), The Rate and Direction of Inventive Activity, Princeton: Princeton University Press, pp. 609-626.

AUDRETSCH, D.B. (1989), The Market and the State: The Role of Government Policy towards Business in Europe, Japan and the USA, New York: New York University Press.

AUDRETSCH, D.B. (1995), Innovation and Industry Evolution, Cambridge: MIT Press.

AUDRETSCH, D.B. (1997), An Empirical Test of the Industry Life Cycle, in: Weltwirtschaftliches Archiv, 123(2), 297-308.

AUDRETSCH, D.B. (ed., 1997), Industrial Policy and International Competitiveness, Volumes I, II and III, London: Edward Elgar.

AUDRETSCH, D.B. and J.A. ELSTON, (1997), Financing the German Mittelstand, in: Small Business Economics, 9(2), April, 97-110.

AUDRETSCH, D.B. and M. VIVARELLI (1996), Firm Size and R&D Spillovers: Evidence from Italy, in: Small Business Economics, 8(3), June, 249-258.

AUDRETSCH, D.B. and M.P., FELDMAN (1994), R&D Spillovers and the Geography of Innovation and Production, unpub. paper, Centre for Economic Policy Research, October.

AUDRETSCH, D.B. and M.P., FELDMAN (1996), R&D Spillovers and the Geography of Innovation and Production, International Joseph A. Schumpeter Society Conference

AUDRETSCH, D.B. and P.E. STEPHAN (1996), Company-Scientist Locational Links: The Case of Biotechnology, in: American Economic Review, 86(3), June, 641-652.

AZARIADIS, C. and DRAZEN, A. (1990), Threshold Externalities in Economic Development, in: Quarterly Journal of Economics, 105, 501-26.

BACKUS, D.K., KEHOE, P. J. and KEHOE, T. J. (1992), In Search of Scale Effects in Trade and Growth, in: Journal of Economic Theory, 58, 377-409.

BALASSA, B. (1978), Exports and Economic Growth: Further Evidence, in: Journal of Development Economics, 5 (2), 181-89.

BALDWIN, J. (1995), The Dynamics of Industrial Competition: A North American Perspective, Cambridge, Cambridge University Press.

BALDWIN, J. and G. PICOT (1995), Employment Generation by Small Producers in the Canadian Manufacturing Sector, in: Small Business Economics, 7(4), 317-331.

BALLOT, G. and TAYMAZ, E. (1997), The Dynamics of Firms in a Micro-to-Macro Model: the Role of Training, Learning and Innovation, Journal of Evolutionary Economics, Vol. 7, 435-457.

BARRO, R. (1991), Economic Growth in a Cross Section of Countries, in: Quarterly Journal of Economics, 106, 407-43.

BARRO, R. and LEE, J. (1993), International Comparisons of Educational Attainment, in: Journal of Monetary Economics, 32, 363-94.

BARRO, R. and SALA-I-MARTIN, S. (1992), Convergence, in: Journal of Political Economy, 100, 223-51.

BARRO, R. and SALA-I-MARTIN, X. (1991), Convergence across States and Regions, in: Brooking Papers on Economic Activity, 107-58.

BARRO, R. J. (1990), Government Spending in a Simple Model of Endogenous Growth, in: Journal of Political Economy, 98, 103-125.

BAUMOL, W. J. (1986), Productivity Growth, Convergence, and Welfare: What the Long-run Data Show, in: American Economic Review, 76, 1072-85.

BAUMOL, W. J., BLACKMAN, S., BATEY and A., WOLFF, E.N. (1989), Productivity and American Leadership: The long view, Cambrigde, MA, MIT Press.

BECKER G. S., MURPHY, K. M. and TAMURA, R. (1990), Human Capital, Fertility and Economic Growth, in: Journal of Political Economy, 98, 12-37.

BECKER, G. S. and TOMES, N. (1976), Child Endowments and the Quantity and Quality of Children, in: Journal of Political Economy, 84, 143-162.

BEISE, M. and G. LICHT (1995), Innovationsverhalten der Deutschen Wirtschaft, ZEW, Mannheim.

BELLMANN, L. et al. (1996), Flexibilität von Betrieben in Deutschland - Ergebnisse des IAB-Betriebspanels 1993-1995, Nürnberg, Institut für Arbeitsmarkt- und Berufsforschung der Bundesanstalt für Arbeit.

BENACEK, V. and A. ZEMPLINEROVA (1995), Problems and Environment of Small Businesses in the Czech Republic, in: Small Business Economics, 7(6), December, 437-450.

BENHABIB, J. and SPIEGEL, M. (1992), The role of human capital in economic development: Evidence from aggregate cross country data, in: Journal of Monetary Economics, 34, 143-73.

BERMAN, E., J. BOUND and Z. GRILICHES (1994), Changes in the Demand for Skilled Labor: Evidence from the Annual Survey of Manufactures, in: Quarterly Journal of Economics 109, May, 367-397.

BHAGWATI, J. N. and KRUGMAN, P. R. (1985), The Decision to Migrate: A Survey, in: BHAGWATI, J. N. (ed.), Essays in Development Economics, 2.

BINKS, M.R. and CH.T. ENNEW (1997), The Relationship between U.K. Banks and their Small Business Customers, in: Small Business Economics, 9(2), April, 167-178.

BLACKBURN, M.L., D.E. BLOOM and R.B. FREEMAN (1990), The Declining Economic Position of Less Skilled American Men, in: G. BURTLESS (ed.), A Future of Lousy Jobs? The Changing Structure of U.S. Wages. Washington, D.C.: The Brookings Institution, pp. 31-67.

BLOOM, H.S. et al. (1997), The Benefits and Costs of JTPA Title II-A Programs: Key Findings from the National Job Training Partnership Act Study, in: Journal of Human Resources 32 (Summer): 281-294.

BOOTH, A.L., and D.M. SNOWER (eds., 1996), Acquiring Skills - Market Forces, Their Symptoms and Policy Response, Cambridge, Cambridge University Press.

BOVENBERG, L.A. and G. SCHMULDERS (1993), Environmental Quality and Pollution Augmenting Technical Change in a Two-Sector Endogenous Growth Model, in: Journal of Public Economics, 57, 369-391.

BRANDER, J.A. and B.J. SPENCER (1984), Tariff Protection and Imperfect Competition, in: KIERZKOWSKI, H., Monopolistic Competition and International Trade, Oxford, 194-206.

BRETSCHGER, L. (1997a), Integration und langfristige Wirtschaftsentwicklung, München: Oldenbourg.

BRETSCHGER, L. (1997b), International Trade, Knowledge Diffusion and Growth, International Trade Journal, forthcoming.

BRETSCHGER, L. (1997c), The Sustainability Paradigm: A Macroeconomic Perspective, Paper presented at Jahrestagung des Vereins für Socialpolitik, Oktober 1997, Bern.

BUCKLEY, P.J. (1997), International Technology Transfer by Small and Medium-Sized Enterprises, in: Small Business Economics, February, 67-78.

BUNDESMINISTERIUM FÜR FORSCHUNG UND BILDUNG (BMBF) (ed., 1997), Zur technologischen Leistungsfähigkeit Deutschlands, Bonn.

BURTLESS, G. (1995), International Trade and the Rise in Earnings Inequality, in: Journal of Economic Literature 33 (June): 800-816.

CABLE, J. (1985), Capital Market Information and Industrial Performance: The Role of West German Banks, in: Economic Journal, 95, 118-132.

CARREE, M. and R. THURIK (1996), Entry and Exit in Retailing: Incentives, Barriers, Displacement and Replacement, in: Review of Industrial Organization, 11(2), April, 155-172.

CAVES, R.E. (1982), Multinational Enterprise and Economic Analysis, Cambridge, Cambridge University Press.

CEPR (ed.), "The Association Process: Making it Work: Central Europe and the European Community," London: CEPR Occasional Paper no. 11.

CHANDLER, A.D.JR. (1990), Scale and Scope, Cambridge, Harvard University Press.

CHATTERJI, M. (1992), Convergence Clubs and Endogenous Growth, in: Oxford Review of Economic Policy, 8 (4), 57-69.

CHENERY, H. B., ROBINSON, S. and SYRQUIN, M. (1986), Industrialization and growth: A comparative study, New York, Oxford University Press.

CLARK, D. E. and COSGRAVE, J. C. (1991), Amenities Versus Labor Market Opportunities: Choosing the Optimal Distance to Move, in: Journal of Regional Science, 31, 311-328.

COE, D. and E. HELPMAN (1993), International R&D spillovers, NBER Working Paper No. 4444, August.

COHEN, W.M. and D. LEVINTHAL (1990), Absorptive Capacity: A New Perspective on Learning and Innovation, Administrative Science Quarterly, 35(1), 128-152.

COHEN, W.M. and D. LEVINTHAL (1994), Fortune Favors the Prepared Firm, Economic Journal, 40(2), 227-251.

COHEN, W.M. and D.A. LEVINTHAL (1989), Innovation and Learning: The Two Faces of R&D, in: Economic Journal, 99(3), September, 569-596.

COHEN, W.M. and R.C. LEVIN (1989), Empirical Studies of Innovation and Market Structure, in: SCHMALENSEE, R. and R. WILLIG (eds.), Handbook of Industrial Organization, Volume II, Amsterdam: North-Holland, 1059-1107.

COHEN, W.M. and S. KLEPPER (1991), Firm Size Versus Diversity in the Achievement of Technological Advance, in: ACS, Z.J. and D.B. AUDRETSCH (eds.), Innovation and Technological Change: An International Comparison, Ann Arbor, University of Michigan Press, 183-203.

COHEN, W.M. and S. KLEPPER (1992), The Tradeoff between Firm Size and Diversity in the Pursuit of Technological Progress, in: Small Business Economics, 4(1), 1-14.

CRESSY, R. and CH. OLOFSSON (1997), European SME Financing: An Overview, in: Small Business Economics, 9(2), April, 87-96.

DAVIS, S.J. and J.C. HALTIWANGER (1992), Gross Job Creation, Gross Job Destruction, and Employment Reallocation, in: Quarterly Journal of Economics 107 (August): 819-863.

DAVIS, S.J., J.C. HALTIWANGER and S. SCHUH (1996), Job Creation and Destruction. Cambridge, The MIT Press.

DE LONG, J. B. (1988), Productivity Growth, Convergence, and Welfare: Comment, American Economic Review, 78, 1138-54.

DE LONG, J. B. and SUMMERS, L. H. (1991), Equipment Investment and Economic Growth, in: Quarterly Journal of Economics, 106, 445-502.

DE LONG, J. B. and SUMMERS, L. H. (1992), How Robust is the Growth-Machinery Nexus?, in: Rivista di Politica Economica, 11, 5-54.

DEUTSCHE BUNDESBANK, 1991, "The Significance of Shares as Financing Instruments," Monthly Report of the Deutsche Bundesbank, October.

DI NARDO, J.E. and J.-S. PISCHKE (1997), The Returns to Computer Use Revisited: Have Pencils Changed the Wage Structure Too?, in: Quarterly Journal of Economics 112, February, 291-303.

DIW (1997), Ausländische Direktinvestitionen in den Transformationsländern, Wochenbericht des DIW 11/97, 183-189.

DOLLAR, D. and WOLFF, E. N. (1993), Competitiveness, Convergence, and International Specialization, Cambridge, Mass.: MIT Press.

DOSI, G. (1988), Sources, Procedures, and Microeconomic Effects of Innovation, in: Journal of Economic Literature, 26(3), 1120-1171.

DOSI, G., K. PAVITT and L. SOETE (1990), The Economics of Technical Change and International Trade, New York, New York University Press.

DOSI, G., O. MARSILI, L. ORSENIGO and R. SALVATORE (1995), Learning, Market Selection and the Evolution of Industrial Structures, in: Small Business Economics, 7, 411-436.

DOSI, G., PAVITT, K. and SOETE, L. (1990), The Economics of Technical Change and International Trade, London: Harvester Wheatsheaf.

DOWRICK, S. (1994), Openness and Growth, in: P. Lowe and J. Dwyer (ed.), International Integration of the Australian Economy, Sydney: Reserve Bank of Australia, September, 19-41.

DUNNING, J.H. (1980), Toward an Eclectic Theory of International Production: Some Empirical Tests, in: Journal of International Business Studies, Vol 11.

EASTERY, W. and REBELO, S. (1993), Fiscal Policy and Economic Growth, an Empirical Investigation, in: Journal of Monetary Economics, 32, 417-58.

EDWARDS, J.S. and K. FISCHER (1994), The German Financial System, Cambridge, Cambridge University Press.

EDWARDS, S, (1992), Trade Orientation, Distortions, and Growth in Developing Countries, in: Journal of Development Economics, 39 (1), 31-57.

EDWARDS, S. (1993), Openness, Trade Liberalization, and Growth in Developing Countries, in: Journal of Economic Literature, Vol. XXXI, 1358-1393.

ERGAS, H. (1987), Does Technology Policy Matter?, in: B. R. GUILE and H. BROOKS (eds.), Technology and Global Industry, Washington, D.C.: National Academy Press, 191-245.

EUROPEAN OBSERVATORY (1993), First Annual Report, Zoetermeer, EIM.

EUROPEAN OBSERVATORY (1994), Second Annual Report, Zoetermeer, EIM.

EUROPEAN OBSERVATORY (1995), Third Annual Report, Zoetermeer, EIM.

EUROSTAT (1995), Enterprises in Europe, Luxembourg, Eurostat.

EUROSTAT (1996), Europa ohne Grenzen, Beilage, Nr. 5.

FAGERBERG, J. (1987), A Technological Gap Approach to Why Growth Rates Differ, Research Policy, August, 16, 87-99.

FAGERBERG, J. (1988), Why Growth Rates Differ, in: DOSI, G. et al., Technical Change and Economic Theory, London, Pinter Pub. 432-57.

FAGERBERG, J. (1994), Technology and International Differences in Growth Rates, in: Journal of Economic Literature, 32, 1147—75.

FAGERBERG, J. (1997), Competitiveness, Scale and R&D, in: FAGERBERG, J. et al., Technology and International Trade, Cheltenham: Edward Elgar, 56-74.

FINDLAY, R. (1973), International Trade and Development Theory, Columbia University Press, New York.

FINDLAY, R. (1985), Growth and Development in Trade Models, in: JONES, R.W. and KENEN, P.B. (eds.), Handbook of International Economics, 1, 185-236.

FISCHER, S. (1992a), Growth: the Role of Macroeconomic Factors, in: Rivista di Politica Economica, 11, 441-470.

FISCHER, S. (1992b), Round Table: Macroeconomic Recommendations, in: Rivista di Politica Economica, 11, 481-484.

FREEMAN, R. B. (1986), Demand for Education, in: O. ASHENFELTER, R. LAYARD (eds.) Handbook of Labor Economics, 357-387.

FREEMAN, R.B. (1995), Are Your Wages Set in Beijing?, in: Journal of Economics Perspectives 9 (Summer), 15-32.

FUENTE, de la, A. (1997), The Empirics of Growth and Convergence: A Selective Review, in: Journal of Economic Dynamics and Control, 21, 23-73.

FUJITA, M. (1995), Small and Medium-sized Transnational Corporations: Trends and Patterns of Foreign Direct Investment, in: Small Business Economics, 7(3), 183-204.

GASTON, R.J. (1989), The Scale of Informal Capital Markets, in: Small Business Economics, 1(3), 223-230.

GEHRKE, B. et al. (1994), Innovationspotential und Hochtechnologie, Heidelberg, Physica-Verlag, 2nd ed.

GEROSKI, P.; MACHIN S. and VAN REENEN, J. (1993), The Profitability of Innovating Firms, Rand Journal of Economics, 198-211.

GERSCHENKORN, A. (1962), Economic Backwardness in Historical Perspective, Cambridge Mass.

GERYBADZE, A. and G. REGER (1997), Globalisation of R&D: Recent Changes in the Management of Innovation in Transnational Corporations, Discussion Paper of International Management and Innovation 97-01, Universität Hohenheim, Stuttgart.

GIERSCH, H., K.-H. PAQUE and H. SCHMIEDING (1992), The Fading Miracle, Cambridge, Cambridge University Press.

GILBERT, R. and C. SHAPIRO (1990), Optimal Patent Protection and Breadth, in: Rand Journal of Economics, 21, 106-112.

GLAESER, E.L. (1992), Growth of Cities, in: Journal of Political Economy, 100(4), 1126-1152.

GOLDIN, C. and L.F. KATZ (1995), The Decline of Non-Competing Groups: Changes in the Premium to Education, 1890 to 1940, Working Paper No. 5202, National Bureau of Economic Research.

GOMES-CASSERES, B. (1997), Alliance Strategies of Small Firms, Small Business Economics, 9(1), February, 33-34.

GOMULKA, S. (1971), Inventive Activity, Diffusion and the Stages of Economic Growth, Aarhus Universtets Okonomiske Institut, No. 24, Institute of Economics.

GOMULKA, S. (1991), The Theory of Technological Change and Economic Growth, Routledge: London/New York.

GRAACK, C. (1997), Telekommunikationswirtschaft in der Europäischen Union: Innovationsdynamik, Regulierungspolitik und Internationalisierungsprozesse, forthcoming.

GRADUS, R. and S. SCHMULDERS (1993), The Trade-off Between Environmental Care and Long-Term Growth - Pollution in Three Prototype Growth Models, in: Journal of Economics, No. 1, 25-51.

GRIES, T. (1995a), Wachstum, Humankapital und die Dynamik der komparativen Vorteile, Tübingen 1995.

GRIES, T. (1995b), Neue regionale Wachstumstheorie und Humankapital als regionaler charakteristischer Faktor, in: B. GAHLEN, H. HESSE and H. J. RAMSER (eds.), Standort und Region: Neue Ansätze zur Regionalökonomik, Wirtschaftswissenschaftliches Seminar Ottobeuren, Band 24, Tübingen, J.C. B. Mohr, (Paul Siebeck), 157-188.

GRIES, T. and JUNGBLUT, S. (1997a), Catching Up of Economies in Transformation, in: P. J. J. WELFENS and H. C. WOLF (ed.), Banking, International Capitalk Flows and Growth in Europe, Heidelberg: Springer.

GRIES, T. and JUNGBLUT, S. (1997b), Catching Up and Structural Change, in Economia Internazionale, Vol. L, 4, 3-23.

GRIES, T. and WIGGER, B. (1993), The Dynamics of Upgrading or How to Catch-Up, in: Economia Internazionale, Vol.XLVI, 4, 3-13.

GRIES, T., JUNGBLUT, S. and MEYER, H. (1998), Foreign Direct Investments in the Process of Transition, Working Paper No. 9801 International Economics, University of Paderborn.

GRILICHES, Z (1992), The Search for R&D Spill-Overs, in: Scandanavian Journal of Economics, 94(S), 29-47.

GRILICHES, Z. (1969) Capital Skill Complementarity, in: Review of Economics and Statistics, 51 (November): 465-468.

GRILICHES, Z. (1979), Issues in Assessing the Contribution of R&D to Productivity Growth, in: Bell Journal of Economics, 10(1), 92-116.

GRILICHES, Z.(1990), Patent Statistics as Economic Indicators: A Survey,: Journal of Economic Literature, 28(4), 1661-1707.

GROSSMAN, G. M. and HELPMAN, E. (1990), Comparative Advantage and Long-Run Growth, in: American Economic Review, 80, 796-815.

GROSSMAN, G. M. and HELPMAN, E. (1991a), Trade, Knowledge Spillovers, and Growth, in: European Economic Review, 35, 517-526.

GROSSMAN, G. M. and HELPMAN, E. (1991b), Innovation and Growth in the Global Economy, MIT Press.

GROSSMAN, G.M. and E. HELPMAN (1994), Endogenous Innovation in the Theory of Growth, in: Journal of Economic Perspectives, 8(1), Winter, 23-44.

GRUPP, H. (1997), Messung und Erklärung des Technischen Wandels, Heidelberg: Springer.

GRUPP, H. (1997), Technischer Wandel und Beschäftigung, in: SCHNABL, H. (ed.), Innovation und Arbeit, Tübingen, Mohr Siebeck, 1-24.

GRUPP, H. (1998), Foundations of the Economics of Innovation: Theory, Measurement and Practice, Cheltenham, Edward Elgar.

GRUPP, H. (ed., 1992), Dynamics of Science-Based Innovation, Berlin, Springer.

GRUPP, H. and S. MAITAL (1996), Innovation Benchmarking in the Telecom Industry, Massachusetts Institute of Technology (MIT), Sloan School of Management, International Center for Research on the Management of Technology, WP # 153-96, Cambridge, Mass.

GRUPP, H. and U. SCHMOCH (1992), Wissenschaftsbindung der Technik, Heidelberg, Physica-Verlag.

GRUPP, H., B. GEHRKE, H. LEGLER and G. MÜNT (1996), Knowledge-Intensive and Resource-Concerned Structures: Strength and Weakness of High Technology in Gemany, in: KRULL, W. and F. MEYER-KRAHMER (eds.), Catermills Guides to Science and Technology: Germany, Catermill Publishing, 46-62.

GUNDLACH, E. (1995), The Role of Human Capital in Economic Growth: New Results and Alternative Interpretations, in: Weltwirtschaftliches Archiv, 383-402.

GUSTAVSON, P., HANSSON, P. and LUNDBERG, L. (1997), Technological Progress, Capital Accumulation and Changing International Competitiveness, in FAGERBERG, J. et al., Technology and International Trade, Cheltenham: Edward Elgar, 20-37.

HAMERMESH , D. S. (1986), The Demand for Labor in the Long Run, in: ASHENFELTER, O. and LAYARD, R., Handbook of Labor Economics, North Holland, 429-473.

HAMMOND, P. J. and RODRIGUEZ-CLARE, A. (1993), On Endogenizing Long-Run Growth, in: Journal of Economics, 95, 391-425.

HARHOFF, D. and G. LICHT (eds., 1996), Die Innovationsaktivitaeten kleiner und mittlerer Unternehmen. Ergebnisse des Mannheimer Innovationspanels, in: Zentrum fuer Europaeische Wirtschaftsforschung, Schriftreihe des ZEW, 8, Baden-Baden: Nomos.

HARRISON, B. (1995), Symposium on Harrison's 'Lean and Mean': What are the Questions?, in: Small Business Economics, 7(5), October, 357-363.

HÄRTEL, H.H. et al. (1996), Grenzüberschreitende Produktion und Strukturwandel - Globalisierung der deutschen Wirtschaft, Hamburg.

HECZOWITZ, Z. and SAMPSON, M. (1991), Output Growth, the Real Wage, and Employment Fluctuations, in: American Economic Review, 81, 1215-1237.

HELLIWELL, J. F. (1992), Trade and Technical Progress, in: National Bureau of Economic Research Working Paper, No. 4226.

HELPMAN, E. and KRUGMAN, P.R. (1985), Increasing Returns, Imperfect Competition, and International Trade, Cambridge.

HORST, TH. (1972), Firm and Industry Determinants of the Decision to Invest Abroad: An Empirical Study, in: Review of Economics and Statistics, August, 258-266.

HUGHES, A. (1997), Finance for SMEs: A U.K. Perspective, in: Small Business Economics, 9(2), April, 151-166.

ISSERMAN et al. (1986), Regional Labor Market Analysis, in: NIJKAMP, P. Handbook of Regional and Urban Economics, 1, 544-580.

IWD (1997), Direktinvestitionen. Schrittmacher der Globalisierung, IWD-Mitteilungen, Nr. 8.

JACOBS, J. (1969), The Economy of Cities, New York: Random House.

JAFFE, A.B. (1989), Real Effects of Academic Research, in: American Economic Review, 79(5), 957-970.

JAFFE, A.B., M. TRAJTENBERG, and R. HENDERSON (1993), Geographic Localization of Knowledge Spillovers as Evidenced by Patent Citations, in: Quarterly Journal of Economics, 63(3), August, 577-598.

JENSEN, M.C. (1993), The Modern Industrial Revolution, Exit and the Failure of Internal Control Systems, Journal of Finance, 68(3), 831-880.

JUHN, CH. and K.M. MURPHY (1994), Relative Wages and Skill Demand, 1940-1990, in: L.C. SOLMON and A.R. LEVENSON (eds.), Labor Markets, Employment Policy, and Job Creation, Boulder, Colorado: Westview Press, pp. 343-360.

JUNGMITTAG, A. (1997), Langfristige Zusammenhänge und kurzfristige Dynamiken zwischen Direktinvestitionen und Exporten, Berlin: Duncker.

JUNGMITTAG, A. and P.J.J. WELFENS (1996), Telekommunikation, Innovation und die langfristige Produktionsfunktion: Theoretische Aspekte und eine Kointegrationsanalyse für dei Bundesrepublik Deutschland, Discussion Paper No. 20, European Institute for International Economic Relations/University of Potsdam, Potsdam.

KENDRICK, J. W. (1976), The Formation and Stocks of Total Capital, New York: Columbia University for NBER.

KING, R. and LEVINE, R. (1993), Finance, Entrepreneurship and Growth, in: Journal of Monetary Economics, 32, 513-42.

KING, R. G. and REBELO, R. (1990), Public Policy and Economic Growth: Developing Neoclassical Implications, in: Journal of Political Economy, 97, 126-150.

KLEIN, M. and P.J.J. WELFENS (eds.,1992), Multinationals in the New Europe and Global Trade, New York: Springer.

KLEINKNECHT, A. (1989), Firm Size and Innovation: Observations in Dutch Manufacturing Industry, in: Small Business Economics, 1(3), 214-222.

KLEMPERER, P. (1990), How Broad Should the Scope of Patent Protection be?, in: Rand Journal of Economics, 21, 113-130.

KLODT, H. et al. (1994), Standort Deutschland: Strukturelle Herausforderungen im neuen Europa, Kieler Studien No. 265, Tübingen, Mohr.

KOHN, T.O. (1997), Small Firms as International Players, in: Small Business Economics, 9(1), February, 45-51.

KRUEGER, A. O. (1978), Foreign Trade Regimes and Economic Development: Liberalization Attempts and Consequences, Cambridge, Mass.: Ballinger Pub. Co for NBER.

KRUEGER, A.S. (1993), How Computers Have Changed the Wage Structure: Evidence from Microdata, 1984-90, in: Quarterly Journal of Economics 108 (February): 33-60.

KRUGMAN, P. (1991a), Geography and Trade, Cambridge, Mass.: MIT Press.

KRUGMAN, P. (1991b), Increasing Returns and Economic Geography, Journal of Political Economy, 99, 483-499.

KRUGMAN, P.E. (1994), The Age of Diminished Expectations, Cambridge, MIT Press.

LAL, D. (1993), Does Openness Matter?, How to Appraise the Evidence, Seminar Paper at Australian National University.

LANDAU, D. (1986), Government and Economic Growth in the Less Developed Countries: An Empirical Study for 1960-80, in: Economic Development and Cultural Change, 35, 35-75.

LEAMER, E. (1984), Sources of International Comparative Advantages, Theory and Evidence, Cambridge, Mass.: MIT Press.

LEVIN, A. and RAUT, L. K. (1992), Complementarities between Exports and Human Capital in Economic Growth: Evidence Semi-industrialized Countries, Discussion Paper 92-14, Department of Economics, Univ. of California, San Diego.

LEVINE, R. and RENELT, D. (1991), Cross-country Studies of Growth and Policy: Methodological, Conceptual and Statistical Problems, in: Working Paper no. 608 (World Bank, Washington, DC).

LEVINE, R. and RENELT, D. (1992), A sensitivity Analysis of Cross-country Growth Regressions, in: American Economic Review, 82, 942-63.

LEVY, F. and R.J. MURNANE (1992), U.S. Earnings Levels and Earnings Inequality: A Review of Recent Trends and Proposed Explanations, in: Journal of Economic Literature 30 (September), 1333-1381.

LICHTENBERG, F. (1992), R&D Investment and International Productivity Differences, in: Working Paper, no. 3161 (NBER, Cambridge, MA).

LICHTENBERG, F.R. (1995), R&D Collaboration and Specialization in the European Community, Discussion Paper FS IV 95-18, Wissenschaftszentrum Berlin.

LINK, A.N. and J. REES (1990), Firm Size, University Based Research, and the Returns to R&D, in: Small Business Economics, 2(1), 25-32.

LUCAS, R. (1988), On the Mechanics of Economic Development, in: Journal of Monetary Economics, 22, 3-42.

MACHIN, S. (1996), Changes in the Relative Demand for Skills, in: A.L. BOOTH and D.J. SNOWER (eds.), Acquiring Skills - Market Failures, Their Symptoms and Policy Responses. Cambridge, England: Cambridge University Press, 129-146.

MADISON, A. (1987), Growth and Slowdown in Advanced Capitalist Economies, Techniques of Quantitative Assessment, in: Journal of Economic Literature, 25, 649-98.

MAHLO, I. (1986), Theories of Migration: A Review, Scottish Journal of Political Economy, 33, 396-419.

MANKIW, G., ROMER and D. WEIL, D. (1992), A Contribution to the Empirics of Economic Growth, in: Quarterly Journal of Economics, 107, 407-37.

MANKIW, N. G. (1995), The Growth of Nations, in: Brookings Papers on Economic Activity, 275-326.

MANSFIELD, E. (1983) Industrial Organization and Technological Change: Recent Empirical Findings," in J.V. Craven (ed.), Industrial Organization, Antitrust and Public Policy, Boston: Kluwer, 129-143.

MANSFIELD, E. (1988), Intellectual Property Rights, Technological Change, and Economic Growth, in: C. WALKER and M.A. BLOOMFIELD (eds.), Intellectual Property Rights and Capital Formation in the Next Decade, New York, University Press of America.

MASON, C.M. and R.T. HARRISON (1997), Business Angel Networks and the Development of the Informal Venture Capital Market in the U.K.: Is There Still a Role for the Public Sector?, in: Small Business Economics, 9(2), April, 111-123.

MATA, J. (1994), Firm Growth During Infancy, in: Business Economics, 6(1), 27-40.

MAYHEW, A.(1992) Fact Sheet on the Association (European) Agreements between the Czech and Slovak Federal Republic, Hungary, Poland and the European Community, CEPR Occasional Paper no. 11, London.

MCDERMOTT, G.A. and M. MEJSTRIK (1992), The Role of Small Firms in Czechoslovak Manufacturing, in: Z. ACS and D.B. AUDRETSCH (eds.), Small Firms and Entrepreneurship: An East-West Perspective, Cambridge, Cambridge University Press.

MICHAELY, M. M. (1977), Exports and Growth: An Empirical Investigation, in: Journal of Development Economics, 4 (1), 49-53.

MINCER, J. (1993), Investment in U.S. Training and Education, Discussion Paper No. 67, Columbia University.

MISHEL, L. and J. BERNSTEIN (1996), Technology and the Wage Structure: Has Technology's Impact Accelerated Since the 1970s?, Washington, D.C., Economic Policy Institute.

MITI (1991), Small Business in Japan, Tokyo: MITI.

MURPHY, K. M. SCHLEIFER, H. and VISHNY, R. W. (1989a), Income Distribution, Market Size and Industrialization, in: Quarterly Journal of Economics, 104, 537-564.

MURPHY, K. M. SCHLEIFER, H. and VISHNY, R. W. (1989b), Industrialization and the Big Push, Journal of Political Economy, 97, 1003-1026.

NELSON, R. (ed., 1993), National Systems of Innovation, Oxford: Oxford University Press.

NELSON, R. and S.G. WINTER (1982), An Evolutionary Theory of Economic Change, Cambridge, MA, Harvard University Press.

NICKELL, S. (1995), The Distribution of Wages and Unemployment Across Skill Groups, Unpublished paper, University of Oxford Institute of Economics and Statistics.

NICKELL, S. and B. BELL (1996), Changes in the Distribution of Wages and Unemployment in OECD Countries, in: American Economic Review, Papers and Proceedings 86 (May), 302-308.

OECD (1993), Frascati Manual 1992, Proposed Standard Practice for Surveys of Research and Experimental Development, Fifth Revision, Paris, 1993.

OECD (1994), Economic Outlook, Paris.

OECD (1996), Globalization of Industry, Paris, OECD.

OECD (1996), The OECD Jobs Strategy; Technology, Productivity and JobCreation; Vol. 2: Analytical Report, Paris: Organization for Economic Co-Operation and Development.

OEKMAN, B.M. and P.C. MAVROIDIS (1995), Linking Competition and Trade Policies in Central and East European Countries, in: WINTERS, L.A. (ed.), Foundations of an Open Economy, London: CEPR, 111-153.

ORDOVER, J..A. (1991), A Patent System for both Diffusion and Exclusion, in: Journal of Economic Perspectives, 5(1), Winter, 43-60.

ORR, L.L. (1996), Does Training for the Disadvantaged Work? Evidence from the National JTPA Study, Washington, D.C., The Urban Institute Press.

PAKES, A. and Z. GRILICHES (1980), Patents and R&D at the Firm Level: A First Report, Economics Letters, 5, 377-381.

PAVITT, K. (1984), Sectoral patterns of technical change: Towards a taxonomy and a theory, in: Research Policy, 13, 343-373

PRZEWOSKI, A. and LIMONGI, F. (1993), Political Regimes and Economic Growth, in: Journal of Economic Perspectives, 7, 51-69.

QUAH, D. (1993), Empirical cross-section dynamics in economic growth, in: European Economic Review, 37, 426-34.

QUAH, D. (1996), Empirics for economic growth and convergence, in European Economic Review, 40, 1353-75.

REBELO, S. (1991), Long-Run Policy Analysis and Long-Run Growth, in: Journal of Political Economy, 99, 500-521.RIVERA-BATIZ, L.A. and ROMER, P.M. (1991a), International Trade with Endogenous Technological Change, in: European Economic Review, 35, 971-1004.

REGER, G. and U. SCHMOCH (eds., 1996), Organisation of Science and Technology at the Watershed, Heidelberg, Physica

RICHARDSON, J.D. (1995) Income Inequality and Trade: How to Think, What to Conclude, Journal of Economic Perspectives 9 (Summer): 33-55.

RIVERA-BATIZ, L. A. and ROMER, P. M. (1991a), International Trade with Endogenous Technological Change, European Economic Review, 35, 971-1004.

RIVERA-BATIZ, L. A. and ROMER, P. M. (1991b), Economic Integration and Endogenous Growth, in: Quarterly Journal of Economics, 106, 531-555.

RIVERA-BATIZ, L. A. and XIE, D. (1992), GATT, Trade and Growth, in: American Economic Review, 82, 422-427.

RIVERA-BATIZ, L. A. and XIE, D. (1993), Integration among unequals, in: Regional Science and Urban Economics, 23, 337-354.

ROMER, P. M. (1986), Increasing Returns and Long-Run Growth, Journal of Political Economy, 94, 5, 1002-1037.

ROMER, P. M. (1987), Growth Based on Increasing Returns due to Specialization, in: American Economic Review, 77, 56-62.

ROMER, P. M. (1990a) , Endogenous Technological Change, in: Journal of Political Economy, 98, 71-102.

ROMER, P. M. (1990b), Are Nonconvexities Important for Understanding Growth?, in: American Economic Review, 80, No. 2, 97-103.

ROMER, P. M. (1990c), Capital, Labor and Productivity, in: Brooking Papers of Economic Activities: Microeconomics, Special Issue, 337-67.

ROMER, P.M. (1986), Increasing Returns and Long-Run Growth, in: Journal of Political Economy, 94(5), October, 1002-37.

ROMER, P.M. (1990), Endogenous Technical Change, Journal of Political Economy, 98, S71-S102.

ROMER, P.M. (1994), The Origins of Endogenous Growth, in: Journal of Economic Perspectives, 8(1), Winter, 3-22.

ROSEN, S. (1968), Short Run Employment Variation on Class I Railroads in the United States, 1947-1968, in: Econometrica, 36, 425-431.

ROTHWELL, R. (1989), Small Firms, Innovation and Industrial Change, in: Small Business Economics, 1(1), 51-64.

ROYAL SWEDISH ACADEMY OF ENGINEERING SCIENCES (1993), Profit from Innovation: A Comparison of Swedish and Japanese Intellectual Property Management, Stockholm: Royal Swedish Academy of Engineering Sciences.

SALA-I-MARTIN, X. (1996), Regional cohesion: Evidence and theories of regional growth and convergence, in: European Economic Review, 40 , 1325-52.

SANTARELLI, E. and A. STERLACCHINI (1990), Innovation, Formal vs. Informal R&D, and Firms Size: Some Evidence from Italian Manufacturing Firms, in: Small Business Economics, 2(2), 223-228.

SAXENIAN, A. (1990), Regional Networks and the Resurgence of Silicon Valley, California Management Review, 33(1), 89-111.

SCHERER, F.M. (1983), The Propensity to Patent, International Journal of Industrial Organization, 1(1), March, 107-128.

SCHERER, F.M. (1991), Changing Perspectives on the Firm Size Problem, in: Z. ACS and D.B. AUDRETSCH (eds.), Innovation and Technological Change: An International Comparison, Ann Arbor: University of Michigan Press, pp. 24-38.

SCHERER, F.M. (1992), International High Technology Competition. Cambridge, Mass.: Harvard University Press.

SCHERER, F.M. (1992), Schumpeter and Plausible Capitalism, in: Journal of Economic Literature, 30(3), September, 1416-1433.

SCHERER, F.M., and D. ROSS (1990), Industrial Market Structure and Economic Performance, third edition, Boston, Houghton Mifflin

SCHMOCH, U. et al. (1996), The Role of the Scientific Community in the Generation of Technology, in: Reger and Schmoch, 1-138.

SCHOTT, TH. (1994), Collaboration in the Invention of Technology: Globalization, regions, and centers, in: Social Science Research, vol. 23, pp 23-56.

SCHUMPETER, J.A. (1911), Theorie der wirtschaftlichen Entwicklung, Eine Untersuchung über Unternehmergewinn, Kapital, Kredit, Zins und den Konjunkturzyklus, Berlin, Duncker und Humblot.

SCHUMPETER, J.A. (1942), Capitalism, Socialism and Democracy, New York: Harper and Row.

SERVAN-SCHREIBER,, J.-J. (1968) The American Challenge, London:Hamisch Hamilton

SHAW, K. L. (1991), The Influence of Human Capital Investment on Migration and Industry Change, in: Journal of Regional Science, 31, 397-416.

SILVESTRI, G.T. (1993), Occupational Employment: Wide Variations in Growth, Monthly Labor Review 116 (November): 58-86.

SIMON, H. (1992), Lessons from Germany's Midsize Giants, in: Harvard Business Review, March-April, 115-125.

SOETE, L. and VERSPAGEN, B. (1993), Technology and Growth: The Complex Dynamics of Catching Up, Falling Behind and Taking Over, in: SZIRMAI, A. et. Al, Explaining Economic Growth, Essays in Honour of Angus Maddison, 101-128.

SOLOW, R. (1956), A Contribution to the Theory of Economic Growth, in: Quarterly Journal of Economics, 70, February, 60-94.

SOLOW, R. (1956), A Contribution to the Theory of Economic Growth, in: Quarterly Journal of Economics, 70 (1), 65-94.

SOLOW, R. (1957), Technical Change and the Aggregate Production Function, Review of Economics and Statistics, August, 39, 312-320.

STEHN, J. (1992), Ausländische Direktinvestitionen in Industrieländern, Tübingen: Mohr.

STEINER, V. and K. WAGNER (1997), Relative Earnings and the Demand for Unskilled Labor in West German Manufacturing, Paper presented at the Third Annual Conference of the American Institute for Contemporary German Studies, Washington, D.C., AICGS, The Johns Hopkins University.

STOCKEY, N. L. (1991), Human Capital, Product Quality, and Growth, in: Quarterly Journal of Economics, 106, 587-616.

SUMMERS, R., and HESTON, A. (1994), The Penn World Table(Mark 5.6)

SVR (1996), Reformen vorantreiben, Jahresgutachten 1996/97 des Sachverständigenrats zur Begutachtung der gesamtwirtschaftlichen Lage, Stuttgart, Metzler-Poeschel.

SWAN, T. W. (1956), Economic Growth and Capital Accumulation, in: Economic Record, 32, 334-361.

TEECE, D. et al. (1994), Understanding Corporate Coherence: Theory and Evidence, in: Journal of Economic Behavior and Organization, 23(1), 1-30.

TEECE, D.J. (1982), Towards an Economic Theory of the Multiproduct Firm, in: Journal of Economic Behavior and Organization, 3(1), 39-63.

TESSARING, M. (1994), Langfristete Tendenzen des Arbeitskräftebedarfs nach Tätigkeiten und Qualifikationen in den alten Bundesländern bis zum Jahr 2010 - Eine erste Aktualisierung der IAB/Prognos-Projektionen 1989/91, Mitteilungen aus der Arbeitsmarkt- und Berufsforschung 27 (1): 5-19.

TIEBOUT, C. M. (1956), A Pure Theory of Local Expandages, in: Journal of Political Economy, 64, 416-424.

TOPEL, R.H. (1993), What Have We Learned from Empirical Studies of Unemployment and Turnover?, in: American Economic Review, Papers and Proceedings 83 (May): 110-115.

TOWNSEND, J. et al. (1981), Science and Technology Indicators for the UK. Innovations in Britain since 1945, SPRU Occasional Paper Series, No. 16.

TYSON, L.D., P. TEA and R. HALSEY (1994), Promoting Entrepreneurship in Eastern Europe, in: Small Business Economics, 6(3), June, 165-184.

UNCTAD (1996), World Investment Report 1996, New York and Genf.

UNITED NATIONS CONFERENCE ON TRADE AND DEVELOPMENT (1993), Programme on Transnational Corporations, World Investment Report 1993: Transnational Corporations and Integrated International Production, New York: United Nations.

UZAWA, H. (1965), Optimum Technical Change in an Aggregative Model of Economic Growth, in: International Economic Review, 6, 18-31.

VEBLEN, T. (1915), Imperial Germany and the Industrial Revolution, London.

VENABLES, A.J. (1985), International Trade, Trade and International Policy, and Imperfect Competition: A Survey, Discussion Paper No. 74, CEPR, London.

VERNON, R. (1996), International Investment and International Trade in the Product Life Cycle, in: Quarterly Journal of Economics, 80(2), 290-307.

VERSPAGEN, B. (1991), A New Empirical Approach to Catching Up or Falling Behind, in: Structural Change and Economic Dynamics, 2 (2), 359-80.

VERSPAGEN, B. and WAKELIN, K. (1993), International Competitiveness and ist Determinants, MERIT Working Paper 93-008, Maastricht, Netherlands.

VON HIPPLE, E. (1988), The sources of innovation,Oxford,

VON HIPPLE, E. (1994), Sticky Information and the Locus of Problem Solving: Implications for Innovation, Management Science, 40(4), 429-439.

WAGNER, J. (1994), Small-Firm Entry in Manufacturing Industries, in: Small Business Economics, 5(3), 211-214.

WAGNER, J. (1995), Firm Size and Job Creation in Germany, in: Small Business Economics, 7(6), December, 469-474.

WEIDLICH, W. and SANIS, M. (1991), Interregional Migration: Dynamic Theory and Comparative Analysis, in: BOYCE; D. E., NIJKAMP, P. Shefer, D., Regional Science, - Retrospect and Prospect.

WELFENS, P.J.J. (1992), Foreign Investment in the East European Transition, Management International Review, Vol. 32, 199-218.

WELFENS, P.J.J. (1995), Telecommunications and Transition in Central and Eastern Europe, Telecommunications Policy, Vol. 19, 561-577.

WELFENS, P.J.J. (1997), Privatization, Structural Change and Productivity: Toward Convergence in Europe?, in: S.W. BLACK (ed.), Europe's Economy Looks East, Cambridge, Cambridge University Press, 212-257.

WELFENS, P.J.J. and C. GRAACK (1996a), Telekommunikationswirtschaft. Deregulierung, Privatisierung und Internationalisierung, Heidelberg: Springer.

WELFENS, P.J.J. and G. YARROW (1997), Telecommunications and Energy in Systemic Transformation, Heidelberg and New York: Springer.

WELFENS, P.J.J. and H. WOLF (eds., 1997), Banking, International Capital Flows and Growth in Europe, Heidelberg and New York: Springer.

WELFENS, P.J.J. and P. JASINSKI (eds., 1994), Privatization and Foreign Investment in Transforming Economies, Aldershot: Dartmouth.

WELFENS, P.J.J. and R. HILLEBRAND (1997), Globalisierung der Wirtschaft: Wirtschaftspolitische Konsequenzen des internationalen Standortwettbewerbs, in: Dikussionsbeiträge des EIIW, Nr. 41.

WELFENS, P.J.J., J.T. ADDISON, D.B. AUDRETSCH and H. GRUPP (1998), Technological Competition, Employment and Innovation Policy in OECD Countries, Berlin, Heidelberg: Springer-Verlag.

WELFENS, P.J.J., J.T. ADDISON, D.B. AUDRETSCH, and H. GRUPP (1997), Research and Development Policy and Employment. Directorate-General for Research Working Document, Energy and Research Series W-25. Luxembourg: The European Parliament.

WILLIAMSON, O. (1975), Markets and Hierarchies: Antitrust Analysis and Implications, New York: The Free Press.

WILLIS, R. J. (1986), Wage Determinants: A Survey and Reinteropretation of Human Capital Earnings Functions, in: ASHENFELTER, O. and LAYARD, R., Handbook of Labor Economics, North Holland, 525-599.

WINTER, S. (1984), Schumpeterian Competition in Alternative Technological Regimes, Journal of Economic Behavior and Organization, 5, Sept.-Dec., 287-320.

WINTERS, L.A. (1992), The Europe Agreements: With a Little Help from Our Friends, in: CEPR (ed.), The Association Process: Making it Work: Central

Europe and the European Community, London, CEPR Occasional Paper no. 11.

WOLFF, E. N. (1997), Productivity Growth and Shifting Comparative Advantage on the Industry Level, in: FAGERBERG, J. et al, (ed.), Technology and International Trade, Cheltenham, Edward Elgar, 1-19.

WOLFF, E. N. and GITTLEMAN, M. (1993), The Role of Education in Productivity Convergence: Does Higher Education Matter?, in: SZIRMAI, A. et. Al, Explaining Economic Growth, Essays in Honour of Angus Maddison, 147-67.

WORLD BANK, (1987), Development Report 1987, Oxford University Press.

WORLD BANK, (1997), World Development Indicators, New York: Oxford University Press.

YOUNG, A. (1991), Learning by Doing and the Dynamic Effects of International Trade, in: Quarterly Journal of Economics, 106, 369-405.

ZIESEMER, T. (1991), Human Capital, Market Struktur and Taxation in a Growth Model with Endogeneous Technical Progress, in: Journal of Macroeconomics, 17-68.

ZUCKER, L.G., M.R. DARBY and M.B. BREWER (1994), Intellectual Capital and the Birth of U.S. Biotechnology Enterprises, NBER Working Paper, February.